URBAN BLUES

URBAN

CHARLES KEIL

BLUES

THE UNIVERSITY OF
CHICAGO PRESS
Chicago & London

International Standard Book Number: 0–226–42960–1

THE UNIVERSITY OF CHICAGO PRESS, CHICAGO 60637

THE UNIVERSITY OF CHICAGO PRESS, LTD., LONDON

© 1966 BY THE UNIVERSITY OF CHICAGO. ALL RIGHTS RESERVED

PUBLISHED 1966

SIXTH IMPRESSION 1970

PRINTED IN THE UNITED STATES OF AMERICA

TO THE MEMORY OF
MALCOLM X

Στὰ περιβόλια μὲς στοὺς ἀνθισμένους κήπους
σὰν ἄλλοτε θὰ στήσουμε χορὸ
καὶ τὸ Χάρο θὰ καλέσουμε
νὰ πιοῦμε ἀντάμα καὶ νὰ τραγουδήσουμε μαζί.
Κράτα τὸ κλαρίνο καὶ τὸ ζουρνὰ
καὶ γὼ θά 'ρθῶ μὲ τὸ μικρό μου μπαγλαμᾶ.

from *Song of the Dead Brother* by Mikis Theodorakis

AUTHOR'S NOTE

All but a few paragraphs of this book were written
before Watts and before our war against the Vietnamese.
Any optimistic passages may be forgiven, laughed off,
or cried over accordingly.

C. K.

PREFACE

I HAVE RESTRAINED a strong impulse to write a soul-baring autobiographical preface for the simple reason that much of who I am comes out in the book; how I got that way is probably irrelevant. The blues, the Negro, and related concepts serve naturally as projective tests; white liberals, black militants, and others of varying pigmentation and persuasion hear in the blues essentially what they want to hear, find in the blues ethos what they expect to find. I claim no exemption from this pattern.

I have, however, tried to keep my interpretations from straying too far from the views of the primary producers and consumers of the blues. I hope that in some measure this work provides an access to the current blues scene for the reader and, more important, a foundation for future students who may attempt to explore the field in greater depth and detail.

To the extent that I have achieved anything here I must thank a great many people who raised me up and equipped me in one way or another.

For having given me an irrationally optimistic perspective on humanity and a broad enough range of experience in which to test and exercise it without losing it, I should like to thank my whole family of origin, particularly my uncles, Henry Keil and Hop Rudd, and especially my parents, Carl and Marcia Keil. As for my family of procreation, my wife Angeliki and daughter Aphrodite sustain and prod me as only they can.

I turn next to a cluster of quasi-ancestors, kindred spirits of preceding generations who have stirred my imagination, shaped my interests, and either shifted or intensified my direction. Whether the influence has been brief or continuous, direct or mediated by a piece of writing, seems unimportant to me for each encounter has forced me to redefine myself and my situation. Rather than pass out inept capsule citations, I will simply list these individuals: Harold Edwards, Kenneth Roberts, Jack London, Robert Peebles, Walt Whitman, Henry Thoreau and many of his transcendentalist-abolitionist, Utopian Yankee contemporaries, Henry Adams, Nietzsche, Ammon Hennacy, Ralph Ellison, Laurence Chisolm, Charles Ives, Norman O. Brown, Janheinz Jahn, Claude Lévi-Strauss, David M. Schneider, Jane Ellen Harrison, Kenneth Burke, Marshall McLuhan,* Herbie Nichols, and Malcolm X.

I had decided to dedicate this book to Malcolm X some months before he was assassinated. Now that he is gone, I find it much more difficult to articulate my reasons for doing so. Our frequent discussions during my senior year in college had a profound effect upon my understanding of the American malady, and his remarkable evolution as a person since that time (1960) was a primary source of inspiration for me during the period when most of these chapters were written. An "invisible man" who was becoming preeminently visible, he represented a perfect target for those powerful and malevolent forces in our society that are unalterably opposed to any black American who seeks freedom. He embodied so many of my hopes for a real cultural pluralism in these less than United States; now that he has been silenced, the loss I feel is immeasurable.

To the above list of writers and teachers I might add a few artists, architects, Charles Ives once again (this time as a composer), and a great many jazz musicians. I came to the blues

---

* Had I come upon the works of Burke and McLuhan before most of this book had been written, I suspect it would have taken a much different shape while retaining the same content. The anecdotal, juxtapositional, fragmented, heavily footnoted style of Burke, and the similar mosaic of aphorisms employed by McLuhan are more in tune with the blues than is the chaptered presentation offered here.

through jazz, with jazz ears and jazz values, and I'm sure that this entrance point has influenced my approach to the material considerably.

A list of all those people who have contributed directly to this interpretation of the contemporary blues world is very much in order and very long, for the special nature of the research has required a high degree of dependence on the cooperation, information, commentaries, and criticisms of fellow students, professors, and of course the blues people themselves.

James Hebel, Calvin Carter, Ralph Bass, the Chess family, Wesley South, Purvis Spann, E. Rodney Jones, Ed Cook, Joe Kotzin, J. B. Lenoir, Cal Cottrell, Mother Ross, Mayne Smith, Freddy King, Billy Boy Arnold, Harold Edwards, McKinley Mitchell, Walt Saveland, John Willis, Sonny Freeman, Elvin Bishop, Willie Dixon, Daniel Scheinfeld, Lonnie Johnson, Al Hibbler, Louis Jordan, Ike Baker, George Rutkowski, Jimmy Witherspoon, Gary Shwartz, Al Braggs, Bobby Bland, T-Bone Walker, Aretha Franklin, Robert and Ariadne Beck, Alan P. Merriam, Helen Sarette, Percy Davis, Esther Newton, Bill Routt, Bishop Dwight Moore, William Henry, B. B. King, Herman Parker, and Stan Karter have all contributed substantially and generously to this undertaking.

I am especially indebted to those people who have taken the time to criticize the first draft of the manuscript: Louis Feldhammer, David M. Schneider, Clifford Geertz, Lloyd Fallers, Linda Wolf, Leonard Meyer, Nat Hentoff, Rodney Vlasak, Mark and Margaret Shaffer, and my indispensable spouse Angeliki.

For the lyrics contained in this book, particularly in Chapter V, and owned by Don Music Company or Lion Publishing Company, Inc., permission was granted for the reproduction of same exclusively for *Urban Blues* by Don D. Robey, President, Lion Publishing Company, Inc., Don Music Company.

For permission to reproduce the song lyrics recorded on Chess Records, grateful acknowledgment is due Mr. Phil Chess of Chess Records.

C. K.

CONTENTS

ILLUSTRATIONS

following page 116

INTRODUCTION

I AM PRIMARILY concerned with an expressive male role within urban lower-class Negro culture—that of the contemporary bluesman.

The terminology of this statement of purpose needs some clarification, for what an anthropologist calls his "conceptual vocabulary" is sometimes labeled "unnecessary jargon" by anyone who is not a social scientist, and might well be considered just plain "signifying" or "off-the-wall jive" by the people I'm writing about. Since I share the points of view of the latter more often than not, my definitions of these terms and others like them that appear in these pages tend to be simple and can usually be taken at face value. For example, urban lower-class people, as far as I am concerned, are those who live in big cities and have very little money.[1]

The term "role" is used here in the conventional theatrical sense for the most part—a person playing the role of Hamlet is supposed to act like Hamlet; a man who calls himself a father, a friend, or a blues singer is expected to act the part or parts. These expectations define each role. An expressive role obligates the person who fills it to express something—the prayer of the

---

1. Some of the implications of urbanism and poverty are spelled out by Louis Wirth, "Urbanism as a Way of Life," *American Journal of Sociology* XLIV (1938), and by Michael Harrington, *The Other America* (New York, 1963).

priest, the joke of the comedian, the composition of an artist. What does the Negro audience expect of a bluesman today, and what does he express for them in his performance?

My attempts to answer these questions in the following pages have forced a confrontation with two problematic fundamentals: Negro culture, and the Negro male. It is the exploration of these components in my statement of purpose and the issues they raise that I would like to emphasize in this introduction.

There are fancier definitions, but essentially a culture is a way of life. In this sense, every individual is a cultured individual. Every child rapidly acquires the language, the eating habits, the religious beliefs, the gestures, the technology, the notions of common sense, the attitudes toward sex, the concepts of beauty and justice, the responses to pleasure and pain, of the people who raise him. These general guidelines for living vary remarkably from culture to culture. What seems pleasurable or just to an Eskimo may seem painful or criminal to me; but once a person has acquired a particular framework of values, beliefs, and attitudes, it is devilishly difficult to modify and impossible to erase entirely. Individuals come and go; cultures remain. To be sure, cultures change—sometimes rapidly—but the process is usually measured, if at all, in generations and centuries.

A basic axiom that underlies anthropological thought is that culture is always learned and never inherited. Anthropologists have long recognized this clear distinction between race and culture. But, judging by the current vocabulary of "race relations," the distinction is still not generally understood. I cannot think of a single respected or self-respecting anthropologist or geneticist who will seriously question its validity. Yet there has been no mass conversion to this principle, no general understanding of its implications; those who have accepted the distinction intellectually sometimes find it difficult to do so emotionally.

The facts on "race" are readily available elsewhere and need not be summarized extensively here. Scientists use the term to denote a shared gene pool—that is, any group of people who breed (exchange genes) with each other more often than they breed with outsiders. Americans, Hawaiians, hillbillies, Asians,

Navahos, Negroes, the inhabitants of most small towns, Catholics, Brooklyn Jews are examples of such groups. Since people who share the same culture or locale are more likely to intermarry, the American race (or any other national gene pool which is in the process of formation) contains a great many genetic puddles and streams. Insofar as we can speak intelligently of a Negro race at all, it is something rather vague and, like the American race of which it is a part, only beginning to take recognizable genetic shape. The scientist's flexible classifications are based upon measurable genetic factors, usually discrete blood and plasma characteristics, since racial classifications based upon appearances have been found to be extremely unreliable. Racists of course employ the latter criteria when they designate groups of people who "look different and act different" as races. This designation reveals a double or compound ignorance for it brings together dubious appearance criteria and totally irrelevant cultural factors—"acting different." This compound ignorance has given firm support to slavery, genocide, imperialism, and all the most hideous crimes of the past few centuries.

I, for one, would like to see the term "race" abandoned altogether and with it the pernicious rhetoric of race relations, racial conflict, race riot, struggle for racial equality, *ad nauseam*. Can a shared gene pool riot? No. Can it relate in any meaningful way to another bunch of genes? No. Nor can races conflict; but cultures can, and in this shrinking world they clash with increasing frequency. Racial equality is an established fact; the struggle is for cultural pluralism.

What are we to make of the "so-called Negro"? The Black Muslim phrase is particularly apropos, for the man called Negro is apparently three men: a genetic man, a cultural man, and a colored man. "Spelled with a capital 'N' by most publications (one of the important early victories of my own people in their fight for self-definition) the term describes a people whose origin began with the introduction of African slaves to the American colonies in 1619."[2] The capital "N" may represent a pyrrhic victory, however, for by insisting upon equality with Caucasians

2. Ralph Ellison, *Shadow and Act* (New York, 1964), p. 262.

(another highly ambiguous category) proponents of the upper case would seem to have further obscured the crucial distinction between race and culture, to the detriment of the latter, as we shall see. There is still a third definition of "Negro" to contend with—the infamous social definition. A man may not fit a geneticist's definition of "Negro"; he may not participate in Negro culture, in fact he may have blue eyes, fair complexion, and a fully developed set of white American middle-class values. Yet American society will still label him "colored" or "Negro" if he has or is rumored to have an African ancestor or two—the proverbial touch of the tarbrush. I don't think it would be pedantic or petty at this point to insist that in the interests of rational discussion we begin to use three different terms in place of the indescriminate (and therefore discriminatory) category "Negro." Perhaps "Negro" best fits the genetic definition, "negro" could be used for the irrational social concept, and in the cultural context "Afro-American" might be considered more appropriate. Since I am writing almost exclusively about cultural matters, I see no reason to force this terminology upon the reader. I would, however, like it to be perfectly clear that I use the term "Negro" in connection with a way of life, a culture, and in no other sense. Note that this usage allows me to include a few so-called white Negroes in my discussion if I care to, while excluding a number of black Americans who identify with the majority culture.

The social definition of the Negro—the fact that he is colored and an outcast—has almost hidden the fact that Negroes have a culture. Twenty-five years ago Melville Herskovits did a rather thorough job of debunking the American myth that "the Negro is a man without a past."[3] Although this myth is still prevalent,

3. Melville J. Herskovits, *The Myth of the Negro Past* (Boston, 1958), p. 2. Much of the myopic ignorance concerning Negro culture and styles that Nat Hentoff and I find so lamentable derives from the premature resolution of a debate between E. Franklin Frazier and Melville J. Herskovits (*The Negro in the United States*, rev. ed., New York, 1957). In his book, Herskovits attempted a thorough comparative study of African-derived cultures in the New World for the insights such a study might provide *vis à vis* "the American dilemma." Unfortunately, Herskovits overstated his case in the area of social organization when he

a much more dangerous revision of it current today is that the Negro has no culture or at least no viable culture worthy of attention. Yesterday's rural Negro may have had something like a folk culture, so the myth goes, but today's urban Negro can be found only in a set of sociological statistics on crime, unemployment, illegitimacy, desertion, and welfare payments. The social scientists would have us believe that the Negro is psychologically maladjusted, socially disorganized and culturally deprived. Others tell us that any Negro way of life that may exist is nothing more than a product of poverty and fear.[4] From an initial assumption that the Negro is only an American, a long

insisted that the matrifocal family, economic independence of women, sexual attitudes, extended kinship patterns, and so on that are found in both contemporary West African cultures and American Negro communities can be seen as evidence of a tenacious, if somewhat generalized, set of familial values that were retained despite slavery. Frazier disagreed completely with this interpretation of the data, and I agree with him in this particular dispute. Slavery, as practiced in the United States at least, obliterated all but the faintest traces of African political, economic, and familial institutions. These aspects of life were rigidly controlled by the white slave masters. On the other hand, basic African predispositions governing religion and esthetics not only survived slavery, but were reshaped, nurtured, and magnified in response to slavery and post-slavery conditions. The facts that support this statement are available in abundance to anyone who will read *The Myth of the Negro Past*. Journalists and social scientists writing about the Negro in the past decade or so have invariably accepted Frazier's refutation of Herskovits' familial theories and have then proceeded to dismiss the rest of Herskovits' painstaking scholarship as well. Therefore, many writers have not even bothered to consult Herskovits' book before labeling the Negro traditionless, cultureless, and made in America.

4. No one can deny these two brute facts of ghetto life, but it is possible to show how a few Negroes have managed to survive and transcend them. I would also like to suggest that affluent white America suffers from spiritual impoverishment and that the suburban child is just as culturally deprived as his urban counterpart. Considering the white anxieties triggered by those unpredictable black forces penned up in the centers of American cities, contemplating the fifty billion dollars poured annually into that monument to terror, the Pentagon, and noting with alarm the growing generation of snipers, bombers, Minute Men, Birchers, and Klansmen, it also seems clear where the designation "culture of fear" belongs.

string of insults and injuries inevitably flows. Remove the assumption, recognize a Negro culture, and many of the alleged pathologies disappear while others become subject to new and difficult verification.

Nat Hentoff writes:

> Not one of the many book reviews I read of Nathan Glazer's and Daniel Moynihan's *Beyond the Melting Pot* took exception to their overwhelmingly ignorant assertion that "the Negro is only an American and nothing else. He has no values and culture to guard and protect." That two such sophisticated social scientists were able to be so myopic is a measure, of course, of how ignorant most of us continue to be about what Ralph Ellison called the Negro American style, or rather, styles. As Ellison persistently points out, the complexity and subtlety of Negro experience in America have produced infinitely more diverse individualities among Negroes than their friends, enemies, and attending sociologists and psychologists have ever recognized.[5]

Ellison's magnificent novel *Invisible Man* and his recent collection of essays *Shadow and Act* establish him in my estimation as one of the most perceptive analysts of Negro culture writing today. Unlike most of the authors considered here, he is well aware of his heritage and the intricate strategies developed by Negroes in an effort to cope with America. Yet even Ellison shies away from Negro culture per se and prefers to speak of "an American Negro sub-culture" or "American Negro styles" with the accent on "American," "styles" and "sub-culture." Some statements from an Ellison essay written in 1958 illustrate this emphasis.

> Thus, since most so-called "Negro cultures" outside Africa are necessarily amalgams, it would seem more profitable to stress the term "culture" and leave the term "Negro" out of the discussion.

> Nor should the existence of a specifically "Negro" idiom in any way be confused with the vague racist terms "white

5. *The Village Voice*, Jan. 7, 1965, pp. 5, 16.

culture" or "black culture"; rather it is a matter of diversity within unity.

> Culturally this people represents one of the many sub-cultures which make up that great amalgam of European and native American sub-cultures which is the culture of the United States.[6]

If Negroes are not the least amalgamated of all Americans, then what is the current struggle all about? The melting-pot tone of Ellison's remarks would lead us to believe that Negro culture is only one minor variation among many on the major American theme. I disagree.

There is an important sense, discussed below, in which the Negro is the most American of all Americans, but I must take strong exception to Ellison's statement that

> Its [the Negro people's] spiritual outlook is basically Protestant, its system of kinship is Western, its time and historical sense are American (United States), and its secular values are those professed, ideally at least, by all of the people of the United States.[7]

These generalizations may have validity when applied to the "black bourgeoisie"[8] and to a cluster of Negro intellectuals, but have little or nothing to do with the vast majority of Negroes living in the Northern ghettos and rural South.

Speaking in tongues, prophecy, healing, trance, "possession," a staff of nurses to assist those "filled with the Holy Ghost," frenzied dancing, hand clapping, tambourine playing,

6. *Shadow and Act*, p. 263.
7. *Ibid.*, p. 262.
8. The Negro middle and upper classes form a special and rather "sick" American subculture according to two highly critical "participant observers." E. Franklin Frazier's *Black Bourgeoisie* (Glencoe, 1957) and Nathan Hare's recent vendetta *The Black Anglo-Saxons* (New York, 1965) do little more than ridicule the middle class as hopelessly trapped and deluded. A more sympathetic and constructive analysis of the difficulties faced by "newly arrived" Negroes, leavened perhaps with some humor, would be helpful and most refreshing at this point, it seems to me.

instrumental groups, fluctuating musical styles, singing-screaming sermons, constant audience participation—these and many other features of Negro church services are completely foreign to the prevailing conception of Protestantism. White Holy Roller churches still exist in many parts of the country, Southern snake-handling cults are occasionally reported,[9] and a few Yale Divinity School students have been dabbling in "glossolaly" recently. But ecstatic communion with "the living God" as practiced in the Negro store-front churches of Chicago is clearly far removed from the staid and stolid Puritanism that has dominated the American Protestant tradition. Significantly, it is only the Black Muslims (approximately twenty thousand in number) and a few other tiny sects who adhere faithfully to the Protestant ethic, and the Muslims are explicitly opposed to all manifestations of traditional American Negro culture (probably the principal reason that their membership isn't closer to the two hundred thousand they claim). The values usually associated with Protestantism—thrift, sobriety, "inner-directedness," strictly codified sexual behavior (better to marry than to burn), and a strong insistence on respectability—tend to be reversed in the Negro cultural framework. Preachers and elderly Negro women love to give these values lip service, but that's usually as far as conventional Protestantism goes.

To say that Negro kinship is Western, Ellison must overlook the most striking feature of Negro social structure—the battle of the sexes. Or, alternatively, he must disregard the essence of middle-class kinship in America—that is, the core concept of marital companionship and the primacy of the nuclear family over all other kinship ties. For the vast majority of Negroes, the battle of the sexes is no mere figure of speech. In the ghetto, men and women are considered to be separate and antagonistic species, and this division "overrides the minor distinctions of creed, class and color."[10] Men are "by nature" primarily inter-

9. Weston LaBarre, *They Shall Take Up Serpents* (Minneapolis, 1962).

10. *The Eighth Generation Grows Up*, John H. Rohrer and Munro S. Edmonson, eds., p. 129. Copyright © 1960 by Harper & Row, Publishers, Incorporated. Reprinted by permission of Harper & Row, Publishers.

ested in sexual satisfaction and independence (money will get you both); they are "strong" sexually, and will take favors from anyone who will grant them. Women are said to be primarily interested in emotional support and their families (money is needed to keep the household intact); they are "weak" sexually, and tend to become attached to one or two men at a time. Men call women self-righteous, money-grabbing, treacherous, and domineering. Women simply say that all men are no good. Relationships between the sexes are usually governed by variations of the "finance-romance"[11] equation that appears in so many blues lyrics. This equation covers a gamut of ties ranging from May-December marriages for security (with a lover on the side for the May partner), through "getting help from my ol' man," to casual, semi-professional and professional prostitution.

The female forces on one side of the battle line consist of units like mother and daughter, sister and sister, niece and aunt, wife and mother-in-law, a matriarch with her daughters and grandchildren. Facing this formidable opposition is the independent Negro male who seeks allies where he can—in the gang, pool hall, blues bar, and barber shop. Moralizing types— Negro women in particular and white Americans generally—see him as lazy, shiftless, and irresponsible. White liberals see him as jobless and demoralized. Norman Mailer[12] portrays him as an existentialist stud, hedonistically at home in a world of violence, drugs, wine, women, and song. Apparently Ellison doesn't see him at all—an invisible man perhaps. However we characterize the anomalous position of the Negro male, he doesn't seem to fit gracefully into a conventional American or Western kinship system. Nor, for that matter, do the basic features of lower-class Negro kinship patterns match well with any non-Western kinship system that anthropologists have encountered. The battle of the sexes can of course be found raging in many slums

11. For a full and excellent discussion of sex role definitions and finance-romance relationships in the Negro community, see Esther Newton's "Men, Women and Status in the Negro Family" (unpublished Master's Thesis, University of Chicago, 1964).

12. *Advertisements for Myself* (New York, 1960), pp. 302–21.

around the world—for example, Athens, Mexico City, Liverpool, Johannesburg—but in most of these "cultures of poverty"[13] the battle tends to be resolved in terms of male authoritarianism rather than "mother-centeredness."[14] The study of lower-class culture (slum culture, culture of poverty, underculture, as you prefer) is in its infancy, and it is hazardous to make comparisons; but it would seem that the Negro male is on the whole farthest removed from both his family of origin —Mama excepted—and his family of procreation. The resultant kinship patterns are different in degree if not in kind from any others.

I do not want to leave the reader with the impression that every Negro is fatherless or that every Negro family is matrifocal, but the patterns sketched above are normative if not normal. That is, working-class or lower-class Negro couples who manage to stick together, as well as families in the emergent Negro middle class, define themselves and their ideals in contradistinction to these well-known ghetto conditions and are, in this antagonistic respect at least, a part of Negro culture. Finally, we can note that every urban culture of poverty is a product of Western industrialization or the beginnings of it, but I don't think that this is the point that Ellison has tried to make.

What about Ralph Waldo Ellison's contention that the Negro's "time and historical sense are American (United States)"? Again I must insist that Ellison speaks for himself but not for the man in the street. The writer-in-residence usually shows up for his literature classes on time. He writes cogent essays relating the past to the present and the future. And he knows that he has two historical traditions to draw upon in his work—the slavery and post-slavery experience of his immediate forebears, and the history in which his namesake Ralph Waldo Emerson played such a prominent part. The black man on the street corner, like most slum dwellers everywhere, lives for the

13. Oscar Lewis, *The Children of Sanchez* (New York, 1963).

14. Compare Lewis' account of the Sanchez family in Mexico with the picture of Rio de Janeiro slums given in *Child of the Dark: The Diary of Carolina María de Jesús* (New York, 1962).

present and tends to drift with events rather than show up for appointments, assuming that he has any. His historical perspective is epitomized in the adage "The white man's heaven is the black man's hell," lyricized so tenderly by the reformed calypsonian and Black Muslim minister Louis X. The heavenly history found in high-school textbooks is mostly meaningless drivel to him, and what he knows of the history of hell he would just as soon forget. To plan for the future is probably futile; Emerson is unknown; and Negro History Week, promoted by middle-class strivers, is a bad joke. His history is American (United States) to be sure, but it is upside down.

The Negro's "secular values are those professed, ideally at least, by all of the people of the United States." The ironic shading of "ideally at least" suggests that the secular values Ellison has in mind are freedom, justice, and equality rather than wine, women, and song. The manner in which these two sets of values coexist and interpenetrate in Negro culture is given some attention in the present book, but I should like to pursue for a moment the notion of freedom, justice, and equality and the related view expressed by many leading authorities that the Negro is the most American of all Americans.

It is certainly true that the traditional American ideals have been given an urgently needed rehabilitation from time to time by a few black citizens audacious enough to blurt out some strong complaints concerning America's long-standing and pervasive hypocrisy. A very small minority within the minority legitimately qualify as most American, I think, when they not only cling to the ideals of the American Revolution but go so far as to act on those ideals in the face of an affluent, complacent populace that, by and large, couldn't care less—throw them a law, a crumb, a prize, or something, 'just get them off the streets! If Negroes try to remind Americans of their spiritual heritage, they also offer an awful parody of the traditional American lust for material possessions. The American status-symbol quest becomes an obsession in the Negro community, where conspicuous consumption—the acquisition of the biggest cars and the flashiest clothes—sometimes takes precedence over adequate food and shelter. Like his fellow Americans, the Negro is addicted to TV, loves baseball, and to a certain extent he even loathes and fears the Negro.

Elkins[15] and many others, including Ellison, have noted the similarities between Negroes in America and the prisoners in a concentration camp who tend to adjust to the brainwashing cruelties and degradations of life there by identifying with the oppressor. They mimic their godlike guards in viewing each other as less than men, and act accordingly. To the extent that Negro culture is a concentration-camp culture—and I am not sure that the analogy is all that valid—the Negro is very American indeed. When so-called Negro spokesmen and white liberals speak of the Negro's Americanness, however, the concentration-camp analogy and ugly facts of slum life are often dispensed with in favor of the dangerous illusion that the Negro is an all-American boy at heart, with a pleasant Protestant outlook and a nice Western kinship system, upholding "our" secular values and sharing "our" sense of time and history.

Almost any Negro in the presence of a white or black bourgeois interviewer or social worker can recite a stream of conventional American values and beliefs without a hitch, halt, or second thought. Yet it is also true that these are rarely the cultural guidelines by which the person reciting them lives. The art of the "put on" has of necessity been developed to an exceptionally high level in Negro culture,[16] and the researcher or leader who reports recited values at face value may be putting us all on twice over.

It is not at all easy to probe beneath the shucking and jiving of Negroes and Negro experts for an unclouded view of Negro culture and man's place in it. My rebuttal to Ellison's generali-

15. Stanley M. Elkins, *Slavery: A Problem in American Institutional and Intellectual Life* (Chicago, 1959).

16. The problem of distinguishing the skillful "put-on" from sincere "wishful thinking" is as important as it is complicated. In either, recited values often conflict with actual behavior. Do the reciters wish to be acceptable citizens, or do they want to push off (put on) agents of welfare colonialism and the white status quo so as to maintain their own way of life undisturbed? I suspect that most urban Negroes have both goals—white acceptance and Negro identity—dimly in view. Question: are these goals incompatible or complementary?

zations, for example, is only a preliminary outline of urban lower-class Negro culture and a slightly lopsided one at that. It could be classified, I suspect, with the grim-reality genre of writing on the Negro problem as exemplified by Charles Silberman's socio-economic study *Crisis in Black and White*[17] and by Kardiner and Ovesey's psychodynamic analysis *Mark of Oppression*.[18] These analysts fail to do what Ellison has done so well. Concerned primarily with the pathological side of Negro life—what whites have done to Negroes—they ignore or obscure what Negroes have done for themselves.

In the late 1940's Abram Kardiner and Lionel Ovesey compiled a thoroughly depressing assortment of psychoanalytic case histories based upon information given by twenty-five residents of Harlem. The individual histories themselves are certainly of value in assessing the impact of oppression upon Negroes in America, but the chapters preceding and following the personal stories are marred by false premises and ignorance of Negro survival techniques. A long concluding chapter on "The Expressions of Negro Personality" dwells on crime and broken homes, devotes a few paragraphs to Father Divine, and overlooks completely such essential forms of expression as jazz, blues, and comedy. The authors' passing comments on folklore, religion, and Negro culture as a whole are indicative:

> He had no culture, and he was quite green in his semi-acculturated state in the new one. He did not know his way about and had no intrapsychic defenses—no pride, no group solidarity, no tradition. This was enough to cause panic. The marks of his previous status were still upon him—socially, psychologically and emotionally. *And from these he has never since freed himself* [emphasis added].[19]

> We have seen little evidence of genuine religiosity among Negroes. They have invented no religion of their own.[20]

17. © 1964 by Random House, Inc., New York.
18. From *The Mark of Oppression* by Abram Kardiner, M.D., and Lionel Ovesey, M.D. Copyright © 1951 by Abram Kardiner and Lionel Ovesey. Published by arrangement with The World Publishing Company, Cleveland and New York. A Meridian Book.
19. *Ibid.*, p. 384.   20. *Ibid.*, p. 385.

> The Br'er Rabbit and Uncle Remus tales are the only remnants of anything that can be called folklore.[21]

> These Spirituals and folk tales do not belong to the contemporary scene, and hence, cannot be used in any way to supplement our study of the present-day Negro personality. Where, then, can we look for such expression?[22]

If the authors had left their offices and gone out into the Negro community, this question as well as a number of omissions and silly assertions might have been avoided.

Charles Silberman, probably the most candid and sensible white American to express himself on "the crisis" in recent years, feels there is little hope for American democracy unless Negroes obtain quality education (particularly at the pre-school and primary-school levels), strong community self-help organizations, and a viable identity. I agree wholeheartedly. Silberman's discussions of Martin Deutsch's revolutionary pre-school program and Saul Alinsky's equally radical self-helping organizational techniques are strong and to the point. But his chapter on "The Problem of Identification" is rather pessimistic and only partly successful, since he too denigrates Negro culture and seems largely unaware of the resources available to the Negro in shaping a positive identity:

> In contrast to European immigrants, who brought rich cultures and long histories with them, the Negro has been completely stripped of his past and severed from any culture save that of the United States.[23]

> Negroes are both more than an ethnic group and less; though their color makes them far more identifiable than any ethnic group, they lack the common history and cultural traditions which the other groups share. The Negro's central problem is to discover his identity, or to create an identity for himself. What history suggests is that when the Negro solves his problem of identity, he will

21. *Ibid.*, p. 340.
22. *Ibid.*, p. 341.
23. Silberman, *op. cit.*, p. 109.

have gone a long way towards finding the means of relating himself to every other American group.[24]

The central problem is not so much to discover or create a new identity as, first, to accept an identity that is already available and, second, to transform into working assets whatever crippling liabilities may be associated with that identity.

Silberman, Kardiner, Ovesey, and many others have neglected that special domain of Negro culture wherein black men have proved and preserved their humanity. This domain or sphere of interest may be broadly defined as entertainment from the white or public point of view and as ritual, drama, or dialectical catharsis from the Negro or theoretical standpoint. By this I mean only that certain Negro performances, called "entertaining" by Negroes and whites alike, have an added but usually unconscious ritual significance for Negroes. The ritualists I have in mind are singers, musicians, preachers, comedians, disc jockeys, some athletes,[25] and perhaps a few Negro novelists as well. These entertainers are the ablest representatives of a long cultural tradition—what might be called the soul tradition—and they are all identity experts, so to speak, specialists in changing the joke and slipping the yoke. An analysis of the Negro's situation in America today, if it is to be thorough and constructive, must take these strategic figures into account.[26]

The entertainment component of Negro culture is significant

24. *Ibid.*, p. 166.

25. I would not contest the usual argument that entertainment channels, broadly speaking, have been the only ones consistently open to Negroes in American society. It is important to note, however, that these ritualized forms developed within Negro culture and were only secondarily, if at all, patronized and appropriated by the American majority. Even when Negroes have contributed to established white American entertainment forms (sports, for example), a distinctively Negro style often shapes or accompanies that contribution. The nothing ball and sucker ball as pitched by Satchel Paige, the base as stolen by Maury Wills, the basket catches of Willie Mays, the antics of the Harlem Globetrotters, the beautiful ritualization of an ugly sport by Sonny Liston and Muhammad Ali—a full list of the symbolic transformations accomplished by Negro magicians in the sporting world would be most impressive.

26. This entertainment-ritual tradition probably does not provide, in itself, a satisfactory solution to the identity problem, and Silberman is

in at least four basic respects. First, it is the one area in Negro life that was clearly not stripped away or obliterated by slavery —the rituals I speak of have an indisputable West African foundation. Second, unlike the immigrant cultural traditions which have been either diluted or dissolved almost completely in the American context, this important cultural legacy linking American Negroes to Africa has not only survived but has thrived on adversity and grown stronger through the years. Third, it is now a full-fledged tradition in its own right. One does not have to be a specialist in African cultures ever on the alert for Africanisms or a psychologist of race relations studiously attuned to the marks of oppression in order to understand a performance by B. B. King, a sermon by the Reverend C. L. Franklin, a Moms Mabley comedy routine, or a John Coltrane saxophone solo. Familiarity (preferably intimate) with contemporary Negro culture and some sensitivity to the particular form of expression in question—music, rhetoric, choreography—are the only basic analytic prerequisites. Finally, and most important, the entertainers are masters of sound, movement, timing, the spoken word. One can therefore find in their performances the essentials and defining features—the very core in fact—of Negro culture as a whole.

The unique and full status of Negro culture is only partly dependent on the basic institutional elements, such as Church and family, that do not fit white American specifications. On another and perhaps more fundamental level, the shared sensibilities and common understandings of the Negro ghetto, its modes of perception and expression, its channels of communication, are predominantly auditory and tactile rather than visual and literate.[27] Sensibilities are of course matters of degree, and

quite correct in stressing the impact of emerging Africa on the Negro's self esteem. But identification with contemporary Africa and the African past must be consciously sought, indeed, created for the most part, whereas the soul tradition is home-grown (with African seeds), already created, and ready to be used. A mixture of indigenous soul and restored ties to West African cultural and historical traditions may ultimately resolve the identity confusion (see Appendix A).

27. To appreciate the many ramifications and implications of this statement, see Marshall McLuhan's fascinating study of print technol-

the sense ratio or "ratio-nality" of a particular culture can't be measured precisely. Nevertheless, the prominence of aural perception, oral expression, and kinesic codes or body movement in Negro life—its sound and feel—sharply demarcate the culture from the irrational white world outside the ghetto.[28] Negro and white Americans share the same general language (superficially a good argument for those who would relegate the Negro to a subcultural corner in homogenized America),[29] but their attitudes toward that language are polarized. In white America, the printed word—the literary tradition—and its attendant values, are revered. In the Negro community, more power resides in the spoken word and oral tradition—good talkers abound and the best gain power and prestige, but good writers are scarce.[30] It is no accident that much of America's slang is provided by Negro culture.[31] Nor is it strange that Negro music and dance have become America's music and dance, a process discussed in the following chapter.

What I have found initially mysterious, however, is the almost universal disregard for the cultural framework that has fostered these forms of expression. Writers, including writers on Negro life, have a vested interest in literacy and the visual world view, to be sure, and some may simply be deaf to the pervasive aural-oral qualities of Negro culture. Then too, real

ogy's impact on the Western world, *The Gutenberg Galaxy*. If McLuhan's thesis is correct, the electronic or post-literate age and its high powered auditory forces that are now upon us ought to give Negro culture a big technological boost.

28. An essay I have written, "Motion and Feeling through Music," *Journal of Aesthetics* (Spring, 1966), considers the kinesic aspect of music and adds a few pieces to McLuhan's "simultaneous mosaic."

29. Englishmen and Americans use the same language, yet references to the American subculture are rare, even in the English anthropological literature.

30. The two writers who have merited most acclaim both served sound apprenticeships: James Baldwin as a preacher, Ralph Ellison as a musician.

31. Approximately 90 per cent of the words that appear in the Sunday supplement slang glossaries can be traced to Negro culture. See also the dialogue in Clayton Riley's "Now That Henry Is Gone," *Liberator* V (July, 1965).

rhetoric and ritual, the pattern and form, heart and soul of Negro expression, are largely unknown in white America.[32] Indeed, the words themselves have taken on decidedly negative connotations—rhetoric: bombastic oratory, trickery, meaningless word play; ritual: dry formality, perfunctory action, unthinking and meaningless behavior. In the literary or typographic world, the labels mere rhetoric and ritualistic are the kiss of death. From this perspective, Negro culture heroes must appear as entertainers at best or at worst as clowns. Finally, a substantial number of influential Americans (politicians, white liberals, the Negro middle class) see Negro culture as a threat, if they can see it at all, for it is bound to make a mockery of hastily legislated integration.[33]

At this point let us look again to the literature on the Negro.

Two studies of the urban Negro have appeared in paperback form recently: *Black Metropolis*, by Cayton and Drake,[34] and *The Eighth Generation Grows Up*, by Rohrer and Edmonson.[35] Both offer a great deal of information on ghetto life in Chicago and New Orleans that the reader may find useful in evaluating and contextualizing the chapters which follow. These studies place justifiably strong emphasis on the cultural difference between lower-, middle-, and upper-class Negroes. The analytic theme of *Black Metropolis* is socio-economic; *The Eighth Generation Grows Up*, following an earlier work, *Children of*

32. A thorough revamping of slum schools along ritualized and rhetorical lines (using the Lancasterian system as a starting point) would do far more to increase student motivation than all the Negro history, Negro contribution, and higher horizon courses combined. What is being taught to Negro children is certainly demoralizing enough, but the typographic manner in which it is being taught is even more destructive. A high degree of literacy should be one goal among many.

33. For the humor involved, listen to Moms Mabley's "Little Cindy Ella" monologue (Mercury LP, MG-20889). Moms' recorded works (at least eight albums) are a singularly rich reservoir of Negro oral expression. When folklorists finally wake up to the fact that the electronic media are making folk of us all, I'm sure this repository of lore will receive the volumes of analysis it deserves.

34. Rev. ed., Vols. I and II (New York, 1962).

35. New York, 1964.

Bondage,[36] uses culture and personality as frames of reference. The two studies complement each other closely. *Black Metropolis* contains an excellent chapter on "The World of the Lower Class" devoted almost entirely to religious activities and attendant values.[37] The case histories presented in *The Eighth Generation Grows Up*, aided by generational time depth and an interdisciplinary approach, are much superior to those found in *Mark of Oppression*, particularly the biographies in which the ramifications of mother-centeredness are elaborated. Again, however, both books treat the entertainment world as peripheral. Drake and Cayton persistently talk about good-timing and pleasure-seeking in the Chicago Negro community, but view such behavior as escapist and nothing more. Rohrer and Edmonson include a ludicrous appendix reporting the statistical frequency of certain psychological variables in a sample of "authentically New Orleanian jazz songs" and "creole folk songs" (no further stylistic specification or sampling criteria given) that must rate as a small but classic example of sterile statistical significance in social science.[38] Nevertheless, these books are indispensable reading for those who want a more complete picture of the existence that nurtures the urban blues.

Rohrer and Edmonson make a sharp distinction between lower-class Negro culture[39] and two shadow cultures: the entertainment world and the underworld. Cayton and Drake are somewhat closer to reality, I think, when they distinguish three extensively overlapping groups within the Negro lower class: "a large group of disorganized and broken families"; "church folk." trying to be respectable; and "denizens of the underworld." "The lines separating these three basic groups are fluid and shifting, and a given household may incorporate

36. Allison Davis and John Dollard (Washington, 1940).

37. The quality of this chapter was an important factor in my decision not to explore the intimate relationship between sacred and secular roles in greater detail.

38. For a book-length classic in the same vein, see Neil Leonard's *Jazz and the White Americans* (Chicago, 1962).

39. Within the lower-class culture they articulate very clearly the opposing value orientations of the matriarchy and the gang.

individuals of all three types."[40] On the basis of my own limited research into lower-class life, I would go further, suggesting that the hustler (or underworld denizen) and the entertainer are ideal types representing two important value orientations for the lower-class Negro and need not be distinguished from the lower class as a whole. Both the hustler and the entertainer are seen as men who are clever and talented enough to be financially well off without working. In this sense, a good preacher can be both a hustler and an entertainer in the eyes of his parishioners and the Negro community at large.

Most ways of making good money without working are illegal, and Henry Williamson has explored many of these ways in *The Hustler*.[41] The most striking thing about his autobiography is not the thoroughly criminal character of his life, from the white American point of view, but that within his culture he is very well adapted, successful (when out of jail), and even enjoys "doin' wrong." Most important, perhaps, "Henry's account is surprisingly free of any signs of racial strife. He wears his Negro image comfortably—neither disgruntled nor proud."[42] Aside from hustlers, entertainers, and rare individuals like Malcolm X (who began his career as hustler) or Reinhardt (the archetypal preacher-hustler in Ellison's *Invisible Man*), few Negroes wear their image in real comfort. Those black men who are comfortable in this sense become logical career models for those who aren't. If we are ever to understand what urban Negro culture is all about, we had best view entertainers and hustlers as culture heroes—integral parts of the whole—rather than as deviants or shadow figures.

Roger Abrahams' aims and techniques in studying Negro folklore are similar to my own in approaching the blues, and, as might be expected, I admire his work immensely.[43] He has

40. *Op. cit.*, p. 600.

41. This is the autobiography of Henry Williamson, edited by R. Lincoln Kaiser, with a commentary by Paul Bohannan (New York, 1965).

42. Bohannan in *ibid.*, p. 215.

43. Roger D. Abrahams, *Deep Down in the Jungle . . . Negro Narrative Folklore from the Streets of Philadelphia* (Hatboro, Pa.: Folklore Associates, 1964).

managed to specify many of the cultural pressures and personal needs that illuminate a limited range of stylized speech forms in a specific community, in this case a Negro neighborhood in Philadelphia. This is a rare achievement and a definite break from the dry and crusty tradition of folklore scholarship. Abrahams persists in yanking texts out of their social context and compiling them, but he for the most part abjures the dissection of archaic forms, and he does concentrate upon cultural processes in his discussion chapters. He lived in the neighborhood, and this fact alone accounts for many of the book's rare qualities.

Abrahams interprets most of the lore he has gathered in terms of the matrifocal complex, the battle of the sexes, and the plight of the disadvantaged, dispossessed Negro male.[44] He argues convincingly that verbal contest skills, good-talking, and word control in general enable a man to play out some of his aggressions and "achieve a kind of precarious masculine identity for himself and his group in a basically hostile environment."[45] Since manhood and the related themes of sex, aggression, control, and identity are basic to any consideration of the blues, the notion of "a kind of precarious masculine identity" and the reasoning behind it deserve close scrutiny.

Much Freudian and neo-Freudian psychological theory has been applied to the predicament of the Negro male. I feel that these applications have suffered from oversimplification and ethnocentrism. Although I do not have much new data to contribute or a full alternative theory with which to subvert the prevailing interpretation of Negro masculinity, I would like to question some of the basic tenets of this interpretation.

Parts of Abrahams' exposition are fairly typical:

> Growing up in this matrifocal system, the boys receive little guidance from older males. There are few figures about during childhood through which the boys can achieve any sort of positive ego identity. Thus their ideas

44. I might add that all the materials were collected from a few men, since the author found the barrier between men and women and the boundaries of alien neighborhoods insurmountable.

45. *Ibid.*, p. 63.

of masculinity are slow to appear under the tutelage of their mothers, and sometimes never do emerge.[46]

Women, then, are not only the dispensers of love and care but also of discipline and authority.[47]

He might, and does to some degree, react against his mother as the authority. But he is emotionally attached to his mother as the source of love and security. This attraction-repulsion paradox is further complicated by the fact that the trauma of rejection is persistently re-enacted for him. He sees his mother sharing herself not only with other children, but also often with numerous men. Finally, rejection comes completely when the boy begins to become the man, and the mother rejects him as a member of that other group.[48]

Having been denied a natural development of his sense of manness, he must constantly prove to himself that he is a man. Throughout most of the rest of his life this will be his major preoccupation, his "fixation."[49]

The spirit of contest . . . is exhibited in nearly every visible facet of the life of the Negro, from gang play to interplay between the sexes to clothes and choice of employment. And through it all the contests are self-defeating because they are never able to give the men a sense of their own identity. They remain throughout most of their lives men *manqué*.[50]

These observations have a certain logical coherence and theoretical validity. Absent or disreputable fathers and loving but authoritarian mothers would seem to foster a formidable set of Oedipal and identity complexities. Indeed, Abrahams' statements are easily related to the aggression and adolescent

46. *Ibid.*, p. 31.
47. *Ibid.*
48. *Ibid.*, p. 32.
49. *Ibid.*, p. 34.
50. *Ibid.*, p. 38.

sexuality that percolate through much of the folklore he gathered.[51] But I take strong exception to the view that lower-class Negro life style and its characteristic rituals and expressive roles are the products of overcompensation for masculine self-doubt. This is simply not true.

To begin with, it is entirely possible that "the Oedipal problem of managing and diverting aggression against the father"[52] may be easily resolved, mitigated, or avoided altogether in families in which the father is absent or weak and where a number of mothering women (grandmothers, aunts) are in or near the household. Even a large set of siblings and a string of visiting "uncles" do not compete for a mother's attention as a potent and omnipresent father might. The "uncles" and other males in the vicinity certainly offer some identity models to a young man growing up, but his sexual development is relatively unimpeded by them.

There is also some evidence which suggests that many Negro mothers do an excellent job of inculcating a strong masculine identity in their little boys at an early age. Esther Newton reports that mothers frequently villify all those "no-good men" and conclude their indictment with the assertion that they are saving all their love and affection for "my little man right here, he's going to grow up and be a real lady killer," in other words, a no-good man.[53] Will Mama reject him when he attains that status, as Abrahams insists? I doubt it. Rather, she will take vicarious satisfaction from the fact that he exploits and mistreats the girls while retaining a basic loyalty to Mama.

The hustling career of "Edward Dodge: Nameless Con," chronicled with wonder and consternation by Rohrer and Edmonson in *The Eighth Generation Grows Up*[54] undermines the logic and theory of those who worry excessively about

51. And most of the lore seems to have been gathered from adolescents.

52. Erik Erikson, "Ego Development and Historical Change" in *Psychological Issues*, George S. Klein, ed. (New York, 1959), p. 29.

53. Personal communication.

54. All the following citations are from pp. 168–85.

Negro masculinity. I would like to include the whole case history here, but a brief summary and a few exerpts must suffice. Edward grew up under classic matrifocal conditions; his mother was on her sixth official husband—a traveling preacher—at the time of the study. She seems to have loved, neglected, and disciplined Edward in random fashion during his formative years. He ran with a gang, spent time in reform school. "At 13 he was having sexual relations 'often' with little girls at school. He started 'doing it,' he says, when he was eight." At maturity, he is a typical hustler, pushing narcotics and apparently using them off and on, in and out of jail, separated from his wife, still living at his mother's flat, leading the fast life.

The authors find him a hopeless case, manifesting masculine insecurity in the worst way:

> Edward has fears about his manliness that seem to be altogether unconscious. Crude defensive methods, such as his beard and the tattoo of a girl's bosom on his chest, are evidences of his conflict about this.

> . . . he sees himself unconsciously as weak and defenseless. He never admits this to himself; rather he idealizes himself as a powerful but misunderstood and mistreated man. He thinks he is a great lover, and even a proper family man, and he maintains this rationalization despite overwhelming evidence to the contrary.

> His morality is external. If he can get away with it, he does it. He is a hedonistic, impulsive man in conflict with a depriving world. He does not understand why this world should not grant him his infantile wishes for a stable of women, a fancy car, and a hundred suits.

> Despite his bravado and assertive masculinity, Edward has never been able to leave his mother, and he has long since internalized her ambivalence towards crime. . . . In his heart of hearts, Edward knows himself to be a failure—weak, nameless, and criminal, and he is unhappy.

Edward's mother, however, sees things very differently:

> Mrs. Burton blames Edward's trouble on bad company and women, explaining that he had to obtain lots of money to be able to entertain his girl friends. She thinks of herself as an exceptionally fine mother, and claims to be proud of her son, but her pride is inconsistent. She praises Edward's accomplishments as a swimmer and boxer, as well as his abilities at outwitting the police, but . . . comments that "jail is just what he needs to straighten him out. . . ." Despite her conviction that women are the cause of Edward's troubles, his mother is exceedingly proud of his prowess as a lover, and delights in pointing out the number of good-looking girls he has had.
>
> The extent of his promiscuous activities can be gauged by the frequent references made to them by his mother and by the pictures of numerous girls in his mother's house. His expensive shirts and suits were proudly displayed to one interviewer by Mrs. Burton. . . .
>
> Edward's mother assures us that he has spent vast sums on whiskey and dope and good times. She is very proud of the fact that he was greatly sought after by the young men and women in his community. Men thought of him as a leader: women were proud to be seen with him.

One incident in particular gives the game away:

> His relation to his current girl friend is similarly structured, and similarly obscure. She also is a nurse, and also proved loyal to him when he was jailed. To some extent, in fact, this girl was able to enlist the cooperation of both Edward's wife and mother in her efforts on his behalf, and remarkably she and his wife shared his attention on visiting days at the jail more or less amicably. Edward expressed no emotion about this girl in any of his interviews, and indicated that he had no expectation

that she would be faithful to him during his prison term. Yet he clearly has some genuine success with women. An even more casual girl friend who worked as a barmaid near his mother's home also tried to help raise money to get him out on bail before his trial.

I don't think there can be any reasonable doubt that Edward's mother, wife, mistress, and assorted girl friends feel that he is a man, and a fairly impressive man at that. Edward thinks so too. Some white middle-class social scientists, enchanted with psychoanalytic theory, disagree. Whose word are we to believe on the matter? Clearly, lower-class Negro culture includes a concept of manhood that differs in kind from the white middle-class definition of a man as a head of a household, who holds down a steady job and sends his kids to college. Measured against this standard, Edward may well be a pathological, amoral deviant with profound psychological problems; but as far as he and his women are concerned, he spends his money freely, dresses well, and is great in bed. That's just the way he is—*a man*—and they like him that way, despite the fact that he's obviously "no good."

Abrahams, like Rohrer and Edmonson, conveniently ignores the culture, and is led to equally disastrous conclusions by the same theory of "masculine self-doubt and ambivalence."

The love-hate ambivalence [toward mother and women generally], on the other hand, is undoubtedly responsible for many of the apparent effeminate traits of this otherwise masculine group. "Don Juanism," the method of hair grooming reminiscent of the handkerchief tying of Southern "Mammies," the importance of falsetto voices in quartet singing, the high prevalence of lisping, the whole "dandy" feeling of dress and walk—all are explicable because of this ambivalence. The "ego ideal" of these men is a confused one; though rejecting women they have accepted unconsciously certain symbols and actions of females.[55]

55. Abrahams, *op. cit.*, p. 33.

All "the apparent effeminate traits" that Abrahams notes are largely figments of his psychoanalytic imagination.

My impression is that those entertainers and hustlers who might be described as Don Juans are simply using their cash and prestige to enjoy a wide variety of women. Although most bluesmen of my acquaintance don't qualify for the supposedly monogamous middle class, they have formed lasting attachments and relationships with their wives; they like to "play around" whenever they can, but are hardly the victims of an insatiable desire to conquer every woman in sight.

The hair-processing techniques that Abrahams finds "reminiscent of the handkerchief tying of Southern "Mammies" are designed to heighten masculinity. Backstage at the Regal Theatre in Chicago "process rags" are everywhere in evidence among the male performers, the same performers who put the women in the audience into states that border on the ecstatic. Prettiness (wavy hair, manicured nails, frilly shirts, flashy jackets) plus strength, tender but tough—this is the style that many Negro women find irresistible. A blues singer is not unconsciously mimicking Elvis Presley's hairdo (the opposite may be true) or Aunt Jemima's when he straightens his hair and keeps it in place with a kerchief. He is enhancing his sex appeal—nothing more.

Falsetto singing comes directly from Africa, where it is considered to be the very essence of masculine expression. The smallest and highest-pitched drum in a West African percussion ensemble or "family" is designated the male drum because its tone is piercing and the role it plays is colorful, dynamic, and dominant. The falsetto techniques of a West African cabaret singer are sometimes indistinguishable from those employed so effectively by Ray Charles, B. B. King, or the lead voice in a gospel quartet.[56]

I have seen no evidence whatever for a "high prevalence of lisping" but "the whole 'dandy' feeling of dress and walk" is

56. I should like to stress again, however, that an Africanism argument may be both relevant and interesting, but it is not necessary to establish this point. If Negro women jump and shout when B. B. King cuts loose with a high falsetto, that is really all we need to know.

again more easily explained in terms of a distinctive masculine style, culturally defined. I see no reason for attributing
such behavior to an underlying love-hate ambivalence toward
women, even if this ambivalence can be shown to be an important factor in other areas of Negro life. Any sound analysis
of Negro masculinity should first deal with the statements and
responses of Negro women, the conscious motives of the men
themselves, and the Negro cultural tradition. Applied in this
setting, psychological theory may then be able to provide important new insights in place of basic and unfortunate distor-
tions.

This is not to say that there are no ambivalent men in the
Negro community or that Negro homosexuality shouldn't be
studied[57]—quite the contrary. But there is an even more press-
ing need for a thorough, extensive, and intimate study of
"normal" lower-class Negroes in a typical slum neighborhood.
Most studies have focused upon abnormal Negroes out of context: those who found their way to the analyst's couch, or
those who were willing to cooperate with inquisitive social
scientists, most of whom were white. It is significant in this
regard that Rohrer, Edmonson, and a large Negro and white
staff found it extremely difficult to get any information from
Edward Dodge, and most of his women and all his male
cronies remained completely inaccessible. James Baldwin's *Go
Tell It on the Mountain*[58] reminds us that some families are
male-authoritarian rather than matrifocal, and undoubtedly
many lower-class households do not fit easily into either cate-

---

57. The nature of Negro homosexuality is a problem that needs to be
explored in depth. A typology of faggots and Lesbians, coupled with the
types of familial organization that tend to promote deviance, might go far
in clearing the haze of illusion and controversy that surrounds Negro
sexuality. I suspect that a surprising number of lower-class Negro men
and women are ambisexual, homo- or hetero- according to circumstances.
I might add that I have noticed a high tolerance of sexual deviancy in
some Chicago blues bars. I would also agree with Gershon Legman (in
Abrahams, *op. cit.*, p. 29) that matrifocality probably produces more
deviancy among daughters than sons. But all these issues need further
study before suspicions will give way to reasonable interpretations.

58. New York, 1953.

gory. The monumental works of Frazier[59] and Myrdal[60] (which need updating) and certain vivid slices of slum life included in *Black Metropolis* and *The Eighth Generation Grows Up* give further indications that the full range, variety, and complexity of day-to-day existence in America's black belts have yet to be fully revealed. It is only when more comprehensive studies of urban lower classes in other countries become available that we will be able to establish more effectively the parts that class, caste, urbanism, and ethnicity have played in shaping Negro culture and the diversity of individuals who are struggling to find identities within it.

Regardless of the forces which have shaped Negro culture, it exists, and within this culture a number of individuals have already found viable identities as men and women. In this respect, the entertainers in general and today's bluesmen in particular are outstanding—they take a firm stance at the center of contemporary Negro culture. If black Americans are to be free and if white Americans are to learn something essential concerning themselves from the Negro's effort to identify himself, a good beginning can be made by attempting to find out what the urban blues are all about.

59. E. Franklin Frazier, *The Negro Family in the United States* (Chicago, 1939).

60. Gunnar Myrdal, *An American Dilemma: The Negro Problem and Modern Democracy* (New York, 1944).

CHAPTER I

AFRO-AMERICAN MUSIC

AFRO-WESTERN MUSIC, as the hyphenated label implies, represents a reflection in sound of massive black and white culture contacts. There are as many Afro-Western idioms as there have been distinctive acculturative situations. In brief, West African music and European folk music are enough alike to blend easily in a seemingly infinite array of hybrids. Or, in Marshall Stearns' words,

> European folk music is a little more complicated harmonically and African tribal music is a little more complicated rhythmically. They are about equal in regard to melody. . . . when the African arrived in the New World the folk music that greeted him must have sounded familiar enough, except for the lack of rhythm.[1]

This statement adequately suggests the general ingredients of any Afro-Western musical style—African rhythm prominent, harmony essentially European, a melodic fusion—but it is important to note that in the blending process the African rhythmic foundation absorbs and transforms the European elements. Analyses of these musical amalgamations have been

1. *The Story of Jazz* (New York, 1958), p. 19. See also chapters i, ii, and iii.

offered by Stearns, the ethnomusicologists Waterman[2] and Merriam,[3] and many others. (My own analytic framework or ethnomusicological point of view is presented in Appendix B.)

In recent years the vigorous hybrids from Africa, Spain, the Caribbean, and the Americas have repeatedly cross-fertilized until the ancestry of any "new" style becomes very complex indeed. For example, the samba tradition in Brazil (itself a complex fusion of Iberian, Indian, and West African elements) is modified by the influx of jazz records from the United States (particularly those of Gerry Mulligan, Stan Getz, *et al.*, whose styles represent another complex synthesis); the resultant jazz samba is labeled "bossa nova," and is in turn picked up by the American jazzmen as a suitable vehicle for improvisation and modified considerably before being redistributed to the world. It is not unlikely that "high life" (itself a synthesis of calypso, European, jazz, and a dozen different indigenous traditions) in Lagos and Accra will begin to show a bossa nova influence; and since high life is just now beginning to interest a few American jazzmen, there is no end in sight to this particular chain.

My only postulate so far is simply that the field of Afro-Western music offers an ideal laboratory for the study of diffusion, acculturation, syncretism, and the emergence, acceptance, rejection of styles through time—all matters of importance to anthropology both theoretical and applied.[4] A few scholars—Herzog[5] and Berger,[6] in addition to the above-mentioned—have

2. R. A. Waterman, "African Influence on the Music of the Americas," in *Acculturation in the Americas*, ed. Sol Tax (Chicago, 1952), pp. 207–18.

3. Alan P. Merriam, "The Use of Music in the Study of a Problem of Acculturation," *American Anthropologist* 57 (1955): 28–34. See also "Music in American Culture," *American Anthropologist* 57 (1955): 1173–81.

4. Alan P. Merriam, *The Anthropology of Music* (Evanston, 1964).

5. George Herzog, "The Study of Folksong in America," *Southern Folklore Quarterly* 2 (1938): 59–64.

6. Monroe Berger, "Jazz: Resistance to the Diffusion of a Culture Pattern," *Journal of Negro History* 32: 461–94.

posed the relevant questions, but few substantial answers have been forthcoming.

In Afro-American music in the United States, three broad subdivisions or genres may be distinguished. In order of stylistic conservatism,[7] these are: sacred music—spirituals, jubilees, and gospels; secular music—blues (country and urban) and most jazz before World War II; "art" music or jazz since 1945. In the past decade a synthesis of jazz, blues, and gospel forms has emerged, and this fusion, "soul music," can be considered a fourth stylistic stream in its own right. Although the blues and the sacred forms are slowly declining in popularity, soul music continues to gain favor among Negroes, particularly with the younger generation. If present trends continue, it may not be long before Negro music will be characterized by the interpenetration of two musical genres: a music of the people (soul styles), and a music for listeners only (advanced jazz styles).

An adequate analysis of any one of the three basic Afro-American genres, whether synchronic or diachronic, cannot be readily divorced from consideration of the other two. In attempting to treat one of the traditions in isolation through time, as in the following chapter (see also Appendix C), I am constantly tempted or forced to point out the areas of overlap. Many blues singers begin their careers in gospel groups, and a few become preachers or gospel singers when the fast life begins to lose its charm. Many blues musicians work their way into the jazz community. Church choir directors are eager to outdraw each other, and try to bring their arrangements up to date by introducing elements from current blues styles. The recent back-to-the-roots trend among many modern jazzmen (one aspect of the soul music resynthesis) has led them to adopt and

7. I hesitate to use the word "conservatism" here, for unlike the music of any conventional Christian church, the sacred music of lower-class Negro churches does not stay put. From month to month and even from week to week new songs may be added and old songs rearranged for maximum impact. It seems clear that when union with a "living God" rather than social status is the motivating factor in church attendance singing styles will change more rapidly. In short, I am not really sure that Negro religious music is much more conservative than the secular forms.

adapt blues, spiritual, and gospel themes for their own purposes. Apparently no shift in one of the three genres takes place without having repercussions in the others. This mutual malleability has been a constant factor—even a defining feature—in any Afro-American style both today and in the past. Harold Courlander, in his recent book *Negro Folk Music, U.S.A.*, makes a similar observation concerning the grass-roots forms of American Negro music that are his special concern.

> But we must recognize that the outer boundaries of some song forms overlap other forms. Some of the criteria established for religious songs apply also to certain secular songs. Worksongs sometimes are recast religious songs. Thematic materials of a certain kind may be found in ring play songs, blues and worksongs. And some musical characteristics are shared by spirituals, gang songs, game songs and blues. Yet these various forms do have elements which, in general, distinguish them from one another.[8]

The Afro-American tradition represents not only a variety of mixtures between European and African elements but a series of blendings within itself.

The flexibility of African cultural systems has been pointed out many times, most commonly in the studies of syncretist religions[9] and perhaps most convincingly in Janheinz Jahn's book *Muntu*.[10] In one art form after another Jahn reveals the African foundation and European overlay—the words in a poem may be English, French, Portuguese, or whatever, but the structure, redundancy, and rhythms usually remain distinctively African. The great flexibility or blending capacity of Afro-American musical forms derives primarily from a rhythmic substructure that can incorporate with ease the most diverse

8. The passage cited is from a review of Courlander's book (New York, 1963) by Frederic Ramsey, Jr., in *Ethnomusicology* 8 (1964): 189.

9. For example, an African may add Christ, Muhammad, the Virgin Mary, and half a dozen saints to his traditional pantheon of gods, assuming that they can't do much harm and may do some good. The most tolerant Christian I know wouldn't even consider reciprocating.

10. New York, 1961.

melodic and harmonic resources. Indeed, jazzmen are constantly on the prowl for new forms to devour, new sources of nourishment, and as a result the world's music is rapidly becoming jazz.

Any attempt to label and define the styles to be found in one of the three main genres while excluding the others in a risky business. The task of placing any individual bluesman (musician or singer) vis-à-vis his forebears, contemporaries, and descendants is still more difficult. Yet if we are to talk about continuities and changes in style, or in culture for that matter, definitions of styles, the placing of practitioners, and perhaps a not completely arbitrary slicing of the continuum are required at some early point in the discussion. (Chapter II and Appendix C represent a first step toward this end.)

The first-step nature of the subsequent classification deserves an explanation. Jazz has been written about extensively; the great bulk of religious music has been ignored almost completely; the blues tradition, thanks to a recent spurt of interest, ranks in an intermediate position, as far as quantity of literature is concerned. Although a number of books and articles have been written about the blues and bluesmen, all the authors without exception refuse to look at, much less discuss, the music as it exists today.

Why this complete exclusion of recent and contemporary blues forms in every treatise on the subject? In trying to answer this question, I find that the men who write books about the blues are often more interesting than the books themselves. Most of these authors exemplify what might be called the "moldy-fig mentality," "moldy fig" being a term formerly used by "modern" jazzmen and their supporters to designate individuals whose interest in jazz was restricted to the prewar period—pre-World War I, that is. Samuel Charters, Paul Oliver, Harold Courlander, Harry Oster, Pete Welding, Mack McCormick—even Alan Lomax until recently—share a number of interests or preoccupations, first and foremost of which is a quest for the "real" blues. The criteria for a real blues singer, implicit or explicit, are the following. Old age: the performer should preferably be more than sixty years old, blind, arthritic, and toothless (as Lonnie Johnson put it, when first approached for an interview, "Are you another one of those guys who wants to put crutches under my ass?"). Obscurity: the blues singer should not have performed in public or have made a recording in at least twenty years; among deceased bluesmen, the best seem to be those who appeared in a big city one day in the 1920's, made from four to six recordings, and then disappeared into the countryside forever. Correct tutelage: the singer should have played with or been taught by some legendary figure. Agrarian milieu: a bluesman should have lived the bulk of his life as a sharecropper, coaxing mules and picking cotton, uncontaminated by city influences.

The writers listed above manifest the moldy-fig mentality in different ways and to varying degrees. Admittedly, their criteria for including a given singer among the "true blue" are slightly exaggerated as listed here. But the romanticizing motive or element *is* omnipresent in blues writing, and the reader must keep this factor in mind when evaluating any book on the subject.

For example, Samuel Charters' best-known work, *The Country Blues*,[11] has a chapter on postwar developments in which the adjectives "crude," "loud," "unsophisticated," "monotonous," and the like are applied liberally throughout. Charters seems to feel that the blues have been diluted and polluted beyond recognition.

> After the war, there were more and more young blues artists who used their new electric guitars at an increasingly high volume. The poorer musicians turned it up to hide their weaknesses and the others were forced to go along.[12]

> The large record companies, within two or three years after the war, had completely lost control of the blues record business. There were hundreds of companies recording blues, many of them Negro owned . . .

11. New York: Holt, Rinehart and Winston, 1959; London: Michael Joseph Ltd., 1960.
12. *Ibid.*, p. 234.

There were long months of insecurity for many of the blues singers and most of the older men were eventually forced into retirement.[13]

The blues have almost been pushed out of the picture; and the singers who have survived at all have had to change their style until they sound enough like rock and roll performers to pass with the teenage audience.[14]

In a paragraph devoted to T-Bone Walker, the greatest single influence on postwar blues before the emergence of B. B. King, Charters says:

T-Bone had grown up around Waxahachie, Texas and had seen Blind Lemon Jefferson two or three times when Lemon was in town or T-Bone was in Dallas. . . . He wasn't much of a blues singer but he was a hard working entertainer.[15]

Charters' comments on an English critic's reaction to a Muddy Waters concert are also revealing.

The critic spent the last half of the concert in the men's room, where the sound seemed a little less shrill. He couldn't hear much of Muddy's singing, but there had been so much din in the stage he hadn't been able to hear much of it anyway. After the refined, sophisticated singing of Brownie McGhee and Big Bill, Muddy sounded a little barbaric, but there was an unmistakable earthiness and vitality in his music.[16]

As for the late Big Bill Broonzy, I wonder why all the blues writers (and Charters is most certainly not the worst of the lot) have failed to notice his terse and logical definition of the field. As reported in *Time*,[17] Broonzy "had short patience with all the folk song curators who insist that a true folk song has to be of

13. *Ibid.*, p. 233.
14. *Ibid.*, p. 240.
15. *Ibid.*, p. 235.
16. *Ibid.*, p. 245.
17. "Folk Singing—Sibyl with Guitar," Nov. 23, 1962.

unknown authorship and come down through oral tradition. 'I guess all songs is folk songs,' he said, 'I never heard no horse sing 'em.'" No neater summary of the present chapter's argument could be found.

English blues concerts afford an interesting opportunity to view the moldy-fig mentality in operation. An affair I witnessed in London featured an array of elderly bluesmen, a few of them quite decrepit; one scheduled performer had just been shipped back to the States with an advanced case of tuberculosis, another's appearance was little more than an exhibition of incipient senility, and some "stars" had all they could do to stave off the effects of acute alcoholism. Aside from a slobbery but impassioned harmonica solo by Sonny Boy Williamson, a couple of numbers in which Howlin' Wolf coerced the dilapidated rhythm section into a more cohesive state, and an all too brief display of artistry by Lightnin' Hopkins, the concert might be best described as a third-rate minstrel show. The same show presented to a Negro audience in Chicago (assuming they could be enticed into watching a parade of invalids in the first place) would be received with hoots of derision, catcalls, and laughter. The thousands of Englishmen assembled for the event listened to each song in awed silence; the more ludicrous the perform-ance, the more thunderous the applause at its conclusion. Even a good blues presentation, yanked out of context, seemed inane. Sonny Boy's usual blues-bar "shuckin' and jivin'" echoed into a void; "Who's the pastor in this here church, huh?"—silence. Howlin' Wolf's performance style—stalking around, rolling his eyes, lunging to and from the microphone—so appropriate to the boisterous atmosphere of a Chicago lounge, made him look like an awkward Uncle Tom. The high point of the evening came when Willie Dixon, the bulky bassist, picked up an unamplified guitar and sang his own ballad on peace, love, and brotherhood in the dulcet Appalachia tones of Joan Baez. The applause was deafening and justly so. Considering this utterly sincere ballad, specially composed for the occasion, and the hundreds of lyrics Dixon has created for his fellow bluesmen—rich in hyperbole, humor, astute sexual metaphors, current slang, and tailored to fit each singer's personality and audience perfectly—I could not help feeling genuine awe in the presence of genius. The concert was brought to a fitting conclusion by the goateed German promoter and master of ceremonies, who noted cheerfully: "These boys just love to play the music; that's all they do, day and night. And, ah, you can be sure that there are lots of empty bottles backstage (laughter). Well, we hope you've enjoyed hearing the boys play as much as the boys have enjoyed playing for you." Applause. Curtain.

Having illustrated the moldy-fig mentality, I have yet to suggest an explanation for the phenomenon. In part, it is simply a semi-liberal variant of the patronizing "white man's burden" tradition that has shaped white attitudes toward Negroes for centuries. Somehow a "we-know-what's-best-for-them" or "we-know-what's-best-in-their-music" attitude helps to alleviate some of the oppressive guilt that many whites cannot help feeling. There is an honest and laudable interest in alleviating Negro suffering or at least to make it known to the world in every blues book, Paul Oliver's *Blues Fell This Morning*[18] being a notable example. Yet I can almost imagine some of these authors helping to set up a "reservation" or Bantustan for old bluesmen; it is often that sort of liberalism. There is also an escapist element in these writings. By concentrating on old-timers and scorning today's blues as commercial or decadent, the writer can effectively avert his eyes from the urban ghetto conditions that spawn the contemporary forms. Similarly, the idealistic undergraduates who flock to a folk blues concert at the University of Chicago are not particularly interested in slum conditions, but can be overheard at intermission discussing last summer's crusade in Mississippi or a forthcoming church reconstruction project somewhere in the Deep South. It is so much easier to reminisce with old bluesmen, collect rare records, and write histories than it is properly to assess a career-conscious singer, analyze an on-going blues scene, and attempt to understand the blues as a Chicago Negro in 1966 understands them. A corollary factor here is historical respectability.

18. London, 1960.

A coarse lyric of thirty years ago has poetic qualities and historical interest; much the same kind of lyric of today is considered frivolous and not worthy of scholarly attention.

Among those who write professionally about music—any music—there is often a feeling of ambivalence or inferiority, a not unfounded notion that only those who can't play music write about it. With Afro-American music, the compulsion to be participating rather than observing is particularly strong; it is simply that kind of music. I suspect that there is great vicarious satisfaction to be derived from discovering and "resurrecting" a blues singer, a satisfaction surpassed only by finding for him a new (invariably white) audience. It's the next best thing to playing the music oneself.

In all fairness, it must be admitted these writers are performing a valuable service when they document, as best they can, the history of the blues and explore its rural resources. A book like Oliver's with its 350 examples of blues lyrics or Charters' most recent anthology of lyrics[19] performs a most useful service. Still, a serious sin of omission has been committed, and anyone who is interested in contemporary blues expression is left largely to his own devices.

One book that stands in a class by itself is *Blues People* by LeRoi Jones,[20] playwright, gadfly, music critic, poet, "the Allen Ginsberg of black nationalism." Unlike the other authors mentioned above—outsiders looking in from a slightly peculiar perspective—Jones is a Negro and takes the stance of an insider looking out. This stance or ethnic pose is certainly more help than hindrance as he sets about proving his thesis that "the one peculiar referent to the drastic change in the Negro from slavery to 'citizenship' is his music." For example, the wild speculations, inconsistencies, misinformation, and absurd arguments that run through his early chapters on blues prehistory should not be immediately discounted as sloppy scholarship but taken, rather, as a new and interesting "myth of the Negro past." The ideological coloring and manifesto prose of the remaining

19. Samuel Charters, *The Poetry of the Blues* (New York, 1963).
20. New York, 1963.

chapters rarely get in the way of the author's good sense, but usually give just the right cutting edge to his incisive observations and hypotheses.

Once Jones begins to grapple with more recent history and can sink his chops into some hard facts, the ethnocentric perspective yields some major dividends. He does a thorough and excellent job of pointing up the ironies of white and Negro musical interaction, and his commentaries on ragtime, minstrelsy, Paul Whiteman, and cool jazz are especially telling. His documentation of the avocational, vocational, commercial, and mechanical stages of various styles as they passed from Negro culture into the culture of white middle-class America—the "mainline" culture, he calls it, borrowing a suggestive term from the heroin addict's argot—is really superb. Probing the schism between the black bourgeoisie and the black masses as reflected in their musical expression, he is equally subtle and informative. In fact, once Jones replaces myth making with reality testing, stimulating ideas follow one another at an accelerating pace that culminates in a masterful final chapter on jazz developments since the war and a consideration of the rebellious avant-garde jazz clique in New York City.

Unfortunately, in his eagerness to demonstrate his point that "Negro music is always radical in the context of formal American culture," Jones inadvertently joins the moldy figs in neglecting the contemporary blues scene and the vital musical role played by the fundamentalist Negro churches during the past few decades. (New York's young jazzmen are certainly radical enough, but they play exclusively to a tiny, predominantly white audience, and the blues people couldn't care less about them.) Although it is a fact that every contemporary blues singer, with perhaps a few exceptions, has received the bulk of his musical socialization in the church and sees little or no conflict between the secular and sacred musical traditions, Jones seems to feel that gospel and blues are worlds apart. He dismisses the church as a force in Negro life: "With the legal end of slavery, there was now proposed for the Negro masses a much fuller life *outside* the church. There came to be more and more backsliders, and more and more of the devil music was heard." Yet there are still at least forty store-front churches for every joint where blues or jazz is played in Chicago, the blues capital of the world, and the influence of gospel music upon blues and jazz has increased year by year since about 1955. Further, there is no discussion whatever of the current big three in blues singing—Ray Charles, B. B. King, and Bobby Bland— or the relation between their music and today's blues people.

Why these basic omissions once again? The downgrading of the Negro church probably reflects an understandable but misdirected Marxist-Freudian disgust with "the opiate of the masses," but the absence of a contemporary blues chapter is rather mysterious. Just possibly Jones wants to keep the "best" music, something of a blood ritual in his eyes, a big, deep, dark secret from his white readers. There are also strong indications that he has picked up some folkloristic values along the way, as when he characterizes "rhythm and blues" (his stylistic desig-nation for B. B. King, Jimmy Witherspoon, T-Bone Walker, and the like) as "a less personal music than the older blues forms, if only because the constant hammering of the over-whelming rhythm sections often subverts the verse, the lyrics, the lyric content of the blues. And too, rhythm and blues, it seems, is more easily *faked*, and only a few of the shouters seemed to be able to vary the mood or mode of their perform-ance, or for that matter, to alter their public image as *perform-ers*."[21] "Folk artists" are valid; "performers" are inevitably suspect. This passage, and many more like it, are but one step removed from the pejorative tone that Charters and the others take on whenever they survey what has happened to the good old blues. The most likely cause of Jones' negligence, however, is probably that he was born and raised in a middle-class Newark, New Jersey, household, and that his exposure to the blues has been less thorough and intimate than he would have us believe and that the ethnic pose is at rock bottom exactly that—a pose.[22]

21. *Ibid.*, p. 172.
22. Perhaps I should both mollify and amplify this accusation slightly with two brief but relevant comparisons. Jones' more recent anti-white tirades and plays have stirred up some needed controversy but lack power

Some remarks Jones directed to the New York "radicals" in a *Down Beat* article reinforce this view.

> All the young players now should make sure they are listening to the Supremes, Dionne Warwick, Martha and the Vandellas, the Impressions, Mary Wells, James Brown, Major Lance, Marvin Gaye, Four Tops, Bobby Bland, etc., just to see where the contemporary blues is. All the really nasty ideas are right there, and these young players are still connected with that reality, whether they understand why or not. Otherwise, jazz—no matter the intellectual bias—having moved too far away from its most meaningful sources, and resources, is weakened and becomes, little by little, the music of another emerging middle class.[23]

With the exceptions of Bobby Bland, James Brown (a great performer if ever there was one), and possibly the Impressions, the singers listed by Jones all peddle variations on the so-called Detroit Sound engineered by Berry Gordy for the massive teenage audience, Negro and white. They appear frequently on those joyous and wholesome television shows *Shindig* and *Hullabaloo*, and this is not exactly "where contemporary blues is," in my opinion. Are "all the really nasty ideas" really there? Diana Ross, lead vocalist with the Supremes, contends: "It's less wild than most of the big beat music you hear today, but it still has feeling to it. We call it sweet music." "Sweet" and

when compared to the pro-black statements of Malcolm X. There is, I think, an important difference between a man who burns up hatred as a fuel and one who parades and peddles the stuff as art—the pragmaticist who holds some things sacred, and the polemicist who finds all things profane. They are perhaps equally capable of dramatizing the terrors and atrocties that currently sustain the "American way of life," but the man who can diminish some of the terror as he exposes it is at a premium. Similarly, men like John Coltrane and Ornette Coleman who attain a certain hard-won serenity through their musical struggles should perhaps be differentiated from musicians like the late Eric Dolphy, whose scrambling, strident, and sometimes brilliant improvisations sounded like those of a driven man looking vainly for solid footing. Like Dolphy, Jones has often produced more fury than sound.

23. *Down Beat* 32 (March 25, 1965): 34.

"nasty" are not necessarily contradictory terms, as used by Negroes, and most Negroes would agree that all these performers have "soul," that is, the ability to communicate something of the Negro experience. The bands of Bland and Brown do have something to offer the avant-garde jazzmen, and the Vandellas have done some "tough" things; but the Detroit sound is a soft-spoken, refined, polished soul music for the most part; the lyrics are usually pleasant, sometimes innocuous; the supporting beat is firm, simple, four to the bar, and highly danceable. Ironically, the Detroit sound is the one Negro-produced style that comes closest to being "the music of another emerging middle class," and a culturally integrated American middle class at that, at least to the extent that white teenagers are committed to it.

Doubts about Jones' ethnicity aside, the general theme of his book—the shifting attitudes of Negroes toward America as seen through the emergence of musical styles—is one that has never before been handled in such detail and with such compassion. Although he does not use the concepts, Jones is really writing about a complex sort of nativism or, more accurately, a musical revitalization movement. Negro music, since the days of the first recordings but especially during the last two decades, has become progressively more "reactionary"—that is, more African in its essentials—primarily because the various blues and jazz styles are, at least in their initial phases, symbolic referents of in-group solidarity for the black masses and the more intellectual segments of the black bourgeoisie. It is for this reason that each successive appropriation and commercialization of a Negro style by white America through its record industry and mass media has stimulated the Negro community and its musical spokesmen to generate a "new" music that it can call its own. In every instance the new music has been an amalgamation of increased musical knowledge (technically speaking) and a reemphasis of the most basic Afro-American resources. This appropriation-revitalization process deserves careful study by anthropologists and ethnomusicologists, because it has largely determined, I think, the present shape of American popular music. *Blues People* not only offers a preliminary analysis of this process but gives us the clearest picture to date of the esthetic ideology that molds the musical explorations of America's leading Negro musicians.

Ralph Ellison, reviewing *Blues People*,[24] praises Jones for spelling out "his assumptions concerning the relation between the blues, the people who created them and the larger American culture," but goes on to voice his disagreement with those assumptions. Although I am primarily interested in the relation between the blues and the people who are creating them today, the Jones-Ellison exchange of views prompts me to make more explicitly a few of my own assumptions concerning Negro music in the larger context.

Ellison argues accurately, but for all the wrong reasons, that American music is American Negro music. From the same review, "Thus, Jones' theory to the contrary, Negro musicians have never as a group, felt alienated from any music sounded within their hearing, and it is my theory that it would be impossible to pinpoint the time when they were not shaping what Jones calls the mainstream of American music." Or, further along in Ellison's line of reasoning, "But his [Jones'] version of the blues lacks a sense of the excitement and surprise of men living in the world—of enslaved and politically weak men successfully imposing their values upon a powerful society through song and dance." Negroes did not impose their values upon white America via song and dance; the song and dance, and just possibly an attendant value or two as well, were appropriated by white America via the white-controlled music business (record companies, music publishers, radio stations). The examples of this process are legion, and the alienation felt by Negro musicians, resulting largely from this process, is very real. Benny Goodman rose to fame on Fletcher Henderson's arrangements, Elvis Presley derived his style from the Negro rhythm-and-blues performers of the late 1940's, Peggy Lee "covers" (the music-business term for a copy or appropriation) many of Ray Charles' most popular songs. And of course the rocking Prince Valiant types from England are notorious plagiarists. These are only a few convenient examples among

24. *Shadow and Act* (New York, 1964), pp. 247–58.

thousands. The Negro innovators in blues and jazz are well aware of this pattern. To greater or lesser degrees they all resent it and, most important, they respond to each appropriation, as Jones has indicated, by reexpressing American Negro identity and attitudes in a new revitalized way.

This revitalization invariably involves a synthesis of new technical resources and a restructuring of the old mazeway. Jazzmen fall back on the blues and reshape it periodically; bluesmen, as we shall see, insert more and more elements from church music into their playing. Jimmy Smith has brought a jazz technique to the electric organ and molded a percussive style so basically rooted in Afro-American tradition as so far to defy any white imitators, though his fellow "soul brothers" Jack McDuff and Jimmy McGriff have succeeded in pushing the style still further back to the roots. Much of the apparent Africanization of contemporary jazz is, however, due to natural evolution rather than to the resurrection of older styles. Elvin Jones and the other percussion virtuosos of contemporary jazz certainly did not learn how to approximate West African polymeter by listening to the simple meter of New Orleans marching bands. Rather, in attempting to create a maximum amount of swing, jazz drummers have inevitably worked toward the crossed triplet rhythms of West Africa. A little less than twenty years ago when bebop was reaching a culmination in Dizzy Gillespie's big band, Gillespie recruited Chano Pozo, a *lucumi* (Yoruba) cult drummer from Cuba, to give his orchestrations a solid African foundation. Other band leaders quickly followed suit. Afro-Cuban rhythms have been an important part of jazz growth ever since and have recently been creeping into rhythm and blues as well. For example, Mongo Santamaria's version of *Watermelon Man*, *Que Será Será* by the High Keys, and the many records that grew out of the dance craze known as "Watusi" all had an Afro-Cuban flavor.

The examples of stylistic revitalization are as common as the instances of appropriation on the other side of the equation. It is simply incontestable that year by year, American popular music has come to sound more and more like African popular music. The rhythmic complexity and subtlety, the emphasis on percussive sound qualities, the call-and-response pattern, the characteristic vocal elements (shout, growl, falsetto, and so on), blues chromaticism, blues and gospel chord progressions, Negro vocabulary, Afro-American dance steps—all have become increasingly prominent in American music. If empirical evidence is wanted, simply turn on the radio or television or sample the best-selling records of the day and you will be immersed in the results of the appropriation-revitalization process.

In light of recent and current events in American music, it looks as if this process may now be entering its final cycles. Once gospel music has been brought to white nightclubs and tambourines have been passed out to patrons at the door, it would seem that there isn't much left to be appropriated. Jazz musicians, sensing that the Afro-American resources (in the United States) have now been thoroughly explored, reintegrated, and appropriated, are turning with increasing frequency to Africa itself and to other ethnic traditions as well for revitalizing force. The incongruous sight of society folks performing dance steps that were developed generations ago in sharecropper's shacks and slum ballrooms can also be taken as a harbinger of universal acceptance.[25] How long will it be before someone compares programs like *Hullabaloo* and *Shindig* to the West African puberty rites they so closely resemble? I suspect that a West African villager viewing *Hullabaloo* for the first time would be delighted to see that Western men and women have at last cast aside the disgusting and lascivious practices of

25. Killer Joe Piro is the remarkable Manhattan dance instructor who played a major role in bringing mambo, meringué, and other subversive Afro-Latin dances to high society a decade ago. Nowadays he is bringing the jet set down to earth with traditional Harlem choreography.

"All that hip movement. . . . It's got new names but you know they were doing that at the Savoy Ballroom in Harlem when I was 17. Remember that boogie-woogie shuffle stuff Cab Calloway used to do? Harlem was doing the Twist 30 years ago and didn't know it. Negroes and teenagers, that's where these new dances come from. . . . I watch them and steal a lot of their stuff. Sometimes I have to clean it up. A little 16 year old can get away with wiggling her hips while her hands are on the back of her head. It's cute. But when I teach it to a 40 year old divorcée I'll keep her hands a little bit lower, just over her shoulders." (*Saturday Evening Post*, March 27, 1965.)

embracing, hugging, shuffling, and grappling in public and have adopted the vigorous, therapeutic pelivc exercise that has always been the pride and joy of his community. Each woman dances for herself and with the other women. Each man demonstrates his strength, agility, and endurance. The musicians are unflagging in their support, though their rhythms are crude by West African standards, and a good time is had by all. The style of the ritual might seem rather mechanical, frantic, and contrived to this "alien" observer, but he would be satisfied that Americans have made some progress, are moving in the right way and in the right direction. If this hypothetical West African reaction is at all accurate, we can infer, I think, that the appropriation-revitalization process has entered its final phase.

It is also worth noting that the white copies of Negro originals show greater skill, sensitivity, and fidelity than ever before. The young Chicagoans Paul Butterfield and Elvin Bishop are well on their way toward mastering the rough city blues idiom typified by Muddy Waters and Howlin' Wolf, much as the young Chicagoans Bix Beiderbecke, Eddie Condon, George Wettling, and friends learned the New Orleans jazz style brought to the Windy City by King Oliver and Louis Armstrong almost fifty years earlier. The popular Righteous Brothers specialize in blue-eyed soul music that is almost indistinguishable from its model, brown-eyed gospel music. Listening to the "big beat" radio stations, I find it increasingly difficult to separate white and Negro performers, largely because many Negro stylists have eliminated some of the coarser qualities from the blues and gospel styles they draw upon for material while a number of white performers have perfected their handling of Negro vocal accent, inflection patterns, and phrasing.

The case history of *Little Red Rooster* is revealing. Howlin' Wolf's original rendering of Willie Dixon's intriguing lyric was strong musically but weak commercially; it is doubtful if more than twenty thousand copies of it have been sold. The late soul singer Sam Cooke did a somewhat more relaxed and respectable version of it, with an organ accompaniment and slightly altered lyrics, that probably sold at least four times as many copies. An English group, the Rolling Stones (the name probably inspired by a Muddy Waters blues *Rollin' Stone*), adhered closely to the original, replete with bottle-neck guitar techniques, and the song became an international hit (sales of more than 500,000). As LeRoi Jones has noted, "They take the style (energy, general form, etc.) of black blues, country or city, and combine it with the visual image of white American nonconformity, i.e., the beatnik, and score heavily. These English boys . . . have actually made a contemporary form, unlike most white U.S. 'Folk singers' who are content to imitate 'ancient' blues forms and older singers, arriving at a kind of popular song, at its most hideous in groups like Peter, Paul and Mary."[26] The moral of the representative *Little Red Rooster* anecdote is simply that it no longer takes much doctoring by commercially oriented Negro singers or clever white imitators to make a ghetto style palatable to a mass audience.

The ever expanding white audience (and here we may include Europeans, Russians, Latin Americans, Japanese, and a substantial number of middle-class American Negroes, too) has been so well conditioned by forty years or so of successive appropriation (and dissemination to the world) that the latest Negro style is no longer dangerous or controversial but eagerly swallowed up in original or slightly diluted form. Howlin' Wolf, known to one white American in a million ten years ago, can now be summoned by the State Department to appear at a Washington festival of the arts and very few eyebrows are raised.[27]

Ellison is perfectly correct in asserting that Negro music has

26. *Down Beat* 32 (March 25, 1965): 34.

27. Judging by the visceral reaction of some Republican Senators to a a "soul music" television program promoted by the Office of Economic Opportunity and entitled "It's What's Happening, Baby!" Negro music is still considered dangerous and decadent in some quarters. Senator Dirksen reported that some of his colleagues "thought it was depraved." Said Senator Gordon Allot of Colorado, "For 1½ hours the intelligence of the public was insulted. . . . If I were a Communist, I would ask for nothing more than to show this film in underdeveloped countries. . . . [The program] made me want to regurgitate." One man's "soul" is still another man's "poison," it seems.

become America's music, and Jones is equally cogent in stressing that Negro music represents the solidarity, the attitudes, the identity of Negro Americans. Thanks to Jones, we have a somewhat better idea of the revitalization aspect of this over-all process. Why whites (excluding a few Senators and their constituents) should consistently appropriate Negro styles as they develop is less clear. Perhaps we might tentatively pair compensation-congruence with appropriation-revitalization. Although Negro musical styles seem to match or reflect current life styles, the demand for Negro-like music on the part of whites, usually of the younger generation, as in the eras of swing and rock and roll, seems to indicate a perceived or felt deficiency of some sort in the American mainstream that the recurrent adoption of Negro or Negro-derived musical expression helps to remedy. The needs of young white Americans to reject and rebel, to dance and blow off steam, have often been cited in connection with various musical fads and crazes, the Beatles (and other British groups) being the latest case in point. Marshall McLuhan's thesis that the Western world is visually lopsided and sorely in need of audile-tactile stimulation is relevant. Norman Mailer's "The White Negro" also provides some potentially useful clues as to the nature of the attraction that Negro music has for many whites. But the motivations involved are complex, and require more attention than can be given here. Were this problem to be explored in some depth, Ray Charles would provide the ideal focus point. Not only does his music embody all the essentials of the Afro-American tradition, but it has been accepted intact by a large mass of white listeners, despite the aforementioned "refinements" of his work offered to the public by Peggy Lee and others. In Ray Charles we have the rare instance of an artist who has enjoyed wide popularity among whites, but still retains the avid appreciation of the blues people. Bobby Bland may be moving into the same sort of position; and B. B. King, though he rejects the possibility, may find that his blues style will in time win for him a substantial white as well as Negro audience.

CHAPTER II

BLUES STYLES: AN HISTORICAL SKETCH

THERE ARE as many definitions of style as there are lexicographers, archaeologists, art historians, music critics, and estheticians. Two anthropological sources on the subject which have achieved a reputation for clarity and simplicity are Meyer Schapiro's essay "Style" and A. L. Kroeber's book *Style and Civilization*. Schapiro states at the outset of his piece, "By style is meant the constant form—and sometimes the constant elements, qualities and expression—in the art of an individual or group."[1] After examining the welter of definitions given for "style," Kroeber concludes: "However, all the more central usages of the word refer first to form as against substance, manner as against content. Second, they imply some consistency of forms. And third, they may suggest that the forms used in the style cohere sufficiently to integrate into a series of related patterns."[2]

These definitions are sufficiently universal, simple, and concise. In keeping with their general import the emphasis in the following discussion falls upon the outer clothing of the blues, the "qualities and expression," "manner as against content." In

1. In *Esthetics Today*, ed. Morris Phillipson (Cleveland and New York, 1961), pp. 81–113.

2. *Style and Civilization* (Ithaca, 1957) p. 4.

speaking of a musical style generally, the analyst is usually well advised to concentrate on form, structural regularities, syntactic rules. Indeed, blues and non-blues can easily be distinguished in these terms. It is also possible to differentiate the rural antecedent blues forms from later phases of development on these grounds. The simplest criterion for classification has turned out to be timbre or texture; the manner in which a given piece is orchestrated invariably identifies it as belonging to one substyle or another. Structure is a useful concept for making gross distinctions, but it is textural variations—voice qualities, instrumental accompaniments—which most clearly define a specific blues style and which make any generic definition of the blues extremely difficult to formulate with any precision. In addition to structure and texture, contextual variables, usually geographic, often play a supplementary role in the classification (Appendix C). In Chapter III, below, some lyric content evidence is brought forward further to support the broad divisions between country, city, urban, and soul versions of the blues.

Holding the textural dimension in reserve as a source of subclassifying distinctions, I shall first define the blues structurally in terms of its characteristic chorus, harmonies, rhyme scheme, and chromaticism. A blues chorus or verse usually falls into a 4/4 twelve-bar pattern, divided into three call-and-response sections with the over-all rhyme scheme of A A B. Occasionally this basic verse unit is contracted to eight bars or expanded to sixteen or even twenty-four, but most recorded blues renditions are based upon this twelve-bar sequence. Typically the singer delivers a line or two in iambic pentameter over the first eight or nine beats, filling the remainder of the four-bar melodic phrase with complementary instrumental figures that usually lead into a word-for-word repetition of the first stanza, sometimes punctuated at the beginning or end with an exclamation like "yeah," "Lord have mercy," "I said"; the third stanza resolves in some way the thought reiterated in the first two stanzas. There is something like a double dialectic to be found in many blues renditions: on one level every sung or spoken phrase is balanced or commented upon by an instrumental response that often carries as important a message as the preceding words. Following this interaction the blues chorus can be divided into six parts or overlapping vocal calls and instrumental responses.

On another level the three vocal stanzas, the statement, its repetition, and the resolution also have a dialectical quality, for a blues lyric rarely proceeds in a narrative fashion. Usually each phrase consists of a fairly simple and concrete image, a trope or Negro idiom of some kind that stands for a complex set of associations and connotations. For example, the phrase "the eagle flies on Friday, and Saturday I go out to play" conjures up in a Negro listener's mind a multitude of activities associated with payday and the pleasures of Saturday night. In the urban blues lyric from which this phrase is extracted, the singer goes on to narrate his prayer for mercy on Sunday, but the concluding phrase, especially in a country blues, might just as well be more disjunct, as, for example, "But I'm sure, baby, you don't mean me no good anyway" or "Well, the sun's gonna shine in my back door someday." In other words, there are many stock phrases in the blues tradition plus slogans of the day that can be played off against each other to illustrate a particular theme or create a general mood. This mood may be sustained throughout the song or shifted from chorus to chorus. Because of the vocal-instrumental dialogue in connection with relationships to be found in the lyric itself, the rhetoric of a single performance can become very complex indeed.

The harmonic pattern underlying this typical twelve-bar structure is:

1	2	3	4	5	6	7	8	9	10	11	12
I				IV		I		V (IV)		I	
Tonic				Subdominant		Tonic		Dominant		Tonic	

A subdominant chord substitution in the tenth measure occurs in almost all non-country blues. Other substitutions of this kind are found with increasing frequency along the folk-urban continuum until in some contemporary blues and in a great many modern jazz renderings of the blues form there is a chord change or a shift in chord voicing with every measure. For some jazz modernists this profusion of chords has become cumbersome, and modes or scales with a blues feeling have been used as a foundation for improvisation. Likewise, in the most "primitive" blues forms a one- or two-chord harmony or drone may sometimes be found.

This blues feeling derives largely from "blue" notes, supposedly "the third and seventh scale degrees which are used either natural or flatted, and which are frequently played deliberately out of tune."[3] The phrase "out of tune" here has misleading connotations, and it is not at all clear that the third and seventh degrees of the scale are the only points where blue notes can be found. The flatted fifth is often referred to as the heart of "funk," soul, or blues feeling, and it has even been said that blue notes can be found in all the cracks between the keys of the piano. The flatting or bending of thirds, sevenths, and fifths into quarter tones is part of a general defining feature, difficult to specify concretely, that may simply be called blues chromaticism.[4] It is this characteristic more than any other that unites the single-chord drones and the vocal moans of John Lee Hooker and Blind Willie Johnson on the primitive end of the blues spectrum with the modal improvisations of Miles Davis, John Coltrane, and other leaders of the jazz avant-garde.

In speaking of the tonal blends, twists, slides, and dips that every blues artist uses, I am moving from structure to texture, from abstract formal prototypes to concrete idiosyncratic qualities of sound. Before I trace the shifts in texture and structure chronologically, two brief statements of the obvious are necessary to complete a preliminary definition of the blues. In terms of context, blues are performed largely by Negroes and for Negroes throughout the South and in the urban North, and usually in a bar, theater, or ballroom environment. In terms of content, most blues lyrics provide the listener with a poetic yet starkly realistic look at relationships between the sexes.

A great many exceptions and qualifications will be made for

3. Willi Apel, *Harvard Dictionary of Music* (Cambridge, Mass., 1961).

4. A short but knowledgeable discussion of "blue notes" by Martin Williams can be found in *Downbeat*, June 20, 1963.

the above generalizations as differences in texture, structure, context, and content are discernible from bluesman to bluesman, area to area, and from one point in time to another. The folk-urban continuum mentioned above refers of course to Redfield's[5] well-known ideal types. Rather than describe the features of each ideal pole, I consider it more efficient and informative to summarize the changes that occur in blues styles from old to contemporary patterns, from the rural South to the urban North and West. The following list of style changes, the diagnostics employed in classification, and the historical sketches of various stages of development are based largely upon casual and unsystematic listening to the odd assortment of blues records at my disposal and interviews with some of the most important blues innovators. The picture presented is rough, not definitive, and represents nothing more than a preliminary ordering of the confusing array of individual styles. In the following chapter I will evaluate the forces at work upon the creation of these styles.

Some of the basic changes that occur in blues styles through time and space are the following. More instruments are used, and the role of each instrument becomes more specialized. Volume and density increase proportionately, especially as first guitar, then bass, and finally harmonica become electrically amplified and public address systems are introduced. Beginnings and endings of songs become more clearly defined, standardized, and instrumental as opposed to spoken (with the recent introduction of gospel effects, endings are sometimes faded to avoid an overt "Amen" ending). A broader spectrum of tempos is found, and the tempo selected is more rigidly maintained. Structure is similarly affected—that is, a broader variety of structures develops (a slight increase in the use of eight-, sixteen- and twenty-four-bar patterns and much greater use of tags, codas, breaks, vamps, and other contrastive sections, analogous to what jazzmen call the bridge or release in standard popular tunes), and these formulas are adhered to without the deviations commonly found in older country blues

5. Robert Redfield, "The Folk Society," *American Journal of Sociology* 52 (1947).

singing, where a beat or two or occasionally whole measures may be dropped from or added to a chorus as the spirit moves. Vocal calls and instrumental responses overlap more obviously. Vocalists begin using a vibrato that tends to become broader. Diction becomes clearer, and voice tones have less nasalization. Singers make greater use of melisma (more than one note per syllable), especially in recent years since the gospel influence on blues singing has become more marked. Singers adopt an identifying shout or cry to climax a song or emphasize a key phrase—for example, Howlin' Wolf's howl, Cleanhead Vinson's "inaudible" falsetto, B. B. King's clear falsetto, Bobby Bland's hoarse cry. There is an increasing emphasis on lyrics that tell a story as opposed to the country practice of stringing together phrases linked only to a very general theme or emotional state.

All these trends would be relatively clear-cut except for the fact that the first blues were recorded in the city (1920) and in a relatively standard form, bordering on a formula. Samuel Charters has given us an accurate picture of the first commercial tin-pan-alley blues productions. A series of women, starting with Mamie Smith, turned out one standardized blues after another. "The accompaniment was usually played by a pianist who accompanied a great many singers," although other instrumentalists were sometimes asked to supply what were then called the "paragraphical phrases." "There were thousands of these blues, the early 'city' blues, recorded and their popularity left a deep impression on the more varied forms of the blues being developed in the rural South."[6]

Charters goes on to describe how record companies in Chicago, the Paramount label in particular, began recording rural singers when they discovered that their mail-order sales were growing in the South. It is difficult to understand exactly what Charters means by the deep impression the early city blues made upon the rural South. Although most Southern singers were certainly aware of the standard pattern, few of them seem to have found it worth emulating, at least during the first fifteen

6. *The Rural Blues: A Study of the Vocal and Instrumental Resources*, RBF Records, Album No. RF 202.

or twenty years after the initial recordings about 1920. Nor does Charters explain why most of the early city or "classic" blues singers were women. The closest thing to an adequate explanation of this initial female dominance in the field of recorded blues is found in LeRoi Jones' book:

> There were several reasons why women became the best classic blues singers. Most of the best known country singers were wanderers, migratory farm workers, or men who went from place to place seeking employment. In those times unless she traveled with her family it was almost impossible for women to move about like a man. It was also unnecessary since women could almost always obtain domestic employment.[7]

Negro women have nearly always been ahead of Negro men in seeking out steady work as domestics and as highly paid night club singers. According to the American mores, it is permissible for white men to be tantalized sexually by Negro women. A Negro man with sex appeal or singing songs with sexual overtones—blues or blues-based material—poses a threat and has only recently been permitted in white night clubs. Although La Vern Baker, Aretha Franklin, and other female singers whose styles are largely church-derived and blues-oriented can work in supper clubs at a high salary, the leading men in the blues world cannot. In other words, much the same sex-economic factor that put a number of Negro women in the spotlight for the first recorded blues now makes it difficult to find a single woman singing blues for a living today[8]—more money can be made elsewhere.

7. LeRoi Jones, *Blues People* (New York, 1963), pp. 91–92.

8. There are few blueswomen around; Mama Thornton and Koko Taylor come to mind, and Big Maybelle is still quite popular. But the latter-day Bessie Smiths can't seem to find the modern style or the contemporary woman's point of view that might get their careers off the ground. There are a number of girls who "could sing blues if they would." Esther Phillips is one of them; Sugar Pie De Santo is another. Little Miss Cornshucks made an amazing album about five years ago (Chess LP 1453) and hasn't been heard from since. Etta James can put more bump and grind into a lyric than any woman alive. Aretha Franklin

The maintenance of rural blues characteristics by rural blues singers in the face of a standardized urban model is not at all surprising. A number of factors contributed to the use of a blues formula in the early city recordings, none of which was present in rural contexts: the three-minute limit of a recording; a desire by performers and record companies to make the blues more "musical" and more familiar or predictable to the widest possible audience; the belief, still held by record company executives, that if one song is a hit a series of records in the same pattern will also make money.

In the rural South, blues singers are usually found in three principal contexts: singing for their own satisfaction and the enjoyment of their immediate family, friends, cellmates in prison, or patrons at the local bar; blind and disabled bluesmen singing in the streets for tips; singing for picnics, barbecues, and dances. Particularly in the first two situations, it is desirable to stretch out each song to the limit. A singer is likely to work his way into a piece slowly via a spoken narration that puts the song in context and his listeners in the mood while he simultaneously retunes his guitar or runs through a few chords. In the course of the song he is likely to add a measure or two to his choruses and "fool around" a bit with the beats between stanzas, thus squeezing a maximum duration from each selection. When such a singer is placed before a microphone with bass and drums accompanying him, invariably such liberties with the structure confuse the accompanists, usually urban musicians accustomed to standard forms. In the "citified country blues" recordings of John Lee Hooker or Lightnin' Hopkins, bass players can be frequently heard shifting their harmonic lines and drummers reversing the beat in their attempts to match the freer forms of the soloists. These records illustrate the principal distinguishing feature of country blues—it is performed by one man accompanying himself, usually on guitar, and as a consequence the "style" is marked by wide diversity and structural deviations. The fact that the country blues is usually a one-man

is great and manages to sound like Aretha even when she is trying to be Patti Page or Nancy Wilson. However, none of these women can really be considered counterparts to the urban bluesmen.

show also helps to account for the broad variety of vocal tones and ornamentations used by a singer to decrease the monotony of his presentation.[9]

The third country context must be regarded as an important phase of blues evolution. In appearing at dances or outdoor affairs like picnics, barbecues, and fish fries, blues singers often found it a help to add one or more instruments for a fuller sound. Even playing by himself for a dance, a bluesman could not take liberties with the tempo and long spoken introductions were largely superfluous. Additional instruments further restricted the amount of structural variation possible but certainly did not eliminate the addition or subtraction of beats and measures entirely, since most picnic ensembles were composed of men intimately acquainted with each other's stylistic idiosyncracies.

Mack McCormick, the Texas blues collector, writing about the sixty-three-year-old rural singer Mance Lipscomb, gives us a clear picture of the musician's role in this context or phase of the blues as well as Lipscomb's own evaluation of the standard city blues form of the period.

> On a subsequent visit Mance talked about other songsters of his generation and described the vital part they played in the life of the communities to which they were bound by church, blood, segregation, heritage, and common circumstances. These men did not think of themselves as blues singers. They were singers whose employment was often to provide music for dancers and thus they thought of its rhythms, not its poetic structure. Thus, to Mance, the ballad *Ella Speed* is a breakdown; the work song *Alabama Bound* is a cakewalk; the bawdy *Bout a Spoonful* is a slow drag. For the most part he thinks of "blues" as a particular slow-tempoed dance that became fashionable around World War I. But of the form, the expression, and the content of the blues, he says, "That was old when my daddy was young. But so far as what was *called* blues, that didn't come till round 1917. One of the first pieces that was

9. See *The Rural Blues*, RBF Records, RF 202.

strictly a blues was *Blues in the Bottle*. What we had in my coming up days was music for dancing and it was of all different sorts."[10]

Interestingly, the young Negroes coming up today still tend to designate musical forms according to the many dance steps that are done to them. Unfortunately, scant attention has been paid to this consistent dance orientation in Negro music, and the categories or labels used by the performers themselves are rarely reported by the blues collectors.

Three geographical regions and three cities are of primary importance stylistically: the Delta, the Territories, the Southeastern seaboard; Chicago, Kansas City, and Memphis. The Delta and hill country of Mississippi and, to a lesser degree, the rural sections of Alabama have produced a wealth of bluesmen, most of whom have migrated north to Chicago, often via Memphis. The Territories—Texas and the adjoining sections of Louisiana, Arkansas, and Oklahoma, plus Missouri and points west—is in many ways more stylistically significant than the Delta. The Southeastern seaboard—principally Georgia and Florida—is probably the least important and least distinctive stylistically, although it has produced some influential bluesmen.

Singers from Mississippi—for example, Muddy Waters, J. B. Lenoir, Jimmy Reed, Little Walter, Howlin' Wolf, John Lee Hooker—rarely move beyond the city phase. The distinguishing features of Delta country blues—drones, moans, the bottleneck guitar techniques, constant repetition of melodic figures, harmonica tremolos, a heavy sound and rough intensity—are usually intensified in the city context.

In contrast to the Mississippi texture, the Texas country blues tradition has usually emphasized a somewhat lighter touch; guitar playing tends to be less chordal, with an emphasis on single-string melodic dexterity; more relaxed vocal qualities and an open rather than a dense accompaniment texture prevail. These descriptive phrases are imprecise and hence inadequate,

10. Mack McCormick, "Tradition Rediscovered," *Rhythm and Blues Magazine* 4 (1964): 14–15.

but no blues singer with whom I have talked has been able to specify the differences between Mississippi and Texas styles except in terms of heavy versus light, dense versus open, although almost all agree that more distinct differences exist. Pete Welding, in a comprehensive article on "The Art of Folk Blues Guitar,"[11] describes the regional variants with the following adjectives: Mississippi—"fragmentary" lyrics, "narrow melodic range," "rudimentary vocal expression," "only slightly removed from speech patterns," "heavily rhythmic," "rough," "clamorous," "stark," "harsh"; Texas—"deliberate," "sophisticated," "higher, clearer voice," "supple," "lean, open, long-lined sound," "refined"; East coast—"harmonically oriented," "easy, infectiously lilting swing," "sweet," "consonant," "smooth," "rich," "fully ordered," "finely wrought." The reader can supply his own adjectives after listening to a sample of recordings by the more representative stylists from these areas. (See "Blues Outline," Appendix C.) Nor should one overlook the many exceptions which prove or disprove the "rules": Mississippi John Hurt, whose name is very misleading; Blind Willie Johnson, a Texan who "ought to be" from the Delta; the rough and tough renderings of East-coaster Peg Leg Howell.

The blues has always been a migratory music. First, it was carried by men roving from town to town and from job to job; later it was disseminated by medicine shows, circuses, and other touring troupes in the South; in the 1930's and 1940's it spread via the itinerant Territory bands; today it is brought to the people by touring package shows, like those of B. B. King, Bobby Bland, and Jr. Parker. When these musical migratory patterns are juxtaposed to the population migrations accompanying the two world wars, from the Delta to the North, and from the Territories to the West coast, the tracing and classification of blues styles become very complex indeed. The constant redistribution of all the more popular blues styles by the mass media increases this complexity still further. For example, one of the most popular blues singers in Texas and the West coast area at

11. *Downbeat*, July 1, 1965.

present is Jimmy Reed, a Chicago city bluesman with Mississippi roots. His style is extremely relaxed, which may account for his appeal in Texas and on the West coast.

In spite of the accumulation of blues styles existing side by side and the increasing homogeneity of the blues during recent years, it is possible to discuss the lines of development leading to the formation of today's modern or urban blues.

Texas and the Territories are the wide open spaces in more ways than one. Although some of the most important developments in jazz, blues, and American music as a whole took place in this area, it has been explored in detail only by the jazz historian Franklin S. Driggs,[12] who restricts himself to a listing of names and dates. The key men of the swing era and the golden age of jazz (Bennie Moten, Walter Page, Alphonso Trent, Troy Floyd, Jesse Stone, Hot Lips Page, Count Basie), the seminal figures in what came to be known as bebop (Buster Smith, Tommy Douglas, Lester Young, Charlie Christian, and Charlie Parker), the leaders of today's jazz avant-garde (Ornette Coleman, Don Cherry, Charlie Mingus, and many other young men whose families migrated from the Territories to Los Angeles), the originators of modern or urban blues and its more commercial offshoots rhythm and blues and rock and roll—all were Territory men.

The refinements leading to urban blues are best viewed in terms of three phases: the period from 1925 to 1942 chronicled by Driggs—that is, the time when big bands of eight pieces and larger toured the Southwest playing blues in arranged form, an era culminating in the Kansas City florescence; the period from 1942 to 1952 when similar bands toured the same terrain usually featuring a blues singer, electric guitar, saxophone solos, and an even stronger emphasis on rhythm and blues; and what might be called the Memphis synthesis, or the foundation of today's urban blues.

Before the folding of the Pendergast regime in 1938 Kansas City was a wide open town and consequently a mecca for blues and jazz musicians in the sourrounding states. In the bands that

12. "Kansas City and the Southwest," in *Jazz*, ed. Nat Hentoff and Albert J. McCarthy (New York, 1959), pp. 191–230.

played the clubs and casinos of the city, jazz and blues styles became so tightly fused that the musicians themselves usually made no distinction between the two fields. Jimmy Witherspoon and Al Hibbler, two currently active singers who began their careers in Kansas City with the Jay McShann band, still see blues and jazz as one entity. The outstanding blues singers of this period (Jimmy Rushing, Joe Turner, Walter Brown) sang with either big bands or boogie-woogie pianists. They developed what LeRoi Jones and others call a "shouting" style, but characteristics besides volume are equally important in discussing the changes that Kansas City blues singers wrought in the tradition. All the best singers were big men with big chest-tone voices, but a heavy vibrato was also an important feature of the style; still more important, the featured singers with big bands began to make greater use of jazz phrasing, placing their lyrics behind the beat or in front of it rather than right next to it. In a recent discussion with Joe Scott, musical director and trumpeter with Bobby Bland's organization, this distinction seemed to be of paramount importance in separating older blues singers from the moderns.

> There's a strong-beat blues where the words are right on the beat, and then you can do it the way "Spoon" [Jimmy Witherspoon] does it, taking your time, pausing and then catching up with the band. As far as I know, Spoon was the first to phrase that way.[13]

Or from Witherspoon himself:

> If I'm working with a band that doesn't know me I won't take liberties, because they're liable to think I've messed up someplace—lost a chord or something. But as soon as I'm sure they know enough to hold on to the chords, I may wait a couple measures or longer with some lines, to make my point.

13. Actually Witherspoon is a postwar Kansas City singer; Rushing and the original K. C. shouters should probably be credited with introducing jazz phrasing.

Many of the singers from the Kansas City phase were not instrumentalists, but relied upon a reed or brass player for responses to their vocal calls. Saxophonists in the McShann band, which once included Charlie Parker, provided the foil to the singing of Walter Brown, Al Hibbler, and Jimmy Witherspoon; many of the instrumentalists in other bands came to be almost as well known as the vocalists they were paired with—trombonist Dickie Wells with Jimmy Rushing, pianist Pete Johnson with Joe Turner. Even singers who had an instrument to play—Louis Jordan, Cleanhead Vinson, Hot Lips Page—would usually let some other instrumentalist fill in behind their vocals. These essential aspects of Kansas City blues singing are found in the styles of urban blues artists today. Bobby Bland, for example, is a big man with a big shouting voice, uses a vibrato judiciously, and, since he himself is not an instrumentalist, uses Joe Scott on trumpet, his guitar player, or a tenor saxophonist in the responsorial role. Kansas City blues singers like Rushing and later exponents within the idiom like Witherspoon are today normally grouped with the jazz community. Witherspoon is low man on the bill at a Regal Theatre blues show in Chicago but is a featured performer at the Monterey Jazz Festival, whereas Rushing has worked only in a jazz context since the 1940's. The modern blues style that these men epitomize was transformed and remolded after the war.

Once again it is Texas and the surrounding states that nurture the new style, but this time all roads seem to lead to Memphis. During and after the war the best-known singers from this area were Smokey Hogg, Peppermint Harris, Floyd Dixon, Amos Milburn, Charles Brown, Roy Brown (not related to each other), T-Bone Walker, Gatemouth Moore, Lowell Fulson, Percy Mayfield, Louis Jordan, and Pee Wee Crayton. Other singers like Cleanhead Vinson, Jimmy Witherspoon, Joe Turner, Wynonie Harris, Arbee Stidham—carriers of the Kansas City shouting tradition—were also appearing in the South and Midwest at the time. Many of these men had records that sold more than a million copies to an almost entirely Negro market—a market that came to be known as rhythm and blues.

The bands these men traveled with were usually dominated

by tenor saxophone and electric guitar, along with string bass, piano, drums, and rarely a trumpet or trombone. The presence of the electric guitar or sax as a responsorial voice, the continued use of a string bass, and the absence of trumpets and brass are the defining features of the accompaniment in the most popular records of the period. It was essentially this sound that set the stage for Elvis Presley, Fats Domino, Bill Haley, Bo Diddley, Chuck Berry, and the other rock-and-rollers during the 1950's.

Although Wynonie Harris, Joe Turner, the Browns, and Percy Mayfield exerted considerable influence in the late 'forties and early 'fifties, T-Bone Walker and Louis Jordan seem to have had the greatest impact on their fellow bluesmen. Jordan, born and raised in Brinkley, Arkansas (about sixty miles from Memphis), is an interesting figure who helped shape the contemporary urban blues style in a number of ways. Primarily a jazz musician earlier in his career, he toured the country as part of the Earl Hines and Billy Eckstine *Blue Ribbon Salute* shows in the early 1940's. Many of the members of these progressive bands (notably Dizzy Gillespie, Charlie Parker, Art Blakey) went on to reshape jazz into an art music during the be-bop revolution, but Jordan decided to remain an "entertainer." "Those guys, except Dizzy, who's the master, the king, really wanted to play mostly for themselves, and I still wanted to play for the people. I just like to sing my blues and swing." The Tympani Five, a tightly knit "jump" band that Jordan formed during this period, backed up the leader's skillfully paced assortment of humorous patter, searing saxophone solos, and remarkably sly and witty blues lyrics, many of which are still featured in the repetoires of singers like Jimmy Witherspoon, Lou Rawls, and Ray Charles. Foreshadowing Ray Charles, Jordan managed to reach a substantial white audience with his diverse talents. He established the saxophone as an integral part of the standard blues ensemble, pioneered in the use of the electric organ (when Wild Bill Davis joined the group), and set high professional standards for the rest of his colleagues to match. At the same time, T-Bone Walker's guitar technique was far in advance of his competitors; when combined with a distinctive voice and a flair for showmanship, his style provided the model for Lowell Fulson, Pee Wee Crayton, the young B. B. King, and many others. At the peak of his popularity T-Bone used a larger band[14] with a brass section and arrangements strongly reminiscent of the Kansas City days. He and Louis Jordan stand as the most important links between Kansas City and Memphis.

Memphis has always been the meeting place for bluesmen from the Delta and the Territories and a center of blues activity. It was here that W. C. Handy began to publish instrumental versions of the blues (usually blues songs in title only) as early as 1912. The Memphis jug bands, prominent during the late 'twenties and early 'thirties, represent another of the transitional phases from country to city, and have been well documented and discussed by Samuel Charters.[15] The city's name also brings to mind Memphis Minnie, a fine post-classic blues singer and formidable guitarist,[16] and Memphis Slim, a gifted lyricist and singer who has been singularly successful in keeping the classic piano-accompanied blues up to date.

Although not a Memphis musician, LeRoy Carr was born and raised in Nashville, Tennessee, not far away.[17] He recorded with guitarist Scrapper Blackwell between 1928 and 1934, and his thoroughly citified and sophisticated blues style was immensely popular; in many ways the Carr-Blackwell recordings foreshadow the Kansas City florescence. Along with guitarist Lonnie Johnson, a thorough musician and technician from St. Louis, Scrapper Blackwell's single-string lines helped clear the way for the first electric guitarists, Eddie Durham and Charlie Christian of the Kansas City era. Carr's songs were used by Basie and Rushing in the late 'thirties; on some early record-

14. Imperial LP's 9210 and 9098 contain examples of T-Bone and his band at their best.

15. *The Country Blues*, pp. 107ff.

16. Bill Broonzy, in his autobiography (*Big Bill Blues: William Broonzy's Story as Told to Yannick Bruynoghe* [London, 1955]), recalls the time he was bested in a blues contest with Minnie but got the last laugh when he ran off with the bottled prize.

17. According to Charters, Carr learned his blues in Nashville and vicinity. According to Duncan P. Schiedt (notes to Columbia LP 1799 *Blues before Sunrise*), Carr's formative years were spent in Indianapolis.

ings, Basie and his rhythm section do two of Carr's blues that show the influence of Carr's piano style as well. Many of today's bluesmen—B. B. King and Jimmy Witherspoon, for example—credit Carr and Blackwell as being two of the first modernists in the field.

After World War II, Memphis became a blues center second only to Chicago. Although older singers in Chicago were for the most part maintaining the country and city traditions in the bars and clubs of the South Side, a younger group of men in Memphis were in the process of creating the blues style that is most popular among urban Negroes today. Johnny Ace, Gatemouth Moore, and Roscoe Gordon were the first major talents; Ace in particular rode the rhythm-and-blues trend to a peak of popularity climaxed by his Russian roulette suicide in 1954. (Gatemouth Moore, by that time Reverend Moore, preached at his funeral.) Ace and Gordon sang in a smooth, polished style similar to the more recent work of the pop blues singers (see Appendix C), and provided inspiration for the younger generation of blues singers coming up in the late 'forties and early 'fifties, especially B. B. King, Bobby Bland, and Jr. Parker.

Born and raised in Mississippi, B. B. King came to Memphis in 1948 as a disc jockey.[18] Bobby Bland, a Memphis boy, was an avid listener and beginning a career before he was drafted in 1952. About the same time Jr. Parker, across the river in West Memphis, Arkansas, started singing professionally while still in his teens, recording first for the Sun label in 1953. B. B. King's first big record, *Three O'Clock in the Morning*, brought him wide recognition in 1950. Although I have interviewed these three men within the past year, I am still confused about developments in Memphis during this period, largely because none of the principal innovators is eager to re-examine the "wild oats" phase of his career. Jr. Parker's comment is typical: "I can't really tell you much about the other blues singers in those days, but I can remember a whole lot of good telephone numbers from my little book."

18. Coincidentally, that same year, Chester Burnett, the Howlin' Wolf, left Memphis, where he had been a disc jockey and performer for some time, and migrated to Chicago.

Putting together various comments from interviews with these singers and examining some of their earlier recordings, I find it possible to reconstruct a general picture of the disparate sources from which these men shaped a new blues style. B. B. King brought to Memphis an intimate knowledge of Mississippi blues styles. His father and a cousin were semi-professional bluesmen, and he was most impressed with the singing of Dr. Clayton and the guitar playing of Elmore James. He also feels that Blind Lemon Jefferson and T-Bone Walker, foremost exponents of Texas country and urban blues styles respectively, were influential early in his career. Add to these influences Django Reinhardt, the French jazz guitarist of Gypsy background, and Samuel McQuery, featured soloist with a gospel group, the Fairfield Four, and we can see that B. B. King's style has a most complex foundation. During his disc-jockey years, when he was developing his performing talents as a sideline, B. B. was in a position to hear almost every blues and non-blues record released between 1947 and 1950 and to select from these recordings the type of music that his radio listeners wished to hear. This intensive and extensive exposure to a broad variety of musical styles must have had considerable effect on the formation of his own style and repertoire.

Bobby Bland credits the gospel singer Ira Tucker of the Dixie Hummingbirds with giving him some key pointers on phrasing; the bluesmen he first tried to copy were Roy Brown (Texas), Lowell Fulson (Oklahoma), and especially B. B. King. Jr. Parker also gives Roy Brown as his first model, but feels that B. B. King is the best and most respected representative of the blues tradition today. Parker insists, however, that most singers make too much of the connection between blues and gospel, and that many who claim to have served their apprenticeship in gospel groups are only saying what they think the interviewer wants to hear. He is quick to admit, however, that although he has never sung gospel professionally he can sing hundreds of religious songs from memory. I think the references made by King and Bland to Sammy McQuery and Ira Tucker can be taken at face value. Although their earlier records are devoid of the more obvious qualities in Negro religious music, gospel is certainly part of the synthesis; in Bland the gospel component has become increasingly prominent since the late 1950's.

The added accompaniment elements in the new style are brass instruments, electric bass, and technical improvements in the electric guitar that enable a player to sustain notes at full volume for longer periods of time. (B. B. King's expressive phrasing—hit a note, hold it, bend it, quiver it, and slide to the next note—would be impossible without this technical assistance.) Trumpets, and perhaps a trombone, give power and a variety of timbre lacking in the earlier city and urban styles excepting of course the Kansas City period. The compact electric bass provides a louder and more sustained harmonic underpinning to arrangements, and permits greater flexibility in the use of other instruments. The usual droning saxophone section background to a vocal becomes superfluous if both electric bass and guitar are present; hence the saxes can be used with greater discretion by an arranger.

All these changes from folk to urban blues have taken place. With the emergence and maturation of B. B. King, Jr. Parker, and Bobby Bland we have the models for nearly all contemporary blues forms.

CHAPTER III

FATTENING FROGS
FOR SNAKES?[1]

LOOKING OVER the preceding historial sketch of blues developments, I think it is possible to offer some tentative explanations, turning first to Aristotle. In terms of the four types of causation distinguished by Aristotle it is possible to show, I think, that a type of "formal cause" is at work. Although the first blues singers obviously had no planned development of their musical expression in mind, many estheticians will agree that incipient forms of a style almost preclude certain further developments and encourage others. This generalization certainly holds for the structural aspect of blues, in that the A A B verse form and I, IV, I, V, IV, I harmonic foundation have been standardized, elaborated, and perfected along lines that might have been predicted from listening to the original rural practitioners. Material cause enters at the instrumental or textural level: the expansion of accompaniment

1. The chapter title is borrowed from a blues lyric of the same name in which Sonny Boy Williamson draws the line on further exploitation:
> It took me a long time to find out my mistake.
> It took me a long time, a long time to find out
>   my mistake. It sure did, man.
> But I'll betcha my bottom dollar, I'm not fattening
>   no more frogs for snakes.

resources and the electric amplification of instruments have had a profound effect upon style through the years. The transition from gutbucket to string bass to electric bass and the effect of these shifts on ensemble timbre are but one example among many of material causation at work. In speaking of "efficient cause," Aristotle had in mind, I believe, the immediate agency or energy needed for the production of the effect. Although it distorts the concept somewhat—record company executives are certainly not the immediate agents of blues production—it is nevertheless true that artist and repertoire men, radio stations, and other commercial interests have been most energetic in reshaping blues styles through the years. In this chapter I would like to assess, if possible, the efficiency of these secondary agents and corporate powers in supplying the demands of the blues audience. The "final causes" of blues development and change in style are of course the predispositions and needs of the blues audience.

Rather than attempt to weigh these causes immediately, let me simply paraphrase Aristotle's well-known dictum "The house is there that men may live in it; but it is also there because builders have laid one stone upon another." The blues exist because some men feel called upon to address themselves to certain basic problems in song and because these songs meet a cultural demand; the blues exist also because record companies and radio stations have delivered one song after another to the public in an effort to make as much money as possible.

Some insight into the nature of the final cause is afforded by an examination of the changes in lyric content, a variable conpsicuously absent in the foregoing discussion, that occur from one major style to another—that is, from country to city to urban to soul music. Even a superficial examination of blues lyrics reveals certain obvious thematic shifts.

In *Blues Fell This Morning* Paul Oliver quotes more than three hundred different blues, nearly all of which are on the country or folk pole of the spectrum. Every conceivable aspect of Negro life is exemplified in one blues or another—mules, boll weevils, highways, trains, boxing, prisons, hurricanes, floods, bloodhounds, lawyers, chauffeurs, Pearl Harbor, fire departments, cities, rivers, gambling, beer, whiskey, voodoo, sex.

Oliver has selected the broadest diversity of topics; his narrative is built around the lyrics, and he wants to show the all-inclusive nature of blues poetry. The point is that he has an extremely wide variety of topics to choose from. And it should be added once again that in a very real sense there are almost as many styles to be examined in the country idiom as there are songs and singers. Admittedly, in the race record catalogues during the 1920's and 1930's most of the titles pertain to love or the lack of it, but there is a large share of blues on such topics as prisons, highways, and natural catastrophes as well.

In the vast majority of city blues, however, sex is the dominant theme and is treated in patterned ways. In the early city blues, lyrics built around *double-entendres* were very popular—*It's Tight Like That, Let Me Roll Your Lemon, Ah Wants to Sell My Monkey*. In the later city blues styles, like those of the best-known Chicago singers at the present time, the accent is either on bravado and virility or—conversely—helplessness. Muddy Waters'[2] many songs (for example, *Hoochie Koochie Man, Got My Mojo Workin', I'm Ready, Tiger in Your Tank*) and some of Howlin' Wolf's[3] material (Hoy, hoy, I'm the boy/three hundred pounds of heavenly joy) illustrate the former boastful type, and Sonny Boy "help me please" Williamson's songs[4] illustrate the latter. In terms of Bales' interaction content categories,[5] most of Waters' best-known lyrics invariably fall neatly into category 12—*"shows antagonism*, deflates others' status, defends or asserts self"; for example, *I'm Ready:*

> I got an ax and a pistol on a graveyard framed
> That shoots tombstone bullets, that's wearin' balls and chains.
> I'm drinkin' T N T. I'm smokin' dynamite.
> I hope some screwball start a fight,
> Cause I'm ready, ready as anybody can be.
> I'm ready for you, I hope you're ready for me.

2. Chess LP 1427.
3. Chess LP 1469.
4. Chess LP 1437.
5. Robert F. Bales, *Interaction Process Analysis: A Method for the Study of Small Groups* (Cambridge, Mass., 1950), p. 59.

Tiger in Your Tank is another classic:

> I can raise your hood.
> I can clean your coils.
> Check the transmissions,
> And give you the oils.
> I don't care what the people think
> I want to put a Tiger, you know, in your tank.

Sonny Boy Williamson's most popular lines, however, clearly belong in category 11—"*shows tension*, asks for help, withdraws from field"—as in *One Way Out:*

> Raise your window; I ain't goin' out that door.
> Raise your window! I ain't goin' out that door.
> There's a man outside, might be your man, I don't know.

According to Bales' key, both men are dealing in "negative socio-emotional reactions," whereas Waters' lyrics reflect "problems of reintegration" and Williamson's "problems of tension reduction." These jargon generalizations oversimplify the situation rather drastically (and parts of the lyrics would be classed in other categories by Bales), but these dominant aspects of the songs do stand out. They suggest, I think, that for today's city bluesmen male roles in the Negro community are confused, anxiety-laden, and in need of redefinition. Muddy Waters' boastfulness is in some respects compensatory and defensive; Williamson's frank appraisal of his inadequacies in song after song gives us another, and perhaps truer, perspective on the same problem.

Urban blues musicians take a different stance. It isn't very often that B. B. King, Bobby Bland, or even Jr. Parker boasts of his sexual potency in public; this quality is taken for granted by both artist and audience, and there is little need to vocalize about it extensively. Nor do the urban bluesmen project themselves as helpless, although pleas for greater understanding do occupy an important place in the repertoire. A typical urban blues lyric frequently contains an analysis of a problematic situation and often a hint of reform or solution as well—for example, Jr. Parker's *Mother-in-Law Blues* or *Sittin' and*

Thinkin', B. B. King's *My Own Fault, Baby*, Bobby Bland's *Your Friends*, Little Johnny Taylor's *Part Time Love*.[6] According to the Bales schema, categories in what is called the "neutral task area" (as opposed to "positive and negative socio-emotional areas") encompass most of the lyric content: category 4, "*gives suggestion*, direction, implying autonomy for other"; especially 5, "*gives opinion*, evaluation, analysis, expresses feeling, wish"; and 6, *gives orientation*, information, repeats, clarifies, confirms." Examples of content in keeping with the complementary categories 7, 8, and 9 can also be found— "*asking* for orientation, opinion, and suggestions"—but the blues lyric by itself is essentially a monologue, so that these questions are largely rhetorical and occur less frequently. I think it is clear, however, that urban bluesmen are coming to grips with the situations that city singers either simply complain about or cover up with bravado.

In urban blues lyrics we can see attempts to understand and patch up the conjugal bond and other problems. In soul music and the most advanced forms of the urban blues today, analysis and understanding are still very important but an increasing emphasis is being placed upon Bales' categories 1 and 2; "*shows solidarity*, raises other's status, gives help, reward"; and "*shows tension release*, jokes, laughs, shows satisfaction." Bobby Bland's feeling-good material and his songs of praise and dependability are perfect examples of this new emphasis[7] and many examples can be drawn from the Ray Charles repertoire as well. Note that this sort of positive socio-emotional content is diametrically opposed to the tension and antagonism lyrics so popular with city bluesmen and their audience.

A more detailed analysis of blues lyrics might make it possible, first of all, to describe with greater insight the changes

6. Taylor's hit prompted the Reverend Edward Blair to record a sermon, *Seeking a Part Time Love* (Mayo Records, Sermon Series II) which includes a long list of those Old Testament figures who had "part-time love" problems. Rather than condemn the Biblical and contemporary philanderers, Reverend Blair sympathetically analyzes the conditions that lead to broken homes.

7. See Chapter V, below.

in male roles within the Negro community as defined by Negroes at various levels of socio-economic status and mobility within the lower class. Certainly the lyric content of city, urban, and soul blues also reflects varying sorts of adjustment to urban living conditions generally. A thorough analysis of a large body of blues lyrics from the various genres would help to clarify these patterns of adjustment and the attitudinal sets that accompany those patterns. On the basis of such studies it might be possible to estimate an individual's upward or downward mobility and life expectations from his choice of a favorite singer.[8]

A re-examination of blues development in terms of the eleven changes noted in Chapter II, above, of the various forces at work on the style, and of these shifts in blues lyric content shows that a degree of rationalization has taken place. Through the years more and more technically efficient and logically structured means have been employed toward achieving blues of maximum expressive power. In Max Weber's analysis of Western musical evolution,[9] emergent rationality seems also to entail disenchantment, demystification, and a corresponding diminution of expressiveness for the sake of order. In the forty years that have elapsed since Weber wrote *The Rational and Social Foundations of Music* an increasing number of mathematically oriented Western composers have abandoned affective goals altogether in favor of music modeled on algebraic equations; "mechanical petrification" has arrived. The blues tradition has evolved in quite an opposite direction, however, since the music has always had to satisfy strong emotional needs. The truth of this statement is greater today than ever before. In the simplest Weberian terms, blues singers have developed more *rational* means, albeit semi-consciously, toward ends that are not only *affective* but somewhat *traditional* and *evaluative* as well. The affective or emotional element in blues remains relatively con-

8. George Rutkowski's "Musical Tastes and Preferences of Male and Female Negro Adolescents" (unpublished manuscript, 1965) is pointed in this direction.

9. *The Rational and Social Foundations of Music* (Carbondale, 1958).

stant through all phases of the blues continuum, and blues listening is certainly habitual or traditional with many Negroes. But in recent years participation in the blues culture has taken on an evaluative aspect—the blues tradition has become an end in itself. For example, Purvis Spann, a Chicago blues disc jockey, frequently tells his listeners, "If you don't like blues, you've got a hole in your soul"—that is, you are not a real Negro or a complete person. To the extent that people heed Spann's warning and similar exhortations, blues adherence becomes something of a sacred duty to one's identity. The recent influx of gospel music into the blues mainstream seems to substantiate this suggested shift from traditional to evaluative concerns.

It is also interesting to note what seems to be a lack of congruence between the changes in style surveyed here and Redfield's folk-urban concept of culture change. Sharecropping and tenant-farming Negroes in the rural South are not far removed from the folk society as an ideal type; yet this fairly homogeneous culture yields a startling diversity of blues styles that cannot be accounted for simply in terms of community isolation. The rural bluesman has not been particularly bound by conventions or traditional restrictions. Largely self-taught and playing for his own amusement or for the secular entertainment of a small group, he is free to develop his mode of expression in idiosyncratic ways. The polar opposites of the adjectives usually applied to dimensions of the folk society concept can easily be applied to forms of rural blues expression; "in the folk society what one man does is the same as what another man does,"[10] unless of course the man is a blues singer. But in certain other respects the country bluesman is quite typical, as in Redfield's description of folk behavior as "spontaneous, uncritical and personal."[11] Conversely, the urban bluesman or soul singer works within a more homogeneous style and places strong emphasis on group solidarity in his lyrics and performance. There are prevailing musical conventions that must be held to if the singer is to maintain any sort of steadfast

10. Robert Redfield, "The Folk Society," *American Journal of Sociology* 52 (Jan. 1947): 298.

11. *Ibid.*, p. 294.

following. And, as will be shown, there are strong sacred overtones that can be observed at any blues gathering. In short, if this admittedly brief and general juxtaposition of the blues spectrum with the folk-urban continuum offers any insight, it is that blues expression tends to reveal a mirrored or reversed reflection of its immediate social milieu.

Stated another way, a bluesman in the country or for the first time coming to grips with city life sings primarily to ease his worried mind, to get things out of his system, to feel better; it is of secondary importance whether or not others are present and deriving similar satisfactions from his music. It is a source of encouragement to know that your complaints and grievances are shared by others, but such support is not essential. An urban bluesman senses a broader and deeper obligation to the community or, rather, to Negro communities across the country, since the urban blues singer is practically by definition itinerant. Individual catharsis is still a *sine qua non* to successful performance, but in an anomic, bewildering urban situation, characterized by shifting values and interpersonal conflicts, people expect something more than a personal lament from a singer. He must not only state common problems clearly and concisely but must in some sense take steps toward their analysis and solution.

In meeting his obligations to these communities the contemporary bluesman is very much dependent upon the record companies and radio stations, as well as on the whole commercial network of managers, agents, distributors, promoters, club owners, and racketeers that surround these two centers. Before he can bring his message to large live audiences across the country these middlemen must put his music on records, and these records must reach his potential public via radio, jukeboxes, and record shops. So described, the business end of the blues seems simple and mundane—there is a demand out there, and a staff of specialists are ready to supply it—but in actual practice the production and dissemination of the blues are accomplished through a maze of compartmentalized complex processes, many of them fascinating and some of them unfathomable to an outsider. The following comments touch only upon a small fraction of the economic, legal, and technical angles that intersect the bluesman's career.[12]

To gain some appreciation for the manner in which the free enterprise system permeates the blues world, we might follow the circuitous route of an imaginary young blues singer and instrumentalist who wants to "make it" with his own distinctive versions of the twelve-bar form. Let us assume that, unlike those of most of the fledgling singers, his blues *are* distinctive; he has moved a step away from his basic B. B. King guitar "licks," his vocal style departs slightly from the King and Bland conventions, and he has a few original lyrics up his sleeve. Let us further suppose that he has been working with some small-time rhythm-and-blues bands in the Negro ghetto of a Midwestern city like Indianapolis. As a ghetto child he has been worldly since the age of five or six, on guard, aware that anyone and everyone, with the possible exception of his mother, will hustle and exploit him given half a chance. In his late teens or early twenties, he knows also that cops habitually dip into the cash registers of club owners, that owners don't pay musicians much and sometimes don't pay at all, and that a business agent of a union doesn't give a damn whether he works or gets paid as long as he pays his dues. Our young bluesman may have considerable *savoir-faire*, he may have paid exorbitant dues, and he may have heard some of the ugly rumors about the big-time operators; but he is still as malleable and helpless as a newborn babe in the hands of the music industry.

He realizes early in the game that he needs a big record if he is to get his career started, so he begins to make the rounds and ask questions. It doesn't take him long to discover that most record companies won't touch an urban blues singer with a twenty-foot pole.

Calvin Carter, A and R man (artist and repertoire executive) at Vee-Jay Records, provides the hard-headed answer to why this is so. He has recorded a number of blues singers for the

---

12. For further information see Nat Hentoff's *The Jazz Life* (New York, 1961), Chapter 3, "The Apprenticeship and the Accounting," pp. 46–59. See also Peter K. Etzkorn, "Social Context of Songwriting in the United States," *Ethnomusicology* 7 (1963): 96–106.

label, and continues to record Jimmy Reed and John Lee Hooker regularly; but "if a young B. B. King with talent to burn walked in here today I'd have to show him the door because there's no future in it." The future, as far as record company executives are concerned, lies with hit singles, and the million seller.[13] Only one group buys that many records—the teenagers, the nine- to sixteen-year-old age group, the same "pimple audience" who have rapidly become the final arbiter of the nation's tastes and fashions in many other areas. In television, radio, and recording, the most successful programs, stations, and products are usually geared to the "adolescents, pre-adolescents and adolescent-minded adults."[14] Business is business—it's the quantity of viewers and listeners that counts; and since the urban blues market is small by comparison, only a handful of companies will bother with it. As has been noted, many a Negro style has caught on with white adolescents; but as yet B. B. King has not struck a responsive chord with this group, and A and R men see no reason why an unknown singer who performs in a related style will be any more profitable.

The businessman's perspective on the blues can perhaps be clarified somewhat by a few rough estimates of the audiences within the Negro community. I would guess that about 90 per cent of the twenty million Americans defined socially as Negroes support some form of Afro-American music, even if it is only to the extent of buying a record or two by Chubby Checker or occasionally attending a Harry Belafonte concert. Taking support or interest to mean record buying and performance attendance, I would estimate that about 70 per cent of the Negro community are interested in soul music—blues, gospel, or some of the many popular and jazz styles derived therefrom—and in a sense this audience defines the outer boundaries of Negro

13. Actually the standard for a big hit these days has slipped to around 750,000.

14. An article by Bill Davidson, "Who Killed Your Favorite TV Show?" (*Saturday Evening Post*, Feb. 27, 1965, pp. 84–87), examines the influence of adolescents on television programing practices. The network tactics he discusses differ little from those used by record companies.

culture. Within it some 25 per cent might be called jazz fans; probably about 20 per cent support the contemporary or urban blues stylist—the Kings (B. B., Freddy, Albert), Bobby Bland, Jr. Parker, Little Milton, Percy Mayfield, Jimmy Witherspoon, Little Johnny Taylor, and perhaps a dozen others; less than 10 per cent are interested in the city blues stylist (Muddy Waters, Jimmy Reed, and so on); less than 5 per cent will buy records in the country blues idioms. Country blues are recorded in albums today, almost exclusively for a rapidly expanded white market, though only a few years ago single records by a Lightnin' Hopkins (with bass and drums accompaniment added) could still be found popping up in ghetto record shops. The average city bluesman's pay now flows from white and Negro sources in about equal proportions. And of course any danceable piece of soul music always has the chance of hitting the adolescent jackpot. B. B. King and the other urban stylists have maintained their popularity with a substantial minority of Negroes— probably about five million have purchased a King or Bland record at one time or another—but I doubt that more than a few thousand white Americans outside the Deep South have ever heard B. B. King's music. If one first-class citizen in a thousand could identify his name, I'd be very much surprised. All this adds up to a lack of future for our hypothetical young bluesman: his potential market is certainly there; but it is not very big and, more important, it is sharply circumscribed.

So what can this aspiring bluesman do? He can present himself to the smaller, often tiny, ethnic companies that will audition just about anyone who walks in the door. Generally the smaller the company is, the more unscrupulous, greedy, and desperate the management is likely to be. Some will listen to him, lift his best musical and lyrical ideas, then pass them on to an artist they already have under contract. If he has a number of good ideas, they may encourage him to hang around the studio with the promise, often false, that any of his material that is used will be copyrighted jointly in his name and the name of the company head, A and R man, or an established staff songwriter. He and his "collaborators" will share future royalties, and he will get a "start in show business." He might copyright in his own name of course *if* he knows how, *if* he has a lawyer handy, and *if* he can afford the litigation necessary to enforce his claim.[15] What's more, should he take offense at this sort of preliminary exploitation and seek justice, he will be immediately branded as a trouble maker and informally blacklisted. Smaller companies in that particular section of the country will not likely even audition him—"nobody loves a smart ass." The larger companies ignore unknowns, and his career opportunities are nil.

He can also start by making a "demo" (demonstration record): renting a studio, hiring musicians, and cutting a record at his own expense—about two hundred and fifty dollars for a cheap one. Some of the more cautious pirates are leary of lifting from demos—music on record, after all—and may try to buy or otherwise obtain the song or the demo itself, again for use by an established artist. A demo improves his bargaining position very slightly, but is more useful to the experienced songwriter who wants to sell his material rather than himself.

The number of ways in which a novice can be seduced and abandoned are legion, and I am not in a position to make a complete list of abuses. The basic factor here is simply that the unknown has nothing whatever to bargain with except his talent and personality, and there are hundreds of talented personalities making the rounds. The field is glutted with both aspirants and companies, all hoping to get rich quick with a few big hits. With nothing to bargain with, and in the absence of good connections, the novice takes whatever he can get.

Suppose that our man finally gets to sign his first contract. Initially all this means is that his exploitation has been legalized. The company signs him up, usually for one year, with options on a second year or two, and promises to record eight sides (four records or two recording sessions of music) each year. In other words, the company will pay for four or five hours of studio time, union scale wages to a group of musicians and about two hundred and fifty dollars in set fees, an advance on possible

15. The legal aspects of the music business are thoroughly documented in *This Business of Music* by Sidney Shemel and M. William Krasilovsky (New York, 1964).

royalties, to the artist. This is the company's only firm obligation. The company has the final say on what material the artist
will record, how he should do it, when and where the recording
will take place, and is under no obligation to release to the
public any of the recordings made. This means that the
company can keep a young man tied up for two or three years at
a cost of less than a thousand dollars a year without doing a
thing to advance his career. They may want to keep him around
for his ideas or to keep him out of the hands of a rival firm.
They may sign him as a blues singer because they like his voice,
and then fail to divert him into the more conventional pop or
ballad field. Sometimes a new singer is signed simply because he
sounds like a particular established performer. If the star is with
the same company the newcomer may be kept on the shelf as a
threatened substitute, thus keeping the star in line when it
comes time to renegotiate his contract. Then again, the novice
may be required to cover the best-selling singles or the general
style of an artist on another label so as to undercut the
competition. Such understudy roles may lead to an independent
career if the young bluesman can surpass his model or gradually
shift to a style and repertoire of his own; but once typed as a
second-rate version of someone else, a singer is usually stuck
and will eventually pass into oblivion.

If the young bluesman manages to avoid being trapped or
disillusioned by the smaller companies and perseveres, he is
likely to wind up attached to either Duke Records in Houston or
Chess Records in Chicago—the largest companies whose primary concern has been the blues or rhythm-and-blues audience.[16]

The Chess family runs a bigger operation by far, and can be
classified as a major independent. Attendance at recording
sessions, interviews with key personnel at the studio and
affiliated radio station, WVON, have given me a vague notion of
the way in which a beginning bluesman might be treated there.

16. ABC-Paramount currently has both B. B. King and Ray Charles
under contract, and Atlantic has recorded a good deal of blues material;
but neither company is dependent on its blues audience or very willing to
experiment with untried talent.

Standards of honesty and integrity seem to be high, considering the industry as a whole. One arrives at an appraisal of this kind with mixed emotions. Stories circulate in the Chicago blues community that are not very flattering. At the same time, most of the performers currently under contract seem to be reasonably well satisfied with the arrangement. Muddy Waters, for example, has been with the company almost from its inception in the late 1940's, *without* a contract. In a sense, this mutual trust in a highly competitive field speaks well for both Waters and Leonard Chess. Yet the arrangement also smacks of the old plantation and paternalism. I suspect that Waters can go to the Chess family with big dental bills or overdue car payments and receive a sizable "advance on royalties" on the spot, with no questions asked. On the other hand, if Muddy were to become "uppity," it is possible that his career might be seriously disrupted. "We're just one big happy family here," say the Chess men when asked about management problems, and I am almost persuaded that they believe it. A large and fairly secure enterprise, the family can afford to be generous with the veterans and reasonably fair in its dealings with new prospects. Then too, Leonard Chess, founder and boss, brother Phil, his right-hand man, and Leonard's son Marshall share among them a solid forty years of experience in the blues business; assisted by a full-time lawyer, they are skillful in avoiding actions that will involve unprofitable legal complications, musicians' union pressures, governmental harassment, and employee resentment.

Phil Chess describes the standard procedure with a new artist in concise straightforward terms:

> We listen to him, and if we like him the first thing we do is to find out if he's recorded before. We check up on it and if not, O.K. If he's under contract to someone else we can't touch him, or if he's recorded for someone they may want to make some money off of our promotion, reissue his old stuff or put out stuff they've been holding, so you got to be careful. If he's O.K., we sign a contract. He's got to be a member of the union, and we clear everything with them. They provide a skeleton contract and the by-law book

spells out our obligations. You file your contract with the
national office, otherwise they can bring pressure to bear.
So when you've got union clearance, you sign him up for a
three year maximum, one and one is standard, one year
outright with a company option on a second year. Then we
listen to his material again, and if it's any good we polish it
up and use it. If it's not so good we find solutions. The
company has the discretion to record whatever it wants to,
but the guy has to like what he's doing or the records are
dead, so you work things out. Then he rehearses at home,
or over at Willie Dixon's basement since he handles most
of our straight blues stuff, or maybe in the practice studio
here. If we think it's worth it, maybe we'll get an
arrangement made. Then when everything's ready, the
session comes off in a couple of hours. We release a couple
of sides in a month or so and then we start hockin'. You
know what hockin' means; we send out about 3,000 d.j.
copies, and to distributors, radio stations, trade magazines
for review, put some ads in Billboard, Cashbox, Music
Vendor and places like that and then see what happens.
Used to know in two or three days if it's going anywhere,
but now it's a couple of weeks to a month before you get a
reaction. Max Cooperstein, our salesman, he stays in touch
with about 40 distributors and starts spreading the word if
something's happening with it. Quick as the first record
fades, you get another one out there, and if the first records
go pretty good you start arranging TV show appearances,
press parties, get him to meet the people any way you can
and all this falls under promotion rather than artist
management, and we pay for it.

In other words, getting an artist started takes time, effort,
and money. Releasing a record that "really bombs" or "doesn't
go anywhere" can cost the company four or five thousand
dollars. Or a moderately successful first release may lead to a
major promotional campaign, expensive arrangements, large
bands, a succession of releases, and a loss of twenty or thirty
thousand dollars when the expected audience growth never

materializes. Considering the investment and the risks involved, the one-sided initial contract can easily lend itself to justification by the entrepreneur.

If the bluesman's first record brings the Chess family a reasonable return on its investment in the form of twenty-five or thirty thousand sales, he's on his way. "His" royalties of two or three cents a record will be absorbed by the company to defray the expenses of musicians, arrangements, and copyists. The company's production, promotion, studio time, and overhead expenses have been canceled by profits, and another session will be scheduled. Ideally, the next few records will expand this audience at a steady rate. One of these pieces may have a catchy lyric or a good sound and, with some strong promotion, become a modest hit—sales of between sixty thousand and a hundred thousand—and a blues newcomer has established himself. At this point our man will still not be cashing any fat royalty checks, but his personal appearance fees will begin to escalate rapidly and he will acquire a personal manager and booking agent, each of whom takes a nice slice (from 10 to 25 per cent) of performance profits while assuming some of the company's promotional tasks and costs. Once associated in the public's mind with a particular song or songs, he is in demand, he can form his own band, he will be approached by songwriters eager to have him perform their works. In short, he is at last possessed of a bargaining lever—popularity—that he may or may not know how to use.

To oversimplify matters slightly, a singer who has arrived can either assert himself and take charge of his own affairs or he can ride with his success. B. B. King is one of the few bluesmen I've encountered who really "takes care of business"; he has learned from bitter experience, and now exercises extensive control over the material he records and the manner in which it is recorded. He knows how to negotiate a contract and how to delegate responsibilities to subordinates. Most of the basic decisions affecting his career are made by B. B. King rather than for him. Ray Charles is beset by his many problems—narcotics arrests, paternity suits, and taxes—and is surrounded by "managers," but he nevertheless retains firm control of his musical productions at all times. Bobby Bland's great talents, on the other hand, are essentially clay in the hands of his business associates; the clay has definite properties that resist molding, but most major career decisions are made for him. Since profits are distributed in rough proportion to decisions made and risks and responsibilities taken, one can guess that B. B. King, though less popular than Bland today, is much better off financially. Bland's clothes, limousine, valet, and plentiful pocket money are image bolsterers from Duke Records (or perhaps a continual "advance on royalties" that keeps him tied to the company) rather than real earnings. He is happy to be singing, meeting the people, and leading the good life, and lets others take care of the business worries. Bland is altogether typical in this respect.

A young bluesman may recognize that Chess records have brought him his fame, a certain amount of fortune, and the opportunity to perform before audiences that will sustain him psychologically and financially. Chances are he will stay with Chess and avoid doing anything that might upset the goose that lays the golden eggs. Unlike the pop artist who may have a smash hit only to disappear in a year or two, a bluesman can make ends meet as a performer on the basis of a few songs that gained wide currency five or even ten years ago. In fact it is this relative stability of the blues audience that has been the key to the Chess success story, a story in which the average blues singer would be happy to play the part assigned to him. Single records by Muddy Waters, Little Walter, Howlin' Wolf, and Sonny Boy Williamson may not sell many copies, but they always sell some. Before and after the boom years in the middle 1950's, when a string of big rock-and-roll hits by Chuck Berry and Bo Diddley facilitated rapid company expansion, the smaller but steady sales of the tried and true city bluesmen paid the rent. Now albums by these men and "old-timers" like Chuck Berry are not only selling well at home but are very popular abroad, and they are still the backbone of the Chess enterprise.

From the time almost twenty years ago when Leonard Chess and son Marshall would tour the South peddling records from the trunk of the car, the family business has steadily enlarged its channels of communication to the blues audience. With the purchase of radio station WHFC in 1963, for approximately one million dollars, this network of connections has been doubled or perhaps tripled in power. If artists have to bow and scrape to record company moguls, they can take some satisfaction from the fact that these companies are usually in a similar position vis-à-vis the radio stations. A singer can't perform effectively without records; a company soon goes broke if no one hears their products. Hence the peon status of most recording artists; hence the recurrent payola scandals; hence the chapter heading, "fattening frogs for snakes." Companies, managers, agents, club owners, and other predators feed upon artists; radio stations receive sacrifices from the companies; radio stations view ASCAP and BMI[17] as parasites; songwriters must give a pound of flesh to the men who publish, record, and perform their works; cops and jukebox mobsters cling like leeches to the club owners—and so it goes in one great chain of devouring. By purchasing WHFC, rechristening it WVON, and programing entirely for the more than a million Negroes in the Chicago area, the Chess brothers have effectively disrupted this balance of nature and established themselves in a new and enviable ecological niche.[18] The Federal Communications Commission doesn't like to hear a record-company–controlled radio station devoting more than 10 per cent of its musical air time to

17. ASCAP and BMI are organizations representing composers, authors, and publishers. They collect about sixty million dollars worth of public performance payments for their membership each year by taking a percentage of the broadcasters' gross receipts; cf. Shemel and Krasilovsky, *op. cit.*, Chapter 11.

18. The following statistics culled (by Walt Saveland) from the local surveys give some indication of WVON's popularity in Chicago. Of the approximately 300,000 Negro radio households in the Chicago area about 25 per cent have a radio on during any given quarter-hour of the normal listening day. About half of these radios are tuned to WVON. During the daytime the station averages between thirty thousand and seventy thousand listeners during any given quarter-hour. In comparison to all other stations in the area, WVON ranks second or third in popularity during the evening and fourth or fifth during the day. A few weeks after WVON first came on the air a "less ethnic" Negro station found itself without an audience, and its owner eventually switched to an "all-news" format.

company products; but this time can be used judiciously by the management, and it is always possible to "buy" a certain amount of advertising time in which to plug a Chess record. Almost every new Chess release in the rhythm-and-blues field is guaranteed a hearing in Chicago—of course a new and important incentive for bluesmen to sign and stick with Chess. Record distributors and other Negro radio stations in Chicago and throughout the land cannot afford to ignore any record that catches on with the WVON audience. Before mailing out a few thousand disc jockey copies and sinking money into nationwide promotion, Chess can expose a record in the Chicago area first in order to estimate its potential. Leonard and Phil Chess produce records; the L & P Broadcasting Company plays them for the people. This neat arrangement cuts down some of the usual risks, but it certainly doesn't eliminate them entirely.

No one can ever be sure that a record will catch on. Certainly a record with Elvis Presley's or Nat King Cole's name on it will not sink below a certain minimal sales level, and the Chess family can be confident that they will at least break even on a single by one of their two or three best-known bluesmen. But generally it is almost impossible to predict sales in the music industry. What little charm and mystery can be found in this frantic snake-eat-frog business derive from this situation. All the free-enterprising machinations alluded to above thrive on consumer demand. But what are consumers demanding today? What record will appeal to them tomorrow? Of twenty-five blues singles released in any one month, about twenty will appear in the accountant's books as losses of varying magnitude, three or four will pass the break-even point, and perhaps one will bring in a solid profit. The blues audience is the powerful final arbiter. It is a somewhat arbitrary and ultimately unknowable force; facing omnipotent arbitrary forces, men invariably turn to magic. The shamans in the music-business tribe are the A and R men, who are blessed with a rare gift called "feel." They are aided by their assistant witch doctors, the recording engineers, who help them "mix" a wild brew called "sound." The abiding anxiety of an executive chief, who usually knows little or nothing about music, is that his shamans will lose their feel and gradually or suddenly go cold. When this happens the magician is banished to the boondocks like a Las Vegas dealer,[19] and a desperate search commences for someone who is hot, has the feel, and can work effectively with the engineer to blend a potent sound.

The way in which a particular A and R man's teen feel or blues feel is translated into sound is a fascinating process that deserves a separate volume of analysis; the following description is highly superficial. The A and R man's first task is to bring together a fertile combination of raw materials—artist, song, instrumentalists, arrangement—for the recording session. This combination can usually be achieved in a fairly rational manner by reviewing the artist's previous work, listening to the recent releases of related stylists that have won acclaim, finding a lyric that fits the performer's personality and an arrangement that fits the lyric. For example, Billy Davis and Willie Dixon, A and R men at Chess, are asked to create a hit for Little Milton Campbell, a recently acquired property who sounds very much like Bobby Bland. Solution: a typical urban blues lyric, something to do with marital cooperation under adverse conditions and hoped-for upward mobility; an arrangement featuring brass, since that sound seems to frame Bland well (economize perhaps by having just one saxophonist for a solo break in the middle); a girl vocal group for Milton to shout at near the end of the record, thus reinforcing the male-female relationship, and also because it has worked wonders for Ray Charles and Bland; use regular studio musicians (who are probably kicking back some of their union scale wages to management in return for being called to the studio regularly), because Milton's own group is likely to use valuable studio time as they master the written arrangement. So much for planning.

19. Erving Goffman, in a lecture on the Las Vegas gambling world, has noted that the owners of casinos disregard statistical probabilities, cherish instead a mythology of "hot" and "cold," and in these respects are no different from their clientele. Thus a dealer who "goes cold" is temporarily replaced or fired outright, long before the laws of chance can come to his rescue. Nothing can rescue an A and R man who has lost his "feel."

The chief assembles the Indians for the session, and the shaman, Billy Davis, prepares to go to work as he listens to the first run-through of a song called *We're Gonna Make It:* "We may not have a cent to pay the rent, but we're gonna make it, Oh yes we will." Knowing that promotional sample records will be tossed into the wastebasket by bored disc jockeys unless the first few bars of a song have ear-catching dynamics or a gimmick introduction, the A and R man first makes sure that a brass flourish from the middle of the song is transplanted to the beginning, followed by a dramatic moment of silence before moving directly into the lyric. Little Milton has the lyric well in hand and delivers with gusto, but he isn't blending too well with the girl vocalists, whose responses seem rather listless. Since they are recording on one track of a multitrack tape, these problems can be ironed out at a second session if necessary.

Accompaniment is the initial concern. Adjustments are made in microphone placement: the drummer's mike is tilted slightly to pick up more snare drum and less cymbal, the trombonist is repositioned, and so forth. Listening to a replay of the second take in the control booth, the A and R man brings in all sorts of disturbing signals on his sixth sense, and he meditates, calls his muse, summons his feel. He returns to the studio and spends twenty minutes or so trying out alternative patterns with the electric bassist and the two electric guitarists. One texture after another is tested and discarded. He may stumble upon a combination of rhythmic figures that suggests the beat of a current dance fad and readjust the drummer's contribution accordingly. (If a blues number can offer some appeal to the younger non-blues audience, so much the better.) Patterns reshaped, the volume of each instrument must be readjusted: more treble on the rhythmic guitar may turn the trick; a flat, whining sound from the melody guitar may be called for; "try playing that figure up an octave at lower volume, and can you put in just a little tremolo?"; and so on until it feels right. The shaman returns to the booth to find that the new balance has somehow diminished the impact of the brass or that the over-all sound is too bright (too many high frequencies) or too dull (low frequencies prominent). The engineer begins boosting highs on one track of the tape, lowering them on another, equalizing, balancing, adding echo to the sax or piano, rendering the guitarists muddy, the drummer more crisp—making adjustments that will facilitate the mixing of tracks at a later date. A slight twist of a dial or the flick of a switch on a control panel that would give a jet pilot pause can mean the difference between success and failure. In the teen or pop field five instruments are sometimes made to sound like a full orchestra, or twenty instrumentalists and a choir can be given the texture of two ukulele players humming to each other in a phone booth. Such alchemy is rarely performed at a blues session, but building and blending the right background for a particular blues singer are often just as subtle and demanding a challenge.

What of the bluesman himself, who presumably has his own feel for what his audience wants? How does he fit his vocalizations to the A and R man's background sound? For illustrative material, let's leave Little Milton and turn to the problems of Bobby Bland himself.

The teamwork aspect of Bobby Bland's artistry described in Chapter V is borne out by brief interviews with sideman Al Braggs and bandleader Joe Scott concerning the preparation of a song before its release on record.

The process starts once again with the lyric for a song and a suggested harmonic pattern; invariably this harmonic foundation is a standard twelve-bar blues, gospel, or ballad chord progression that has established itself as a proved money-maker. Braggs, Scott, or an independent songwriter may supply this lyric-harmonic formula. If Scott, Bland, and the powers that be at Duke Records feel it has potential, Scott will write an arrangement for it, revising the lyric if necessary with Bland's strengths and weaknesses (e.g., his inability to sing long phrases) in mind and searching for orchestrational devices that will most dramatically heighten the lyrics. The accompaniment is then recorded, leaving one track open for Bobby's vocal. Scott then turns the tape over to Bland, teaching him the basic melody line and giving him a few ideas as to the treatment he feels the song should receive. Braggs may also work it over, as he says, singing along with the tape and looking for places where a change of lyric, a twist of phrase, or a few spoken words may work some magic. A single phrase or punch line can make all the difference. Thanks to the multiple-track tape, Bobby can sing it over and over again or can lift out a phrase or word that doesn't fit and insert another. When a satisfactory meshing of Bland and band has been accomplished, the tape can be put away for two months to a year, unless of course the song is designed to follow up a previous hit, in which case immediate release is essential.

After one brief and abortive meshing or dubbing session at Chicago's plush Universal Studios, it appears that Bobby has to first hear himself singing a new song before he can actually sing it. More magic? No—just hard work.

Bobby, Scott, and Brother Dave Clark, publicity man, enter the studio, as the engineer finds the tape of the song they plan to complete. Bobby, amiable and cooperative, stations himself at the mike with the lyrics before him on a music stand. Scott, bored but businesslike, seats himself on a stool next to him. Brother Dave, though he appears to be pushing seventy, has on his stylish black leather suit and is full of boyish enthusiasm as he heads for the control booth after slapping Bobby on the back. The engineer puts on the tape, and Bland listens attentively, frowning, nodding, and closing his eyes from time to time as Scott sings and hums the lyric softly over the slow and rich band accompaniment. The lyric has something to do with a girl who is like an angel, a dreamy creature who "must be from another world," and represents one more futile effort to launch Bobby into the lucrative teenage market.[20] Bobby clears his throat of the gravel accumulated during his four shows a day at the Regal Theatre as the engineer puts on the tape again. Scott drops his arm to cue Bland's entrance, but Bobby fails to negotiate the first phrase. "I guess I'll have to try to stretch it out more." A few more false starts and a great deal of throat clearing follow.

20. Almost all Bland's albums include a few of these monstrosities. S. I. Hayakawa's article "Popular Songs vs. the Facts of Life" (*Etc.*, Vol. 12, pp. 83–89) is required reading for those who would dwell on the ironies inherent in the juxtaposition of "teen angel" and "you done me wrong" lyrics.

"Man, we're still just goofing. I'm too damn hoarse." Bobby bursts forth with his characteristic cry and seems to feel better for it. Brother Dave vigorously nods his approval. Scott suggests that they get the whole first verse on tape and then work on it. He cues Bobby on every phrase, and they stumble through it. Bobby paces around the studio during the playback and evaluates his performance as everyone exchanges pained expressions. As Bobby goes back to the mike for another try, Brother Dave offers lots of encouragement: "You can do it; you'll make it; you've got it now." Bobby, half in jest, signals him to come into the studio for further support. The next take is a big improvement, Bland is confidently spacing out each line, but Scott still needs to cue every other phrase. Things fall apart when the bridge of the song presents a whole new set of problems. Bobby calls a halt: "I know what you want, but I just ain't got it this morning." Brother Dave is still sending inspirational messages, but Scott looks resigned. They decided to try again in a few days.

If I hadn't been present, Scott would probably have wheedled, cajoled, and browbeaten a respectable rendition from Bland while Brother Dave offered ever stronger moral support (which Al Braggs could do equally well)—but this is only conjecture. I suspect that much less cueing and coaxing are required when Bland settles into a blues lyric. Still, there may be something to be learned from the fact that Bland, an original, has such trouble working his way through a lyric whereas his "imitator," Little Milton, seems to soar through a first take with relative ease.

The method used in putting together a blues record varies of course with the performer and the recording studio. There is a great deal of interesting material to be gathered from observing the men who make the music as they interact in the recording studio with the men whose job is to sell records. The blues record dates that I attended have revealed one eye-opening fact after another. A singer whose style sounds completely uninhibited on record or in person can be the same man who must be prodded and coached note by note through a song in the recording studio. Jimmy Reed often has each phrase of a new lyric whispered into his ear just before he drawls it into the microphone. Another bluesman may come to the studio with his own band perfectly rehearsed, every word in place, and ready to resist with his dying breath any suggested change in his presentation. The lead singer of a rhythm-and-blues vocal group embellishes the melody in a very different manner on each of the first five run-throughs or takes, and the best of these versions is selected; after listening to it once, the singer proceeds to sing in unison with himself the second time it is played back (multiple-track tape again), matching each involved inflection with perfect split-second precision, thereby increasing the power of the piece immeasurably. This virtuosity, to which the adjective "incredible" can be applied impresses upon the observer as nothing else can the fact that long years of training and practice go into every apparently effortless melismatic phrase. One afternoon at a productive recording session can often reveal more about a current style than all the books, interviews, and performance observations put together.

How are we finally to assess the services and disservices rendered by the music industry to the bluesman and to the blues audience? It is easy to overlook the fact that the electronic mediators—record companies, radio stations, television—are performing something of a miracle.

Let us look again at A and R shamanism. The sound of currently successful records in a particular idiom and the special requirements of single records designed for broadcasting to car and transistor radios[21] set a few basic limitations and guidelines for the A and R man. Nevertheless he is faced with an infinite array of choices (and precious little time in which to make them) on at least four different levels: the initial organization of session components, adjustments in the studio, readjustments in the control booth, the final post-session mixing of the multiple-track tape. A man who feels his way through these four levels to a successful teenage formula can become a millionaire in a matter of months—witness, for example, Berry Gordy's Detroit Sound,

21. The engineer tries to boost the "upper register" or overtones of bass notes so that they will be heard on tiny transistor radio speakers; other compensations are made by engineers at the radio station.

Phil Spector's Spector Sound—but a string of unfortunate
judgments and adjustments at any and all levels can bring ruin
just as quickly. An inept A and R man can destroy a budding
career or tarnish a star's luster; a good one can boost a minor
talent to celebrity status. It is no wonder that artists and
management attribute mystical powers to these men or that they
themselves assume they have such powers.[22] The increasing
speed and magnitude of the cycles by which individuals rise or
fall, succeed or fail, in the music business are matched by an
increase in mystery, myths, superstitions, and magical techniques.

Judged by the vocabulary of "sound" and "feel," Marshall
McLuhan's thesis that electronic media herald a rebirth of tribal
conditions and a return to our audile-tactile senses is most
persuasive, especially when applied to the emergence of an
international culture (or is it cult?) of adolescents. The disc
jockey's stream-of-consciousness chatter; the popularity of Detroit, Spector, Liverpool, and other sounds; the bizarre "beach"
movies; the writhing bodies and pounding beat of TV shows like
Hullabaloo and *Shindig*—what do they all herald? Are we
witnessing the escapist circuses of a sick and dying Western

22. Aretha Franklin, for example, feels that some A and R men have
as much "soul," the ability to create and communicate, as the artists they
record. In statements reported by *Life* (May 21, 1965), pp. 93–94,
Spector and Gordy present contrasting versions of their creative-commu-
nicative functions. The egocentric Spector explanations are psychological: "My job is to get that emotion into a record. We deal with the
young generation, with people lacking identification, the disassociated,
the kids who feel they don't belong, who are in that 'in-between' period in
their lives." "Soul means yearning . . . the yearning to be free, to be
needed, to be loved. Singers like the Beatles and the Righteous Brothers
have caught this need. The whole world is in tune with one kind of
music. This was never true before. . . . Ingmar Bergman makes movies
of our times. I make records of our times." While Spector sees himself as
the musical prophet meeting the needs of a new era, Gordy, a Negro,
stresses cultural and historical forces, suggesting that he is but a channel
for the collective consciousness. Our sound "is basically gospel because
most of us involved here were raised in the church. Most of us involved
here have struggled a great deal. We've had the rats and the roaches—
and the problems. Our sound was never calculated technically. It is just
something we feel. We've never stopped to think about it."

culture, or are these events rituals of passage and rebirth, resurrections of the body,[23] harbingers of a nonmechanical, anti-work and highly sensational post-civilization?[24]

The world of teen feel may be mysterious, but I think that what has happened to blues feel in the midst of this electronic business is quite clear. The strands of a folk tradition have been brought together; the music of a people has been unified, energized, amplified, and disseminated with an efficiency that seems fantastic. The bluesman and the businessman share the same objective—they want to reach the people.[25] And they do. If the singer is exploited in the process, he can sing the blues with a little more fervor. But is the opportunity to tell your story to hundreds of thousands of people an exploitation? Many bluesmen would pay for the privilege.

With every record that reaches out, the bonds that tie B. B. King to his audience and the members of that audience together are tightened. In a sense every record released creates and defines a new subculture, a new set of shared sensibilities. B. B. King is able to "appear" in five hundred different bars across the country each night. Thanks to magnetic tape, the long-playing record, and the record player, any man who so desires can listen to *B. B. King Live at the Regal*[26] whenever he wants to, and his friends can share that therapy with him. It's the next best thing to being there.

23. Norman O. Brown, *Life against Death*.

24. Kenneth Boulding.

25. Of course, when confusion or conflict arises as to which people to reach, Bland's "teen angel" songs and similar misfortunes are likely to result.

26. ABC-Paramount, ABC-509. This recent "in person" recording is the first to capture some of the "commitment" that B. B. King can inspire (See Chapter VI, "Role and Response"). ABC-Paramount has performed the same fine service for Ray Charles: *Ray Charles Live in Concert*, ABC-500.

CHAPTER IV

B. B. KING BACKSTAGE

WHILE MORE THAN two hundred thousand black Americans assembled in Washington to claim their long-anticipated freedoms one hot August afternoon not long ago, a visitor sat backstage at the Regal Theatre on Chicago's South Side eagerly looking forward to an encounter with B. B. King, possibly the best of the big name blues singers. Before going to the Regal I had been watching another King on TV as he stirred the throng of marchers with his final appeals. Now as I waited for B. B. to come off stage I began to draw comparisons in my mind between the two Kings—the preacher and the bluesman—both leaders in their respective fields, both eloquent spokesmen for their people, both from the Deep South. Recalling Martin Luther King's effective oratory and the artistic devices he used to stretch out and strengthen his delivery, I was struck by the stylistic common denominator that binds the sacred and secular realms of the two Kings into one cultural unit. The preacher used two phrases over and over again as he improvised the conclusion of his address, "Let freedom ring from . . ." followed each time by a different range of American mountains, and then "I have a dream . . . that someday . . ." used to introduce each item on the list of promises to the Negro that have yet to be kept. This relentless repetition of phrases, the listing of American landmarks and the long enumeration of Negro goals, gradually moved the audience to an emotional peak, a fitting climax to a stirring demonstration. Employing a standard twelve-bar blues form, repeated over and over again in song after song, turning out well-known phrases in every chorus yet always introducing novel combinations and subtle new twists in each performance—in short, using the same patterns— B. B. King rarely fails to give his listeners much the same kind of emotional lift.

This formula may be stated in a number of different ways; "constant repetition coupled with small but striking devia- tions"; "similar wails and cries linked to various tumbling strains and descending figures"; or simply "statements and counter-statements"—all of which equal "soul." It is a pattern that a Negro child in the rural South or the urban ghetto learns by heart, normally in a church context, and it is as old as the oral traditions and call-response patterns of West African poetry and music. In the hands of an amateur or someone attempting to squeeze cash profits from the formula, the net musical result can often be extremely dull and monotonous; but when the formula is handled with care by a sincere and experienced artist (or minister), whose sense of timing is sure and whose imagination never lags, the cumulative effect can be devastating. It's the magic formula that is the emotive key not only to the Rev. C. L. Franklin's sermons and parables, but to Jimmy Smith's incredibility and Ray Charles' genius, or even John Coltrane's hypnotic quality. To the uninitiated—and a surprising number of music critics are included in this category —Jimmy Smith's funky runs,[1] Coltrane's sheets of sound, or B. B. King's clichés seem monotonous, tiresome, or just plain boring; but to the people who have been exposed to the music for the longest time and who have listened to it with care and attention, these artists never lose their freshness and vitality.

Part of the continued respect which a blues singer like B. B. King enjoys is due to his successful manipulation of the time-

1. LeRoi Jones' definition of "funky" is apt: "Even the adjective 'funky,' which once meant to many Negroes merely a stink (usually associated with sex), was used to qualify the music as meaningful." (*Blues People*, p. 219) The term "funky runs" describes rapid arpeggios that are liberally sprinkled with "blue notes."

tested formula in a style full of nuances and shadings that are distinctly his own; but part of this respect stems from the fact that he is more than a singer or a guitarist—he is a personality, a spokesman, a culture hero, perhaps. His problems are every man's problems; and when he sings about those problems and the guitar talks back or echoes his exposition, everyone present feels that he is taking part in the conversation. At some of B. B.'s ballroom performances I have talked with people in the audience. A few always claim to be relatives. A lady who has put away a few drinks will say, "Yeah, I used to be his ol' lady, a few years back, when I was sweet sixteen." People like to think of B. B. as a friend, a lover, or one of the family. It is at this point that the comparison between the two Kings shows more contrast than similarity. Both men are airing the grievances of their people: but with Martin Luther King, the complaints are general, political, and phrased in terms of a call to action; B. B. King's concerns are specific, deeply personal, and have little or nothing to do with social protest.

The blues boy can't resist preaching to the people occasionally, but his politics are always familial. He may pause in the middle of a song to say:

> I'd like to tell you a little story now. Ladies, if you got a man, husband, or whatever you want to call him, and he don't do exactly like you think he should, don't cut him, because you can't raise him over again you know. Don't hurt him. Treat him nice. And fellas, I want to say to you, if you got a woman, a wife, or whatever you want to call her, and she don't do like you think she should, don't go up side her head. That don't do but one thing: that'll make her a little smarter, and she won't let you catch her the next time! So all you do is talk to her softly, real sweet, and you know, and you tell her, "I know you'll do better"— [and into the lyric of the song again][2]

Those who suspect that the driving force behind the blues will disappear in the harmonious and fully integrated society

2. *B. B. King Live at the Regal*, ABC-Paramount, 509.

that the Reverend King envisions are probably mistaken, because it is conflict between the sexes more than conflict between cultures that motivates the blues artist to bring his troubles before a sympathetic audience. It can be argued, I suppose, that the impact of slavery and centuries of discrimination have so demoralized the Negro male and disorganized the Negro family that the battle of the sexes is particularly fierce in this segment of American society; the blues, according to this line of reasoning, are simply a musical reflection of this sad state of affairs. All sorts of fearsome statistics on illegitimacy and desertion rates can be mustered to support this view, and the inevitable conclusion is that a decade or so hence, when slums, poverty, and bigotry are largely a thing of the past, the blues will die a natural death along with the environment that produced them. There is an element of truth in this view of course, but I wonder, first, whether the poverty and prejudice that have nurtured Negro culture will be removed or intensified in the future, and, second, whether a substantial increase in prosperity and tolerance will erase the culture or strengthen it. A rich man can still be a soul brother, and a blues man like B. B. King can adhere to some basic middle-class values without diminishing his authenticity one iota. Whatever the future holds, I suspect that men and women will have little trouble in finding excuses to fuss and fight. These basic conditions of friction are enough to ensure the continued existence of the blues for many generations to come, if only because no form of music yet evolved has been able to express so simply and directly the frustrations, satisfactions, and reversals of the mating game. In *Baby, You Lost Your Good Thing Now*,[3] Mr. King makes the point more concisely.

It is illuminating to place B. B. King in perspective vis-à-vis the blues world as it has developed in the past fifteen years, since his present position is unique in a number of respects.

In 1949 when Riley B. King, "the Beale St. Blues Boy" gave up spinning records as a disc jockey in Memphis and began making records instead, three new and distinct blues audiences

3. *My Kind of Blues*, Crown, 5188.

were also beginning to emerge. Since at least the turn of the century, there has always been an adult Negro audience for blues, although since the death of the race labels in the 'thirties this audience seems to have been slowly but surely dwindling in size. There are many reasons for this shrinkage, but the two principal ones are easy to understand: increased competitiveness in the record industry, leading companies to emphasize the pop market to the exclusion of artists with limited appeal; growing class-consciousness on the part of Negroes and a corresponding reluctance to be identified with that "nasty," "gutbucket," "bottom," "in-the-alley" music "from slavery days." Beginning in the late 1940's however, a blues renaissance took place on three fronts at once. Bluesmen who had been scuffling for a living found themselves billed as rhythm-and-blues artists, and their record sales began to grow. Ralph Bass, formerly A and R man at Chess Records, remembers touring with various blues shows in the South during this period and noticing the larger numbers of younger patrons at the gate, predominantly Negroes still, but with increasing numbers of whites turning up at every show. At first they just listened and watched, but soon a section of the dance floor had to be roped off to accommodate white teenagers. This new thirst for blues on the part of white youth spread quickly to the North and West; Elvis Presley made some records, and the rest of the rock-and-roll story needs no retelling here. Shouters like Wynonie Harris and Joe Turner set the pace, but it is not often recognized that many of the early rock-and-roll singers, white and Negro, were influenced also by what might be dubbed the postwar Texas clean-up movement in blues singing led by stylists like T-Bone Walker, Amos Milburn, Charles Brown, and Lowell Fulson, who sang with a lighter, more relaxed feeling and worked in larger bands with saxophone sections and arrangements. While the rock-and-roll specialists were distorting and reshaping this style to meet teenage demands, Mississippian B. B. King adopted this cleaner Texas or Territory-band style and refined it still further.

Not long after the rock-and-roll craze began to spread, white intellectuals, college students, liberals, cognescenti, and later the beatnik-folknik crowd rediscovered the blues in their quest for "truth," "vitality," and "authentic ethnicity." Singers who had long been in partial retirement or in total obscurity were unearthed and recorded for posterity. Musicians still active like Bill Broonzy, Brownie McGhee, and Sonny Terry were quick to adapt their styles to this new audience. Considering the premium placed on authenticity, it is rather ironic that many musicians who had been living in the city since their childhood found it convenient to let themselves be labeled country singers, primitives, or folk singers, unhooking their electric amplification and cleaning up their diction a bit to fit the new roles demanded of them. Samuel Charters' book *The Country Blues* added fuel to this particular revival fire, and it is still burning strong today.

The third new audience can really be considered a part of the second in some respects, but European blues fans form an important audience that has the added virtue of being extremely catholic in taste; blues artists who are neither folk heroes nor rock-and-roll stars in this country—for example, Shakey Jake, Sonny Boy Williamson, Little Brother Montgomery, Lonnie Johnson—will be enthusiastically received abroad. Europe thus fills a big gap in the American blues market, and many a bluesman has found to his surprise that his biggest following is in France or England.[4]

In view of all these new resources from which a blues artist can earn a livelihood today, it is interesting to compare the recent activities of John Lee Hooker and B. B. King. One month Hooker can be found working around joints and bins in Detroit; then he may move to a "folk" nightclub in New York, where he entertains the college set; then on to the Newport Jazz Festival or a European tour; and he occasionally records a tune that becomes a hit rock-and-roll item among teenagers, like his potent *Boom, Boom, Boom*. From one record or personal appearance to the next, Hooker has at least four different audiences to choose from—and choose he does, going around the

4. J. B. Lenoir, one of the lesser known and semi-retired blues singers in Chicago's South Side, was quick to point out that of the four interviewers who had visited him during the last few years I was the first American, the others being either French or Belgian.

circle from one group to another, modifying his style and material slightly to suit the tastes of his listeners.

With Hooker's example in mind, it is astounding that B. B. King has never been to Europe, has never done a college concert or appeared at a folk club; he has never been on a jazz festival stage and, aside from a few obscure records with strings and trimmings, he has never directed his efforts toward a pop or teenage market. In other words, he is still singing to the same audience he has always had—that is, the people who know best what the blues are about. Further, unlike Ray Charles and Bobby Bland, he has never attempted to enlarge this audience by using gospel chord progressions or other churchy effects. Certainly B. B. sometimes looks like a preacher when he sings; like that of so many blues artists, his earliest musical training was in the church; but no trio of "Amen" girls like the Raylettes or the Bland Dolls plays a part in his presentation; and there are few if any songs in his repertoire that can be traced directly to the church.[5]

All these observations and facts lead to one striking conclusion: B. B. King is the only straight blues singer in America with a large, adult, nationwide, and almost entirely Negro audience. If the adjectives "unique," "pure," and "authentic" apply to any blues singer alive today, they certainly apply to B. B. King.

Upon being ushered into a small and crowded dressing room, I settled myself in a corner while B (as he is known to his friends) climbed out of his clothes and into a dressing gown. On the TV set in the corner Senator John Stennis from Mississippi was reading some remarks on the freedom march from a prepared text. B went over and turned up the volume, and everyone quieted down. "I'm sure the Congress will not be

5. An album recorded some time ago for the Crown label, *B. B. King Sings Spirituals* (Crown, 5119), was extremely popular, but this represented a clear and distinct departure from the usual blues output that has not been repeated since. Like Louis Jordan, T-Bone Walker, and a number of other established bluesmen I've talked with, B. B. believes in "keeping things separate."

pressured by any minority group into passing legislation that is not in the nation's interest. This march is going to backfire on the people who organized it," the senator drawled. I was embarrassed and muttering to myself. No one spoke. When the senator disappeared from the screen, B shook his head slowly and said simply, "I was born in Mississippi."

From this starting point we talked about blues and related topics late into the afternoon. Constant interruptions at the rate of about one every three minutes proved almost as informative as the interview itself, since B. B. King is many things to many people. The little sister of an old Memphis girl friend dropped by to say hello, and five or six other fans and folks from home found their way past the police sergeant at the stage door and into B's dressing room. Singers Gene Chandler and Chuck Jackson, the disc jockeys Purvis Spann and E. Rodney Jones,[6] and various band members stepped in for a minute or two, each with a different problem: to borrow a razor or a radio; to inquire when, where, and how to fix an amplifier; to pick up ice cubes, paper cups, Cokes; to discuss the party at Lee's Lounge the night before; to arrange a party for the coming evening; to ask for a stack of autographed pictures. One after another people "fell by" in a never ending stream, it seemed. No one was turned away; no favor was refused; all invitations were accepted that didn't conflict with the Regal's scheduled three shows a day —and, at this point, according to his own estimate, he had had less than twelve hours' sleep since arriving in Chicago six days earlier.

K: Seems like every time I talk to a touring blues singer backstage here or at a club, people from home keep showing up. Like I tried three different times to talk with Percy Mayfield when he was here with the Ray Charles show, and each time a hometown reunion shaped up and I couldn't get a word in.

6. On his all-night radio show, Spann invariably introduces B. B. King as "the President of the Amalgamated Blues Association, Incorporated," while Jones refers to B. B. as "the boss hoss—like Sea Biscuit, he never lost a race!"

B: Percy's a buddy of mine—a real stylist. His voice isn't great, but he can put a song over better than anybody. You know you can never afford to snub anybody in this business. Especially if you haven't been to town for a while, people will want to come on by and say hello. Turn your back on your friends, and the word spreads fast that you're snubbing people; and besides most of them you like to see anyway. Even if you can't remember the names the faces are familiar, and these are the people who like your music and respect you enough to come by and say hello. So unless I'm about to drop and need an hour's sleep to pick me up, my door is always open.

K: How do you get by on so little sleep?

B: I don't know. I catch an hour or two between shows and on the bus. Whenever there isn't something happening I drop off for a few minutes or a few hours, whatever I can get. It isn't much, believe me—there's always a little party somewhere or some piece of business to take care of. Like at Lee's Lounge last night, Chuck Jackson and I sang *Sweet Sixteen* together and it was something to hear. If somebody had a tape recorder there, they'd have gotten a hit single for sure. It's those good moments you hate to miss. Would have been quite a night if that bomb scare hadn't broken things up early [big laugh].

K: Somebody planted a bomb in the place? Sounds like Birmingham.

B: No. I think maybe one of his competitors was mad about all the business going to one place, so he decided to scare off some of the customers. Then somebody was telling me it was just some guy's old lady calling up to get her juiced husband home. "Get that bum out of there," she yells, and the barkeep thought she said "bomb," and that's how it got started. Anyway my wife and her mother were with me, and I didn't want to take chances, so we left early.

K: Sounds like a wild night. I've got a question here that I've had trouble getting an answer for. How come all the big blues singers used to be women—Bessie Smith and the other Smith girls, Ma Rainey, Alberta Hunter, and so on—and now it's all men?

B: That is a teaser. It's hard to say.

K: I've had some people tell me that the women don't have anything to be blue about any more, so just the men sing.

B: No . . . seems to me like any girl in a choir who's got any kind of voice at all can make more money as a pop singer or in the good clubs, or even calling herself a jazz singer, than she can by going into blues. It's mostly economics, I think. A female will make more money in other fields if she has any kind of voice, because blues singers are left out of the big clubs. Even Ray Charles won't get near the money that Nat [King Cole] will at the big clubs, Las Vegas, hotels and like that.

K: Why's that? He's selling more records, isn't he?

B: But Ray has still got the rock-and-roll label, even though he's following the Elvis Presley, Bobby Darin pattern, doing all he can to get rid of the label and into the big money—the big club money I should say, because the kids still buy most of the records.

K: I've heard a few things you've done with strings and things; are you trying to get into the pop market and out of the blues field?

B: No. I'm me. I sing blues, and that's what I do best. I won't ever get into the big money. *You Know I Love You* —I felt that all right, and it was sort of commercial. But most of the time I feel forced, hemmed in with all that stuff behind me. Strings are O.K., and later on I might be able to fit them into songs and still be myself, but not yet. Do you follow me?

K: I think so; a contrived context like that puts you off your stride.

B: Yeah, that's it. Let me put it this way. Frankie is Frankie, and he's the greatest. That doesn't mean I want to sing like him, but I would like to be called a singer, a musician, an artist, rather than a blues singer, and be given the same kind of respect for my style that Sinatra gets for his. When I go to a jazz club, sometimes the leader or the M. C. will say "B. B. King, the well-known blues singer, is in the audience tonight," and the way he says "blues" you know he really means "nasty." I'm a blues singer all right. And I don't mind being called a blues singer just so long as the tone of voice is right, you know. When a lot of people say "blues singer," you know they're thinking of some ignorant lush moaning in a gutter some place. I believe that if a bluesman leads a pretty straight life and really studies—I mean learns music—he can gain the respect of the people. Like Sonny and Floyd, they stick to their thing, they keep at it, and they get respect. If you're doing something as well as you can and working to improve, people shouldn't put you down. There's no reason why a man can't sing blues as a profession and still be a gentleman. That's the main reason I'm sticking with blues because I'd like to show people that it can be done.

K: What do you think of Lou Rawls? He sings blues and is given a lot of respect by jazz players.

B: I don't know . . . I guess I'm just a little critical about everybody, myself too; lots of records I hear today, mine too, don't move me much. I haven't heard him yet, really, but the sides I have heard gave me the same feeling as when I hear *Stardust* sung much too fast—do you know that feeling? He jives things a little too much for me, but I want to hear him more before I give an opinion. Sometimes you have to listen a long time before something gets to you.

K: Can you tell me a little about how you put your singing style together? Everybody seems to start out copying someone else, like Ray Charles copying Nat King Cole, and when I talked to Bobby Bland a few months ago, he said he used to copy you so hard he got hoarse, and that's how he found his own sound. Who did you copy at first?

B: Well, Dr. Clayton was the man that I used to idolize; just about everything he did, I used to sing along with it for hours. And Sammy McQuery, as a spiritual artist; that's Samuel H. McQuery of the Fairfield Four. I think he's gone back to preaching now. And Blind Lemon Jefferson is tied in there too. I used to listen to him on my aunt's Victrola, and he sang a style I really liked. Those three guys in about equal parts shaped my style, but I don't think I ever sounded like any one of them—more of a mixture plus my own contribution.

K: These were your only real influences?

B: I can list all kinds of singers that I've liked, like, well, Leroy Carr for one, Bumble Bee Slim, Gene Autry, and Jimmie Rodgers, Peetie Wheatstraw, Tommy McClennon, Tampa Red, and Lonnie Johnson—there's one of the greatest, a real musician. I like 'em all. But those three are the ones that I really wanted to sound like at first.

K: How about guitar playing—who appealed to you most when you were beginning to learn?

B: T-Bone [Walker] and Elmore James and that Frenchman, Django Reinhardt. Those three combined to one is the basis of my playing. And a little Charlie Christian too—I liked him a lot but never went out of my way to copy him.

K: When did you first hear Django?

B: I've had his records for a long time. His last record— just before he died, I guess—he plays electric guitar with an American-style rhythm section, all Frenchmens but they sound American, and Django plays some beautiful things.

K: He's one of my favorites too. While we're on the subject of copying, how do you feel about being copied so much? It's hard to find a guitarist in the clubs around Chicago that doesn't sound like you, and some of them are carbon copies. I've even heard of a B. B. King, Jr., playing around town. Does all this bother you?

B: Man, there are at least four little B. B.'s or B. B. King juniors running around now—one in New York, one in Chicago, one in California, I even heard of one back in Mississippi. If the name helps them get started, I don't suppose I mind much. I just hope they grow out of it. But it makes me feel good to be copied, makes me think the fourteen years I've spent in this business haven't been in vain. Being an influence makes me happy, and keeps me on my toes too. I always have to stay a little ahead of them. You know, some bluesmen are right where they were ten or twelve years ago, like a petrified forest. I like to keep improving and perfecting my way of playing so that every time I go on stage there's something different about the way I play. Back when I was featured with Tiny Brad- shaw, the guys in the band used to say, "Just sing, B, and you'll do all right; just keep singing and playing the way you are now and you've got nothing to worry about." I used to say, "Fine, O.K.," and then I found myself at an off-hours session one night out in California, and a man who really played guitar changed my mind. I heard Barney Kessel, and he shamed me. It made me want to study, study hard to better myself as a person and as a musician.

K: Self-improvement seems to be a big thing with you.

B: The ninth grade was as far as I ever got in school— started the tenth grade and quit. I've always regretted that, at least since my d. j. days, I've missed the lack of education. I keep taking correspondence courses on this and that, read when I get the chance, and I've even been working on a pilot's license. I've only been up a few times with the instructor, but I sure am proud of my hours. Man, people think the average blues singer is stupid, and I'd like to get that out of their heads, set things straight. It really hurts me to hear my people put blues down. It's our big contribution—something to be proud of. Some people don't want to lower themselves to listen, or they think they're lowering themselves if they listen; they're afraid of what people will say—that is, the people they think are better class. Some people like to copy the class above them, and they're the ones who won't listen. There have been times when I go out to sing and give it all I have—people just sit there, chin resting on one hand, staring into space. I mean they couldn't care less. When that happens, sometimes I walk off and cry. I'm serious—I really do cry. It's emotionally upsetting to see people hate my music who should like it.

K: How do you work with an audience? Do you have any tricks or techniques to get people on your side, ways that you build things to a climax? I think you know what I mean.

B: Sure—you're asking how I get across. Are people giving me a chance is the question. It's like hypnotism. If you don't want to be hypnotized, Houdini himself hasn't got a chance of putting you to sleep. But if you're the least bit willing, a good hypnotist can put you under in no time. Same thing as going with a woman; if she won't let you get started, keeps saying no, no, no, no, no, every time you open your mouth or make a move, you're not going to get anywhere. One little yes, and then it's up to you. If you can get an opening, then you try to draw an audience in to what you're doing little by little. Usually I try to build each song from the beginning and reach a climax at the end, but sometimes I'll make a strong pitch to the audience with one line that I know will get a reaction—depends on the tune. Like there's one tune I do where I say in the middle of it, "I gave you seven children, and now you want to give 'em back." I really punch that line and it always gets a big reaction. But I've never had people screaming their heads off when I come on, like the school girls do for Gene [Chandler] or Chuck [Jackson]; if people like it, they sit and enjoy it—that's all. Some yell out occasionally, and that gives me courage, but there's never a big crowd reaction for me even though we usually outdraw the competition.

K: The times I've heard you, the first phrase you sing or the first thing you do on guitar usually gets a big reaction or at least applause and some shouting.

B: Yeah, I guess the people like to show that they recognize me. The way the guitar equals the voice, people like that—the two make one, and it fits together. They like my funky guitar; there's slightly more response for a familiar phrase on guitar than when I sing. I work hard every time I go out there, and they usually appreciate the effort. You can feel completely helpless on stage if there's no response. It's frightening. I'll take a nightclub over the stage every time.

K: What kind of music do you like besides blues?

B: I like to think I'm open to all kinds of music. You should listen to everything, take each man as he comes. I've got about fifteen thousand records in a collection at home, cylinders, lots of 78's of the older singers, and a lot of things besides blues, little bit of everything. Spanish music I like, and there's a Japanese instrument that sounds something like a guitar that knocks me out.

K: I'll bet you're thinking of koto music.

B: I think that's it. It has a movable set of bridges, and they hit one note at a time, slow and hard. I didn't hear it at first, and then it began to reach me after I listened a few times. That's soul all right.

K: Do you have any specific plans for the future?

B: Well, like I said, I don't think going commercial is the answer. I've been studying arranging, reading Schillinger, because what I would really like is a band that echoes my guitar—like Ray's [Charles'] band sets off his piano playing. I've had guys do arrangements for me that weren't bad; and my musicians are O.K., but they play standard things behind me. I won't really feel like an artist —you know, gone as far as I can go—until I get me some arrangements that really add a third part to my guitar and voice and make everything fit together just right. And I'm the only one who can do it, because nobody else is me.

B. B. has appeared in Chicago a number of times since August, 1963, and my visits with him on these occasions have reaffirmed my initial impressions. His involvement with the blues life remains total; sleep is still a scarce commodity, a flux of details need personal attention, and B is still omniavailable to band members, promoters, friends, fans, and the intermittent interviewer.

When last I saw him he was sitting on a bed in the Evans Hotel, sorting out the contents of the miniature filing cabinet that is his wallet. In the midst of the myriad slips and cards spread over the blanket, B pointed with pride to a pilot's certificate, acquired that same morning, saying, "Now I can fly solo." A lady dropped in—a friend of a friend of a friend—and asked B. B. if she might ride on the bus to Los Angeles, the band's next destination; after some discussion with road manager Cato Walker, B acquiesced even though the vehicle was already overcrowded. The Beale Street Blues Boy may be flying high in more ways than one, but he is still a man of and for the people.

Recently B. B. seems to have assumed a slightly different position in the entertainment world. Some months ago he signed up with ABC-Paramount. Judging by the notes on the jacket of his first album for this company, Paramount hopes that he will gain a larger audience during the next few years, in the manner of Ray Charles. A recent hit record called *Help the Poor* includes a female vocal group in the responsorial role—another indication of a shift in King's repertoire in the direction of the Charles model. Lest the reader conclude from the title of this song that B has abandoned his usual personal appeal in favor of protest lyrics, the opening line is "Help the poor; baby, help poor me." Most of his currently popular numbers, however, are still reworkings of older blues materials. I suspect that he will continue to utilize the blues almost exclusively in the foreseeable future, but will also continue to experiment in his recording efforts from time to time, testing different arrangements, band instrumentations, and vocal group backgrounds as frameworks for his voice and guitar.

As for the distant future, B. B. King has more definite plans than most bluesmen. Bobby Bland intends to sing for a living "as long as anyone will come to hear me"; should his popularity decrease drastically, he will probably have to scuffle and "hustle" for a living like any other unskilled Negro. Jr. Parker foresees the day when he will give up the fast world, like a number of bluesmen before him, for the more secure and sedentary profession of preaching, although Parker is not sure at present whether he will become a Black Muslim or Baptist minister. B. B., on the other hand, is investing his earnings in a number of different enterprises and plans to maintain his association with music in one capacity or another. He has partial interests in two small record companies, owns a farm in Tennessee, where he hopes to build a small motel. When his touring days are over, he would like to have his own nightclub, do some promoting on a small scale, go back to spinning records at the local radio station, run the motel and a service station—in short, if his plans work out, B. B. King will be as busy as ever but free of the perpetual travel that is both the bane and balm of the blues life.

CHAPTER V

BIG BOBBY BLUE BLAND
ON STAGE

BOBBY BLUE BLAND has been variously described by his fans (mostly female) as a "big sweet boy," a "lovable slob," and "one of them handsome brutes." And on the back of one of his albums we find: "Bobby is a quiet easy going modest young man, who likes to go to the movies and baseball games. He is also an ardent admirer of good gospel music . . . a smart conservative dresser and shy guy around the girls."[1]

All these descriptions fit not only his public image but his personality in private life as well. They only hint, however, at the paradoxical qualities of the man. On stage and off he manages to convey the impression of being helpless, naïve, childish—yet he also seems to be in control, well groomed, self-assured, reliable, and a gentle taskmaster. This baby-boss combination adds up not only to irresistible sex appeal but to charisma of a kind that may be peculiar to Negro culture.[2] In Bobby Bland's performance the baby-boss duality is subtly dramatized in a number of different ways, as we shall see.

But first, an introduction to the key members of the Bland organization is in order. Behind Bobby Bland the performer are

1. *Here's the Man!* Duke, 75.
2. On the other hand, the Democratic Kennedys and Republican John Lindsay seem to share this quality of boyish command.

mastermind Joe Scott, and business manager John Green. In front of Bobby are Al "T.N.T." Braggs,[3] his foil and alter ego, and Brother Dave Clark, publicity man.

Joe Scott leads the band, does practically all the arranging for it, and plays fine trumpet as a complement to some of Bobby's vocals. According to some insiders, Bobby Bland is Joe Scott's creation.

This is something of an exaggeration, but it is certainly true that Scott is very much the show's director and that without Scott's original and coordinative talents, Bland would probably be just another blues singer. Yet Scott prefers to remain in the background. He is often conspicuous by his absence as the band plays with no one sitting in the first trumpet chair. Even when he is on stage, other members of the band usually count off the tempo or signal the cut-off point at the conclusion of a song. Only Scott's goatee and his trumpet, a horn with two bells (a unique instrument that apparently helps to extend his range of notes and timbres), mark him as someone out of the ordinary when he is on stage.[4]

Although Scott is the omniscient and somewhat mysterious figure behind the scenes, Braggs is very much out in front, a veritable stereotype of the show business personality. Braggs is skinny, nervous, and constantly performing. Backstage at the Ashland Auditorium he will usually be found playing at the piano and singing to himself or to anyone who will listen. If Bland is in his dressing room, Braggs will occasionally run in to demonstrate a variation on a song that he has worked out. He drapes himself over Bobby's shoulder and sings the lyric into Bland's ear, imitating Bobby's sound and phrasing so perfectly that without visual cues the listener would swear that Bland is singing to Braggs and not vice versa. On stage he is dressed in pegged pants that are almost skin tight and a short bus-boy-type jacket. The net effect is of a scrawny José Greco. He does the

3. For some reason the pluralization of last names is a common practice in the Negro community. For example, jazz pianist Horace Silver is often referred to as Silvers; Sam Cooke becomes Sam Cookes.

4. In recent appearances Scott has restricted himself to leading the band and his double-barreled trumpet is no longer in evidence.

currently popular dances (the monkey, twist, flea, or whatever) in a jerky, energetic style, throwing around his processed hair with flicks of his head like a self-propelled puppet. From the moment he steps onto the stage he is always moving and exhorting his audience to move with him. His most crowd-pleasing dance steps are invariably those in which it looks as if some sections of his body do not know what outlandish things the other parts of his body are doing. It is the same sort of technique that middle-aged men employ when they dance a short solo at the blues bars around Chicago; the torso remains stationary while feet, knees, and legs, gyrate in a dozen different directions. As a singer, Braggs can imitate anyone (see above) but usually restricts himself to a number or two in B. B. King's style, in which Wayne Bennett, Bland's guitarist, provides the King-like accompaniment. Or he may do a few songs that are currently popular, sounding exactly like whichever artist it was that made the song a hit. In short, Scott is a creator, but Braggs is an imitator—a flexible and dynamic shell into which a variety of contents can be poured as they are needed. Because of his great eagerness to please both his employers and his audience, Braggs is a handy man to have around. He can fill any required role—and does—but the question of who Al Braggs really is, is almost as perplexing as the question of what Joe Scott really does. In very different ways, they are indispensable to Bobby Bland, the star, polishing and completing his performance every step of the way.

Two other important components in the Bland organization are the band itself and the Bland Dolls (see note 7, page 118).

Over the past few years Scott has brought together an impressive group of eleven musicians, all of whom are well trained and—as musicians go—enthusiastic about playing in the band. Most of the musicians[5] were band leaders in their own

5. The personnel of Bland's band: Wayne Bennett, guitar (Chicago); Plummer Davis, trombone (Houston); Melvin Jackson, trumpet (Nashville); John Starks, drums (Mobile); Charles Crawford, baritone sax (Memphis); Hamp Simmons, electric bass (Houston); Johnny Board, alto sax (Chicago); Jimmy Beck, tenor sax (Cleveland); Bobby Forte, tenor sax (San Francisco).

Bobby Bland

So you take it
  where you find it,
Or leave it like it is.
That's the way
  it's always been,
That's the way love is.

PHOTOGRAPHS BY
STANLEY KARTER

Lightnin' Hopkins

The older "boys"
deliver this material directly
with an important
but subtle use
of gestural or dramatic
ornament.

PHOTOGRAPHS BY RAEBURN FLERLAGE

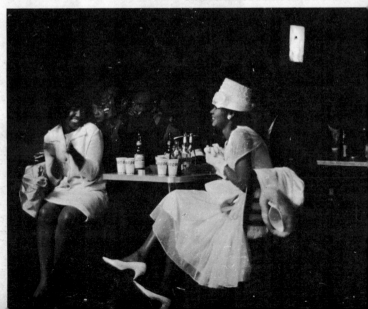

*Al
"T.N.T."
Braggs*

Skinny, nervous,
and constantly
performing.

Ray Charles

The rare instance
of an artist
who has enjoyed
wide popularity
among whites
but still retains
the avid
appreciation of the
blues people.

B. B. King

"If you're
the least bit willing,
a good hypnotist
can put you under
in no time."

Muddy Waters

A minority group
still like the dirtier down-and-out styles
of Muddy Waters and Howlin' Wolf.

PHOTOGRAPH BY RAEBURN FLERLAGE

Little Jr. Parker

"The blues
is based on somebody's life;
it hits 'em in the heart,
and the love comes out."

PHOTOGRAPHS BY RAEBURN FLERLAGE

Howlin' Wolf

Known to one white American in a million
ten years ago, he can now be summoned by the State Department
to appear at a Washington festival of the arts
and very few eyebrows are raised.

PHOTOGRAPHS BY RAEBURN FLERLAGE

right before joining the group. The nucleus of the present band has been together for almost eight years, and was directed by Hamp Simmons until Bland and Scott took over the operation. Some of the musicians in blues groups are usually malcontents who are either simply working for a living or biding their time until they are proficient enough to gain access to the jazz community. One of the chief complaints of bluesmen concerns their lack of security. It is true that while a bluesman is popular his work is steadier than that of the average jazz player who goes job hunting from one night, week, or month to the next, but the long-term rewards from working a few years behind a touring blues singer are negligible. As one musician put it, "If B. B. King were to retire tomorrow, or get killed in a car accident or something, we'd be nowhere, but like when Glenn Miller gets hisself killed in a airplane crash, the guys in his band can go right along without him on his reputation, on his sound. But without B, we've had it." By comparison Scott's men are secure—a number of performers would be happy to have Scott and company take care of their musical settings. The band is a unit, not simply an accompanying group, and they know it and show it at every performance. There are a number of soloists in the band, besides Scott and Bennett the guitarist, who can step to the microphone and deliver just the right melodic lines in response to Bobby's vocals. When necessary the band can sustain interest by itself with a sax battle (there are two first-rate tenor players in the band) or a series of better-than-average jazz solos. When Bland is playing an engagement without other singers on the bill, the band plays for dancing for an hour or two before the show itself or between shows if necessary. The band, then, is both the foundation and the sustaining force in any Bobby Bland appearance. Like any rhythmic music, whether martial or dance, it unites all the people within listening range through a steady irresistible pulse.[6] As long as the band is playing, people are necessarily

6. The difference between white and black culture can, however, be summarized concisely as the difference between white march music, in which the accents fall on 1 and 3 of a 4–4 measure, and Negro dance music, which emphasizes 2 and 4, the "off beats" or "back beats." Some

involved with each other via a common rhythm and are kept in a state not only of active participation but of keen anticipation as well, for everyone knows that when Bland steps into the spotlight this is the kind of band that will frame him perfectly.

The Bland Dolls, a singing trio of girls, were for a short time part of the troupe[7] and were clearly patterned after the Raylettes, the three girls who are an integral part of the Ray Charles package. The girls in trios of this kind usually come directly from church choirs and are used in those songs that have a gospel chord progression. They usually repeat one phrase over and over again (usually the title of the song) in response to the cries and shouts of the male vocalist. They are the frame within the frame, so to speak; although they are usually positioned at the opposite side of the stage on a separate microphone, they surround the big man with sound and provide the vocal springboard from which he can "jump and shout."

Let us examine in some detail what actually happens at a Bobby Bland performance.

Imagine yourself at the Ashland Auditorium on Chicago's West Side about ten o'clock on a Saturday night. Climbing the stairs and entering the hall, you survey the scene. About two thousand people are present; there are perhaps one or two white faces in the crowd. Tables are spread on the ground floor, and groups of ten or twelve are sitting around them drinking and having a good time. Waitresses in party hats are wandering around taking orders and bringing ice, beer, mixers, and the like from the long bar in the lobby behind the stage. People are meeting and greeting each other here and there in the ritualistic manner so common all over the Chicago ghetto: a shout of recognition, "Hey, how you feelin'?" "Wha's happenin'?"; the slap-

---

Negro artists who find their way into white concert halls still find it necessary to "hip" those "stiffies" in the audience who insist on clapping their hands in a martial manner.

7. Today the Bland Dolls are no longer part of the show. According to Braggs they were a source of much dissension in the band and rather than fire the musicians involved, the girls were dismissed. Miss Elvira Campbell is now the only girl vocalist.

ping of hands and a shake that may last as long as a minute; hands remain clasped, arms flop over shoulders, heads shake in disbelief, and the patterned banter appropriate to such occasions will go on for some time before the greeters disengage. In the tiers of seats surrounding the ground floor and in the balconies, young men sit by themselves or in pairs looking for friends and stray chicks. A number of couples, some of them getting along in years, also watch the proceedings from these vantage points, waiting for the action to begin. Almost everyone is very well dressed—red outfits are especially popular among the women. Noise reverberates, and loud, long laughs echo noticeably in the large hall.

The band members file onto the stage. They warm up their instruments, and a few dozen patrons gather around the stage and shout their greetings to old friends in the band. Happy reunion scenes, similar to the greeting ritual described above, take place on the stairs leading up to the stage and behind the band stand; it is a long time before everyone is assembled and ready to begin. Joe Scott's chair is vacant—he is probably off somewhere working on an arrangement or renewing acquaintances with one of his many female admirers. The band usually opens with a flag waver in the Count Basie tradition, showing off and letting everybody know that things are underway in earnest. (At the Regal Theatre the band usually begins with a different tactic; a slow, relaxed blues tune sets the mood, as the movie screen is rolled up.) Usually no one dances during the first few numbers, but some couples take to the floor when the band does the first twist number. Cries of "work it on out" are heard as a large lady and her partner really begin to move. More dancers move out to the floor with succeeding pieces, as the spirit moves them, but most of the people stay seated or wander around without dancing throughout the evening.[8]

8. The fact that dancing is not an integral part of a blues party atmosphere was brought home to me in my visits to Indianapolis blues clubs. There is a city ordinance forbidding dancing at any place where there is a bar, and consequently people sit for hours while the musicians on the platform play violent, danceable music, acting out the various dances for an immobile but attentive audience.

The band pauses, and the M. C.—usually a local disc jockey —makes his appearance. He bellows into the microphone a few questions on the order of "Is *EV*erybody happy?", and the crowd answers with a drawn out "Yeah" each time. The M. C. introduces Al Braggs with a string of adjectives; Braggs bounces and skips his way to the center of the stage, gives the M. C. a big hug and a hand slap, then immediately plunges into his routine. Usually his first song is a fast and vigorous call-and-response number in which Braggs strides back and forth across the stage, microphone in hand, shouting, "Are you ready?" or "Everything's all right," with the full band answering back each time he repeats the phrase. The A section of this type of song consists of these repeated calls and responses, whereas the release or B section usually consists of phrases describing the ongoing events or, as noted above, the dances of the day: "Now the band really starts to blow, Come on, everybody, let's go"; or "When the band begins to play, everybody shout hey-yay"; "Let's everybody do the flea, do it right along with me"; "We do the monkey, yeah, we do the monkey"; or "Do the bulldog, do the hound dog, do the bird dog." And so forth. Braggs usually saves his dance demonstrations for the second number, which is otherwise much like the first. As he encourages everyone to do the dances, he performs them simultaneously: the flea—he scratches madly at various parts of his twitching body, and the audience yells its encouragement; the monkey—he climbs an imaginary coconut tree, does a King Kong imitation, and peels an imaginary banana as a couple near the stage picks up the cue and monkies along with him; the dog—he mimics the motions of a copulating canine, the audience laughs, and a few band members cover their eyes in mock horror. If circumstances permit, he will encourage two or three women in the audience to come onstage and participate in the dancing. Finally, he does some of his special twist variations to finish the song and receives warm applause.

One of Braggs' most interesting routines is based on a blues associated with Little Jr. Parker and entitled *Drivin' Wheel*. The first and last verses are:

My baby don't have to work,
She don't have to rob and steal.
(repeated)

I give her everything she needs;
I *am* her drivin' wheel.

Every time she walks
She's like a leaf shakin' on a tree.
(repeated)

I want you to come on baby,
Here's where you get your steak, potatoes and tea.

Braggs uses the song as a vehicle for a great deal of graphic sexual imagery and *double-entendres*. After the first verse he tells the girls, "I want you to walk like this for your man," and does an exaggerated bump-and-grind strut; the girls squeal. Suddenly the band stops, and Braggs calls like a combined Baptist preacher and auctioneer: "Do you want a hot dog with lots of relish on it?"; crowd answers "Yeah!"; "Well, you can get it right here (pointing to the tenor sax player). Do you want a big hamburger with plenty of catsup and onions with it? Get it right here (points to guitarist). Do you want some hot pastrami on rye? Do you want a twelve-inch hot dog with all kinds of mustard?"—and so it goes until all the members of the band have been accounted for except the little bassist Hamp Simmons. Braggs makes a big fuss about bringing him out front into the spotlight and then asks, "Do you want a sardine sandwich?" As the laughter dies down, Hamp walks dejectedly back to his place and the band begins to play. The trombone player comes forward as if to take a solo, but instead puts the instrument between his legs and manipulates the slide in a most sensuous manner. He then tucks his large white handkerchief into Braggs' belt, and as Mr. T.N.T. sings the final chorus of *Drivin' Wheel*, he dances all around a motionless pendulum.

Braggs may also do one of B. B. King's best-known vocals, word for word, phrase for phrase, but this is not such a crowd-pleaser; most of the audience have heard the real thing, and an imitation, no matter how exact, is still an imitation. Nevertheless, Braggs' mimicry is something like an invocation to an absent god or gods; intentionally or otherwise, Braggs' reiteration probably leaves the audience thinking, "Wouldn't it be nice if B. B. King were really here." And if Braggs faithfully renders a song identified with the late Sam Cooke, Freddie King, or Ray Charles, to name but a few other figures in the pantheon, I suspect the effect is much the same. Although these mimed invocations offer certain important but limited satisfactions in themselves, perhaps their most important function is to highlight the importance of the genuine article: Bobby Bland in the flesh. Braggs' homage is a strong reminder that in a little while they will be hearing a singer who is his own man, with songs and a style that are personal and even unique.

Braggs usually concludes his part of the show by pulling out all the vocal and choreographic stops with a cry routine in the general manner of James Brown or Little Richard. Normally this is a direct orgasmic appeal to the fairer sex but, as Braggs does it, pleading plays a secondary part to gymnastics. He screams; he groans; he crawls rhythmically across the stage on his stomach dragging the microphone behind him; he leaps over, under, and around the microphone cord; he lies on his back and kicks his feet in the air; he does some syncopated push-ups; he falls halfway over the edge of the stage and grabs the nearest hands; initiating a few unfinished dance steps, he does the limbo; he bumps and grinds; and gradually maneuvers himself off stage with a flying split or two, still twitching and shouting. A big ovation follows, and the M. C. appears saying, "Al Braggs, ladies and gentlemen." Braggs takes his curtain call, still bobbing and weaving, and disappears again in perpetual motion.

Even if a fan has been doing nothing more than sitting at a table, bending his elbow occasionally, Al Braggs' carrying-on leaves the viewer limp, exhausted, and sighing a mixture of relief and satisfaction. This sort of catharsis contributes a great deal to the feeling of mellowness, and "mellow" is the adjective most frequently used by participants to describe a good blues scene.

Bobby Bland's introduction is a set piece with band accompaniment. A loud drum rim-shot, a chord from the saxophones, a trumpet flourish, and the M. C. says, "Ladies and gentlemen, here's the man (trumpet fanfare). I mean the MAN (fanfare), the sensational (band chord sustained), the incomparable (chord), the dynamic Bobby (silent pause by band, and screams and cheers from audience), Bobby Bland!" (fanfare leading immediately into the introduction of the first number).

Bobby ambles on stage in a well-tailored white suit that contrasts markedly with Braggs' tight black outfit. He wanders about slowly, microphone in hand. He seems to have something on his mind, and—sure enough—it's a woman. Typically he will begin with a slow blues in the analytic vein, like *The Feeling Is Gone*.

> When I needed you, to stand by my side
> All you did, was laugh while I cried.
> And now you want me, to take you back in my arms.
> Oh-oooo-oh, it's too late, baby
> I'm here to tell you that the feelin' is gone.
>
> I remember, the look on your face,
> Oooow, when you told me, that I was being replaced.
> Now you're beggin' me, you say you wanna come back home.
> Oh-oooo-oh, it's too late baby.
> I'm standin' here to tell you that the feelin' is gone.
>
> You told me to hit the road, and I did just that.
> Now you find out that you need me, but ooh, I ain't comin' back.
> And now you say you want me, to take you back in my arms.
> Oh-oooo-oh, I say it's too late baby
> Loooooorrrd, I tell you the feelin' is gone.

This song is delivered in a relaxed, easy-going style for the most part. Aside from a brassy introduction and ending and some soft masses of sound by the full band at carefully selected points in the second stanza, the accompaniment consists of droning electric bass, a loose triplet rhythm on drums, sustained guitar chords and piano adornments. All the distinctive features of Bland's vocal style are in evidence, notably the hoarse cry and his use of melisma on key words. Bland's cry usually consists of a twisted vowel at the beginning of a phrase—going from a given note, reaching up to another higher one, and coming back to the starting point—as in the "Oh-oooo-oh's" of the lyric above. He is likely to treat any vowel in this way: ah-oowl-ways, day-ee-ay-ee-ays, cry-eee-eyes. The first few times he does this, and from time to time as he climaxes other songs with this device, women sprinkled throughout the audience yell back at him, shaking their heads and waving their hands on high. Almost without exception Bobby uses more than one note per syllable on the concluding word of each phrase. For example, in the last stanza of the above lyric, "road" and "that" in the first line get two notes each; "ooh" and "back" in the second line get the same treatment; in the third line, "back" has five notes and "arms" has three; the last words of the concluding lines receive four- and five-note treatment respectively. At slower tempos he will stretch out syllables with even more melisma, using as many as ten or eleven notes over a two-syllable word. Melisma of this kind is not found in many of the older blues styles, but is derived directly from the intensely emotional services of the Negro fundamentalist churches. Bland and Aretha Franklin use more melisma than almost anyone else,[9] and it is no coincidence that they are designated as the king and queen of the soul singers by many of the blues people.

Another analytic song is *Your Friends*, a classic in the modern blues genre. Only trumpet and rhythm section accompany Bland here, but the interweaving of vocal and instrumental lines in the recorded version of this song is the closest thing to a perfect example of contemporary blues singing that I have encountered in my research. (Unfortunately, Bland doesn't do

9. *Aretha*, Columbia, CL 1612.

this tune very often in person.) At the conclusion of *Your Friends* there is an excellent example of the intentional hang-up or calculated stutter, another stylistic feature shared by some preachers and a few bluesmen. Older bluesmen have employed stuttering and other speech-impediment imitations to good effect —for example, Lightnin' Hopkins' long narrative introduction to *Mr. Charlie*[10] or Champion Jack Dupree's many versions of *Harelip Blues*.[11] John Lee Hooker—and perhaps other singers— stutters in conversation but is free of this handicap when he sings. The calculated stutter is not a novelty effect, an attempt at humor, or an actual impediment, but is rather a device used by preachers and bluesmen to convince an audience that they are trying to verbalize an emotion too big for words. This stutter also serves a structural purpose as well as an expressive one, since the stutter or intentional hang-up delays the arrival of an important word in the phrase and/or note in the melodic line. Bland rarely uses this device, either on records or in person, but when he does stumble over a word it lends just the right touch of conviction. On the other hand, some preachers may overwork the stutter until it is just another mannerism.

In Bland's stage show, he is likely to turn from a relaxed analysis of the situation in his opening song to an energetic plea for assistance in the second. During the first number he talks to the audience, asking, "Do I have a witness out there?"; they always respond in the affirmative, using many of the same phrases that would be used in church; "Tell it like it is," "Lord, have mercy," "All right, brother." Now he sings the same sort of request rather than speaking it between stanzas. Not too many years ago, *Loan a Helping Hand* was his best-known song in this category:

> Well, somebody, yes, somebody,
> Please, somebody, before I go insane,
> Won't somebody
> Please lend me a helpin' hand.

10. Candid, 8010.
11. King, 735

I've got money, and I've got a place to stay,
I've got money, and I've got a place to stay,
But everybody needs a friend, both night and day.

Well, I walk, talk—but all by myself,
Well, I walk, talk—but all by myself,
I'm so afraid, it's gonna wear me to death.

Well, somebody, yes, somebody,
Please, somebody, oh, baby,
Please, somebody,
Won't you lend me a helpin' hand.

More recently *Turn on Your Love Light* has been one of the most popular up-tempo songs in this genre, and the pleading has been more overtly toward the women in the audience. This is a full production number and is done at a fast twist tempo. In the middle section Bobby is accompanied only by drums. He effectively builds his cries and pleadings to a tenor sax solo with trumpets riffing in the background and brings the whole development to a frenzied climax in the third section. Notice that the lyric begins with Bobby blue and broken-hearted and ends with "I feel all right," a fine example of a blues catharsis.

Without a warnin', you broke my heart.
You shook it darlin', and you tore it apart.
You left me sittin', in the dark cryin'.
You said your love, for me was dying.
I'm beggin' you baby, baby please,
I'm beggin' you baby, baby please.
Turn on the light, let it shine on me.
Turn on your love light, let it shine on me.
Let it shine, shine, shine, let it shine (screaming brass).
(drums) I get a little lonely, in the middle of the night.
I need you, darlin', to make things all right.

Come on baby, come on please.
Come on baby, baby please.
Turn on the light, let it shine on me.

Turn on your love light, let it shine on me.
A little bit higher (enter rest of rhythm section)
A little bit higher now,
A little bit higher,
Yes, a little bit higher,
Just a little bit higher (sax solo, trumpet riffs).

Come on, baby,
Come on, please,
I'm beggin' you, baby
I'm down on my knees
Turn on the light, let it shine on me.
Turn on your love light, let it shine on me.
I feel all right.
I feel all right.
I'm feelin' all right (begins to fade out).
I feel all right, baby.
Let it shine, mmmmmmmm.

From this point, Bland may vary his program in a number of ways, using songs from four other fairly distinct genres within his repertoire: songs of praise, songs of good feeling, songs of vengeance and despair, and songs of dependability. Bland and Scott mix their presentation differently from show to show and from night to night. Sometimes, like a good quarterback, Bland may shift the format at the line of scrimmage, announcing a number that may suit his mood and the mood of the audience, waiting momentarily for the band members to dig out the arrangement from the book. Bland may decide to sustain the concluding mood of *Turn on Your Love Light* by doing a song of good feeling: *Don't Cry No More* or *Ain't It a Good Thing*.

Forget about your troubles; forget about all your sorrow,
You're a beggar today, a king tomorrow.

Baby, don't you worry, when things go wrong,
Lift up your voices,
And help me to sing this song.

Now ain't it a good thing,
Ain't it a good thing
Loooord—one more time
Ain't it a good thing—good thing
That trouble don't last always.
Oh, yeah.

Honky Tonk, one of Bobby's hits, begins in the feeling-good genre, goes on to develop an important urban blues theme, and concludes with the carefree stance. The refrain implies that Bland is not class-conscious and is happy to perform for all people; subsequent verses also concisely emphasize his essential reasons for singing. When a good man is played for a sucker and made to look like a fool, he bounces back by singing the blues.

Well, I'm tired of being abused,
I'm tired of feeling low,
I'm gonna have myself some fun,
Oh, I'm not gonna worry no more.

(*refrain*):
'Cause I'm gonna play the high class joints,
I'm gonna play the low class joints,
And, baby, I'm even gonna play the honky tonks.

Well, I've always been true,
I never told you a lie.
  (refrain)

No matter what I say
I just can't satisfy.

I'm gonna . . .
  (refrain)

I haven't been runnin' around,
I just been playin' it cool.
I thought that you would change
Yet, you treat me like a fool.

Well, I'm gonna . . .
    (refrain)

Now if you want to leave,
You can just help yourself.
Yes, I've woke up now, baby,
And I'm no longer on the shelf.

Although these lyrics focus once again on the tensions and bitter frustrations that accompany the breaking up of a good thing, Bland's delivery and the band's forceful accompaniment paradoxically create a feeling of release and resiliency, even of satisfaction.

When a mellow mood has been established and everything's all right, Bland may slow up the tempo and take the soft and tender approach as only he can. As the liner notes to his most recent album say, "If there ever was a singer of the truth, here is one who has the drive, the voice and control to tenderly caress the words of a song as if he was actually caressing a loved one, and on the other hand, scold her with veracity when she has wronged."[12] There are many examples in the caressing category, or what I have called praise songs, notably *You're the One That I Adore*, *Ain't That Lovin' You?*, and *You're Worth It All*.

Soft tears that I shed for you,
The little favors that I loved to do,
The quick response to your every call,
Oh, darlin', oh, darlin', you're worth it all.

The lonely nights leave me so blue,
The little white lies you know are true,
I know I'm headed for a fall,
But oh, darlin', oh, darlin', yeah, you're worth it all.

But I know you're, I know you're worth it all, baby.

The half-spoken, half-sung conclusion to this song (only parts of which are quoted here) is still another piece of evidence for

12. *Bobby Bland*, Duke, 77.

the close stylistic ties between today's blues singers and preachers. The broken phrase and repetition are the functional equivalent of the intentional hang-up or calculated stutter, and are even more commonly used by Bland, especially at slower tempos. Aretha Franklin[13] is the outstanding exponent of this technique today, and her father, the Reverend C. L. Franklin, also handles it well in his sermons and parables.[14] Particularly in the chanted parables, Reverend Franklin relies on the repetition of phrases and parts of phrases to keep up the momentum of his "deliverance."

Bland can also scold. Between songs of praise, feeling-good material, and pleadings to the fairer sex, what I have called songs of vengeance and despair are sometimes inserted for a change of pace. They show the less satisfying side of the mating game, and probably have a stronger appeal to the men in the audience. These songs bear a closer affinity to traditional blues material than do most of the songs in Bland's repertoire, and are usually spiced with folk sayings and folk wisdom. When Bobby first started, these songs were his biggest hits, but they have since become only one small part of a balanced program.

Farther Up the Road (or, more recently, *Twistin' Up the Road*) was one of Bobby's first big hits, and he still answers many requests for it every time he appears in Chicago:

> You got to reap just what you sow;
> That old saying is true.
>   (repeat)
> Like you mistreat someone,
> Someone gonna mistreat you.
>
> Now you're laughin', pretty baby,
> Someday you're gonna be cryin'.
>   (repeat)
> Further on up the road
> You'll find out I wasn't lyin'.

13. Hear especially, *Maybe I'm a Fool* on Columbia, CL 1612.
14. Any one of his albums for Chess or Battle Records will furnish a number of fine examples.

Farther on up the road
When you're all alone 'n' blue
  (repeat)
You're gonna ask me to take you back, baby,
But I'll have somebody new.

The "fool" songs—*I Pity the Fool* and *Who Will the Next Fool Be?*—are also of this type. The former is the only song I have heard Bobby sing that stresses anger and outrage from beginning to end. The full band plays staccato quarter notes on every beat of the measure, and Bobby screams:

Look at the people.
I know you're wondering what they're doing,
They're just standing there
Watching you make a fool of me.

Oh, I pity the fool,
Oh, I pity the fool
That was in love with you
And expected you to be true,
Oh, I pity the fool.

Or in *Who Will the Next Fool Be?*:

After all is said and done,
You won't be satisfied with anyone,
So after you get rid of me, baby,
Tell me, who will the next fool be?

On his latest album, Bland takes his cue from the radio quiz show and reworks the vengeance theme as follows:

From mink to rabbit,
Ain't it a shame,
It's your own fault, baby,
Lord, you have yourself to blame.

So don't cry tomorrow,
Don't cry tomorrow when you hear me say
Well, I want you to tiptoe down offa that throne, baby,
Because you were only Queen for a day.

Having given some vicarious satisfaction to the men in the audience, while at the same time having warned the women that he's not a man to be trifled with, Bobby usually works toward the conclusion of his program with a song or two of dependability. To this point, Bland has worked largely with his audience, discussing his problems and theirs, occasionally voicing encouragement to various members of the band as they take their solos or respond to lyrics, but for the most part simply singing his songs as straightforwardly as possible. But now the drama begins to unfold, with Big Bobby Blue Bland as protagonist, the protector, the man who can be relied upon through all adversity, the center of attention who gathers everyone around him into a tight unit.

Lyric segments from *Ain't That Lovin' You?*, *I'll Take Care of You*, and *Call on Me* illustrate the mood of confidence that Bland creates as he moves to the finale.

Ain't That Lovin' You?

You build my hopes so high,
And then you let me down so low,

It makes no difference, darling,
I just love you more and more.

And every time you smile,
You know I'm smiling with you.

Every time you cry
You know I shed a few tears, too.

Ain't that lovin' you, baby,
Ain't that lovin' you,
Ain't that lovin' you,
I know that's lovin' you.

I don't believe, I don't believe
You know what I'm talkin' about.
(Joe Scott comes to the microphone and literally converses with Bobby via his muted trumpet, reassuring him melod-

ically that indeed he knows exactly what Bobby is saying.)

I don't believe, I don't believe
You know what I'm talkin' about.

I'm talkin' about love, love, love,
I'm talkin' about love, love, love,
I'm talkin' about love, love, love,

You know I told you, darling,
That I'd never let you down.
And no matter what you do
I'd always be around.
You treat me like a school boy
That you know is true,
It makes no difference, darlin',
I'll take care of you.

Ain't that lovin' you, baby? (saxophone answers)
Etc, etc. (band echoes saxophone)

I'll Take Care of You

I know you've been hurt by someone else,
I can tell by the way you carry yourself,
But if you'll let me, here's what I'll do—
I'll take care of you.

I've loved and lost, the same as you,
So you see, I know, just what you've been through,
But if you'll let me, here's what I'll do,
Oh, I just got to take care of you.

Call on Me

You needn't be lonely
You shouldn't be blue,
I'll design a life of love for you.
And here's all you got to do.

> When you need a good loving,
> When you need a good kissing,
> When you need a good hugging,
>   Yeah, yeah, yeah,
> Won't you call on me?

On the cover of one of Bland's albums,[15] there is a picture of Bobby well groomed, down to his manicured and polished fingernails, and so relaxed that he hasn't bothered to flick the long ash from his cigarette. He has a big warm smile on his boyish face and is surrounded by four telephones in pastel shades. The title reads *Call on Me*. There are smaller pictures of four women, phone receivers in their hands: a *femme fatale* in the upper left-hand corner, a shy adolescent girl in the upper right, a stylish young matron in the lower left, and a high society lady at his right elbow. Obviously Bobby appeals to all classes and age groups, and still more obviously he is a ladies' man.

On stage, Bobby stresses his dependability and then calls on the Bland Dolls to assist him in a number or two. The three girls strut out in flesh-fitting sheath dresses and group themselves tightly around the microphone at the other side of the stage. At the same time they heighten Bobby's image as the ladies' man they offer definite visual pleasure to the men in the audience. The best-known song that Bland and his Dolls do together gets directly to the core of a fundamental problem in the Negro community: the instability of the conjugal bond. *Yield Not to Temptation* is church music, and recognized as such by all present. Bobby plays the preacher role, the girls represent a choir, and the audience is the participating congregation. But the problem being symbolized is as usual, completely personal. The touring blues singer is invariably separated from his wife or sweetheart during most of the year; will she be true while he is away, and can he withstand the temptations that his many female admirers present as he travels from town to town? The conflict—the temptation—cuts both

15. Duke, 77.

ways; although the conflict is practically universal in Negro ghetto life, the blues singer, by the very nature of his profession, is exposed to this difficult situation to a greater extent and with greater intensity. Before discussing its implications, I shall examine the lyric itself and the interplay between soloist, singing group, band, and audience.

Yield Not to Temptation begins with a rocking medium-tempo rhythm by the drummer and a figure repeated over and over again in unison by electric bass, piano, and electric guitar. The rest of the band sets up an intricate off-beat hand clapping pattern that is quickly picked up by members of the audience who are familiar with the rhythm from church services they have attended since childhood. (If it is a Saturday night, some in the audience will be participating in the same way Sunday morning.) In the following, chorus parts are in parentheses and other features are in brackets.

[rhythm section introduction and hand clapping]
Yield not
To temptation
Oh, my love
While I'm away.

Don't you know (ooooo—girls hold chords softly in back-
  ground)
You got to be strong (ooooooo)
Leave all the other guys alone (ooooooo)
One bright sunny day (ooooooo)
I'll be back home to stay (ooooooo)

Yield not (yield not)
To temptation
And let no one
Lead you astray (yield not)

So many times (so many times) [trumpets in unison with
  girls throughout]
You're gonna be lonely (but yield not)

So many times (so many times)
You're gonna be blue (but yield not)
But yield not (yield not to temptation) [some women in the
    audience sing along]
Yield not (yield not to temptation)
Oh, yield not (yield not to temptation)
Yield not (yield not to temptation)

Don't you know (ooooooo)
You got to be strong (etc.)
Leave all the other guys alone
One bright sunny day
Oh, I'll be back home to stay
Yield not (yield not)
To temptation (yield not) oooooooh-aah!
    [tenor saxophone solo, spoken encouragement to soloist
    from Bland]

Don't you know (ooooooo)
You gotta be strong
Leave all the other guys alone
One bright sunny day
I'll be back home to stay.
Yield not (yield not)
To temptation (yield not)
(Yield not to temptation)
(Yield not to temptation)
(Yield not to temptation)

I got to know
    [the verse is repeated by the Bland Dolls with every
    measure twelve more times while Bland shouts his lines
    in and around the responses]
I said I want to know
And I gotta know
Without a doubt
You got nobody
Takin' you out

I want to know
Oooooooh, baby,
I want to know
I said I got to know
One of these days
I want to know, baby
I just got to know, baby [band begins to fade out and girls
  march off stage still singing]
I got to know [Bland waves goodby].

Bobby is "moralizing" and preaching not from any superior
vantage point but out of empathy. The command "Thou shalt
not commit adultery" is there, but it is also a plea, a request,
even a hope or prayer that the relationship will not fall apart as
it has so many times before. Bland's repeated shouts of "I
want to know," "I got to know" at the end have a feeling of
helpless desperation. The chorus can be seen as supporting and
reinforcing the protagonist in his frenzied call for loyalty, or it
could also be interpreted as giving a counter-commandment—
women asking their men to be faithful. This latter interpretation
accurately reflects the matrifocal pattern of so many lower-class
Negro families. At the same time that the basic male-female
conflict is musically symbolized in the dialogue between Bland
and the girls, their overlapping call-response patterns intertwined with the intricate band and audience accompaniment
form a carefully planned and extremely effective aesthetic unity.
The sight and sound of a common problem being acted out,
talked out, and worked out on stage promote catharsis, and the
fact that all present are participating in the solution creates
solidarity. The constant repetition of phrases and driving
intensity of the rhythm reflect the redundant patterns of ghetto
life and all the persistent anguish that goes with it. As the song
comes to an end and the girls go off stage, Bobby Blue Bland
has the audience in the palm of his hand. Whatever distance has
existed between artist and audience to this point has been all but
eliminated. Bland and his listeners are one unit.

As if to emphasize this fact beyond all shadow of a doubt,
Bland concludes his show with two pieces that chronicle the

vicissitudes of the Negro week. *Yield Not to Temptation* serves
as an excellent example of a musical style mirroring life style. In
Bland's treatment of *Stormy Monday* and *That's the Way Love
Is* the musical mirror is dispensed with and the Bland organization presents a distillation of reality itself.

Stormy Monday is a blues with a long history. T-Bone
Walker first made it famous, but the lyric goes back to blues
prehistory for its source material, to work songs and spirituals,
to the literal facts of day-to-day post-slavery existence. The fact
that the lyric is more powerful and popular today than ever
speaks for itself—unfortunately. Bland handles the words slowly,
deliberately, and with humility. The accompaniment consists
simply of piano, bass, drums, and electric guitar; the guitar
plays all the countermelodies and solos. There are no frills or
flourishes here; the simple words tell a story that every member
of the audience knows by heart.

> They call it stormy Monday
> But Tuesday's just as bad.
> (repeated)
>
> They call it stormy Monday
> But Tuesday's just as bad.
>
> Wednesday's worse
> Lord, and Thursday's oh, so sad.
>
> The eagle flies on Friday,
> And Saturday I go out to play
>
> Yes . . . the eagle flies on Friday
> And Saturday I go out to play.
>
> Sunday I go to church
> And I kneel down 'n' pray.
> . . . And this is what I say, baby (spoken).

Bobby kneels on the stage as he delivers this line and then
talks to the audience. People shout encouragement and words of
understanding as he bows his head.

Lord have mercy,
Lord, have mercy on me.
You know I cried, Lord, have mercy (shouted)
Lord, have mercy on me (whisper).

You know I'm trying, trying to find my baby,
Won't somebody please send her home to me . . . Yeah
(spoken).

Bobby gets up, walks over to the guitarist and praises him as he bends over his instrument to extract the long-drawn-out whining phrases that are as much a part of the song as the lyrics. Suddenly the guitarist doubles the tempo and repeats a particularly funky phrase a few times accompanied by "oohs," "aahs," and "yeahs" from the audience. Bland says, "Play it one more time, brother," and the guitarist takes another chorus, finishing with the same double-time figure while Bland shakes his head in wonderment. Bland puts his hand on the guitarist's shoulder and beckons to the audience for applause, making a comment like "Ain't that the truth?" A third and even better chorus by the guitarist follows, and Bland wanders slowly around the stage, head cocked to one side, making clear his appreciation with a "yeah" between phrases. At the end of the chorus he turns abruptly to the audience and cries with all his might:

Well, I cried, Lord, have mercy
    (women wail in the audience)
Lord, have mercy on me (whisper).
I said I cried, Lord, have mercy,
Lord, have mercy on me.

You know I'm trying, trying to find my baby,
Whooa . . . send her home to me.

It should be noted here that Bland makes a special point of his dependencies during these final selections. Unlike most blues singers, who are instrumentalists capable of supplying their own melodic counterpoint, Bobby plays no instrument, though he once tried to learn guitar and is now interested in the tenor sax. This deficiency forces him to rely heavily on soloists within the band. He turns this liability into an advantage, however, when he acknowledges his debt and works with his solo countervoice; he thereby makes a show of teamwork, cooperation, and respect for another that enhances the binding-together mood of his performance.

This feeling of solidarity is further strengthened with the reappearance of Al Braggs and the Dolls for the final selection of the evening. Bobby is a big man and not exactly graceful; so it is difficult for him to enact his lyrics in the manner of, say, Chuck Berry, who often dances as he sings and plays guitar. In *That's the Way Love Is* (and in some other numbers as well) Al Braggs choreographs the lyrics, and Bland works with him in the same way that he cooperates with soloists in the band. Because the lyrics of this song are so similar to those of *Stormy Monday* it is not often that they are used in tandem to climax a performance. Usually one or the other brings the show to an end.

> Monday's so good;
> Tuesday's so cruel,
> One day you're sooo happy now,
> The next day you're in tears.
>
> So you take it where you find it,
> Or leave it like it is.
> That's the way it's always been.
> That's the way love is.
>
> Wednesday's all right
> But Thursday's all wrong
> One day, you are with your baby,
> The next it's all gone.
>
> So you take it where you find it,
> Or leave it like it is.
> That's the way it's always been,
> That's the way love is.
>   (band interlude)

While the band plays, Al Braggs and two of the Bland Dolls enter from the wings doing a little dance step. They dance up to and around the microphone. At the end of each of Bland's lines they shout, "That's the way it is!" then do circular steps in different directions; their bodies wheel, and the three heads converge at the microphone at the exact instant when the vocal response is called for. This separation-and-reunification pattern is repeated during the next few verses.

> Friday you'll beg her, Saturday she'll plead,
> One day she'll say she loves you,
> The next day she might leave.
>
> So you take it where you find it,
> Or leave it like it is.
> That's the way it's always been,
> That's the way love is.
>
> It seems so fair sometimes
> But that's the way love is
> It makes you want to cry . . .
> But that's the way love is.
>
> I know you don't know what I'm talkin' about, baby,
> Because I don't believe you ever been in love,
> But that's the way love is.

Braggs breaks away from the microphone at this point and begins to inch across the stage on one foot in time with the music. The audience applauds, and Bland holds out a hand to Braggs, who is slowly but surely propelling himself to center stage. Bland goes on singing, "I see you comin'," "You're doin' all right," "Don't stop now, baby," "You're lookin' good." Each time he is answered by the girls with "That's the way it is." Finally, Braggs reaches out his hand, achieves his goal, and falls exhausted into Bobby's arms as the curtain closes and Bobby sings,

> That's the way it's always been,
> That's the way love is.

It is difficult to imagine a more simple and direct way of dramatizing solidarity and the basic idea that we're all in this thing together. It is interesting that *all* the instances of direct unification and cooperation are man to man—Bland in relation to Al Braggs and vis-à-vis various soloists in the band. These ritualistic acts certainly have an aesthetic *raison d'être:* Bobby needs these choreographic and instrumental extensions of himself to round out his image as the complete blues artist and unifying force. But there are probably other reasons for these displays of brotherhood. Obviously, if a woman were to be united with Bland before the world, it would tarnish his reputation as a man for all women; but it is more important, I think, that he be perceived by the Negro community at large as a man among men, or, better still, as a leader among men. Braggs' final pilgrimage across the stage and the feeling of mutual respect that Bland creates with his supporting soloists contribute to this effect. The more Bobby initiates and integrates successful teamwork on stage, the easier it is for men to identify with him, the greater his sex appeal for women, and the higher his status within the lower-class Negro community as a whole. The "lower-class" label may be misleading here, however, since Bland fans tend to have middle-class aspirations, and in a sense Bland's success and his appeal are functions of each other.

In the foregoing description, the familiar concepts of charisma, catharsis, and solidarity have been illustrated in passing but are of central concern. Bland's performance represents a dramatic synthesis of these forces as they are welded together in the more potent aesthetic patterns of Negro culture. In the following chapter, these concepts and others will be applied to an analysis of the role of the blues artist, the responses of his audience, and the emergent soul movement.

CHAPTER VI

ROLE AND RESPONSE

IN THIS CHAPTER I shall attempt to bind together some of the analytic strands left dangling in the preceding descriptive sections by viewing the blues artist and his audience from a somewhat more theoretical perspective. Since there are little data but my own to draw upon, and since a unified socio-cultural theory of music has only just begun to take shape,[1] this analysis is of necessity fragmented, disjointed, and incomplete.

The role of blues artist holds particular interest for the anthropologist in at least two respects. In spite of the fact that blues singing is ostensibly a secular, even profane, form of expression, the role is intimately related to sacred roles in the Negro community. Second, the role is all-encompassing in nature, either assimilating or overshadowing all other roles an adult male may normally be expected to fulfill.

As professions, blues singing and preaching seem to be closely linked in both the rural or small-town setting and in the urban ghettos. We have already noted some of the stylistic common denominators that underlie the performance of both roles, and it is clear that the experiences which prepare one for adequately fulfilling either role overlap extensively. Participation in the musical life of the church and intimate knowledge of and passionate living within the Negro reality provide both

1. See Appendix B.

the mold and the raw materials for blues lyrics and sermons. This observation is further strengthened by the not uncommon occurrence of the same person's fulfilling both roles at different phases of his life. The pattern remains essentially unbroken when the rural Negro migrates to the urban centers. The number of important male roles which are possible in the city increases; these two roles, however, remain completely contained within Negro culture. A person must go to a white university (for that matter, any university is white) in order to become a doctor or lawyer, but no such contact with white middle-class culture is essential to the aspiring bluesman or preacher. If anything, such contact would tend to decrease the authenticity of such roles, granting that they could be possible at all under such circumstances. For a bluesman like Ray Charles who does reap considerable financial rewards from a white audience, the connection with this particular audience segment is rather inessential to the role. Charles manages to retain his cultural identity even when singing a hillbilly song with chorus and string section accompaniment; further, Negro listeners tend to ignore these more commercial efforts in favor of his more representative work. In most other instances to date, whenever the audience for a male singer shifts from black to predominantly white, the blues role ceases to apply as far as the Negro audience is concerned. Another point of interest is that whereas in the rural South itinerant preachers are paralleled by traveling bluesmen, sharing all the traditional socio-economic weaknesses of the Negro male role, in the urban context the emergence of patriarchs[2] in the churches is paralleled by still traveling but decidedly strong blues singers who wield both economic power and prestige.

Evidence for the interplay between blues and preaching roles

2. Though the years a number of the better known Negro churches in Chicago have developed into family empires. The patriarch's children serve in administrative capacities, relatives start branches of the church in other neighborhoods, members of the congregation marry into the heirarchy, a son may take over the ministry upon his father's death, and so forth. In short, a "church family" can present a picture that is just the opposite of a "matrifocal complex."

is plentiful. Some of the best-known blind street singers, such as the late Blind Willie Johnson and the currently popular folk artist Reverend Gary Davis, are often classed stylistically as bluesmen but have always been willing to preach whenever the opportunity presented itself and are still best known for their religious songs. In his youth Big Bill Broonzy would earn his way as a bluesman one week and preach the nest, until his father insisted that he "stop straddling the fence."[3] "Be what you are," said the father, and the son, seeing more ready cash and excitement on the blues side of the fence, decided not to preach. Georgia Tom gave up a promising blues career, after recovering miraculously from a serious illness, to devote himself to the propagation of gospel music, and today Mr. Thomas A. Dorsey is the leading writer and publisher of gospel music in the country.[4]

J. B. Lenoir (Lenore) says that his father and brother in Monticello, Mississippi, "used to play nothin' but blues" but now devote themselves exclusively to preaching and church affairs. J. B. himself has given up the fast world "to follow the Lord," although he keeps his hand in by occasionally recording a number for Chess Records. He regards his own talents and those of other prominent bluesmen as God-given gifts, as when describing Jr. Parker as "blessed to blow harp" (harmonica), and hence feels that every blues artist should be true to his talent and to its spiritual source. It is on the basis of these criteria that he judges the current crop of bluesmen: B. B. King is true to himself and therefore his soul; Bobby Bland doesn't play an instrument, sometimes follows commercial trends, and therefore isn't as good a singer as he might be. Lenoir doesn't label blues "devil music" as many in the church do, but feels that all valid music has a sacred source (his best lyrics come to him in dreams) and a singer strays from this source at the risk of losing his soul. Many of the other singers I have interviewed share this same general point of view.

3. *Big Bill Blues: William Broonzy's Story as Told to Yannick Bruynoghe* (London, 1955).
4. George Robinson Ricks, "Religious Music of the United States Negro" (Ph.D. Dissertation, Northwestern University, 1959).

Concerning the transition from a blues role to a ministerial one, there are two significant stories that a number of singers have told me: the first concerning Gatemouth Moore, the second, Little Richard. Gatemouth, at the peak of his popularity, was playing an engagement at the Club DeLisa, one of Chicago's leading blues rooms during the 1940's.[5] One night, in the midst of a rocking blues rendition, he brought the proceedings to an abrupt halt, sang a chorus of *Shine on Me*, announced his retirement, and "he just up and walked off the stand." The Reverend Dwight Moore served his apprenticeship with Reverend Cobbs, and has been preaching the gospel in Chicago ever since.[6] He is fondly remembered and much respected by all the bluesmen I've interviewed. Little Richard was one of the first well-known cry singers, and his pioneering work earned for him a considerable amount of money. He also renounced the stage to become a religious leader, but was less successful than he had anticipated. His recordings of spirituals didn't sell too well, he ran out of capital before he could set up a functioning church, and so he tried to make a comeback in the entertainment world. The consensus among bluesmen and blues lovers at large is that once an entertainer returns to the fold he should stay there. "If he had the money," said one well-known blues singer, "he should have set up a nice little church and recreation center and he would have been set, although with these college educated

5. As I write, the Club DeLisa has just reopened and is now called The Club. E. Rodney Jones and other WVON regulars are promoting the revival and have mustered an impressive array of talent, including a chorus line, to insure its success.

6. Reverend Cobbs is the well-known leader of the largest Spiritual church in Chicago. His philosophy exalts life and tolerates "sin" as part of the natural order of things. "This is one church," says Moore, "where high livin' is not frowned on." All men partake of the spirit, and people "from all walks of life" (including all the less legitimate walks) are welcome to join the congregation. Reverend Moore, resplendent in the robes of a Catholic cardinal, teaches his version of this gospel of acceptance at "Wesley Chapel," next to the Maxwell Street "flea market." But he still spends a few months of each year making appearances at Spiritual churches all over the country. "I've always been nervous in one place; I like to *go*, even if it's just across the street."

pastors comin' along, it's tough to set up anything but a storefront these days."

Similarly, Little Jr. Parker speaks of the switch from blues to preaching: "I know why they stop singing the blues—their conscience troubles them. But why anyone starts again I can't figure out. Myself, I promised God that in eight more years, whether I'm popular or not, I'm going to show my appreciation and devote myself to his service, 'cause he made it possible for all the other people to dig me." The transition, then, from a blues role to a preacher's position can normally be made only once.

There is a strong prodigal-son pattern here: a set of related concepts or common understandings that allow a man to move from a most decidedly secular role to the sacred role without a strain or hitch. First of all, in the Negro community few expect a young man to be saintly—in fact many mothers inculcate a particularly strong sex-role identity in their little boys of the stud, rogue, lady-killer type. John Lee Hooker states it neatly in one of his blues soliloquies as he tells of his parents' reaction to his incipient blues career: Father disapproved, but Mama said, "It's in him, and it's got to come out." It is understood and expected that every boy will sow some wild oats—something's wrong with him if he doesn't—and his wild period will not be held against him in later years. The Negro woman's concept of the no-good man (sexually desirable but domestically intolerable —good lover but bad provider), as reported by Esther Newton,[7] closely parallels the defining expectations most fans verbalize when considering the blues singer's role or what Nadel might call the role's "halo effect."[8] The converse concept of the good man is severely restricted in its application—some women claim there is no such creature—but clearly the preacher as an ideal type at least offers an approximation or model of what a good man might be like: steady, reliable, above the sexual strife (in theory though not often in fact)—a man of God after all.

7. "Men, Women and Status in the Negro Family" (Master's Thesis, University of Chicago, 1964).

8. S. F. Nadel, *The Theory of Social Structure* (Glencoe, 1957), p. 26.

Bluesman and preacher may be considered Negro prototypes of the no-good and good man respectively.

It should be obvious that a reformed bluesman is not only an acceptable preacher, but may even have an advantage over his fellow clerics. I would suggest that the most exciting, attractive, and charismatic preachers are often those who have been big sinners in their prime. To absolve sins successfully, you may find it helpful to have been a transgressor yourself once upon a time. The prodigal returned to the fold is living evidence of God's power to redeem and is better qualified than most to lead the flock. He knows what life is all about.[9]

The transition, then, from blues role to preacher role is unidirectional but peculiarly appropriate and smooth for anyone who cares to make the shift. Gatemouth Moore's "call" must be respected; Little Richard is ostensibly a backslider of the worst order.

There is a firm economic foundation to this transitional pattern. It is possible to get rich quick in the blues or rhythm-and-blues field; a few hit records in succession, a corresponding boost in personal appearance fees, and a singer can find himself on easy street. Usually a blues artist builds a following over a period of years, and his popularity is not likely to vanish as suddenly as that of some teen-age idol. Nevertheless, there invariably comes a point when the financial returns no longer compensate for the tremendous amount of time and energy spent in singing the blues, and the smaller (perhaps) but steadier income of the collection plate looks very appealing. Some bluesmen persist in their prodigal ways—"I love the life I live, and I live the life I love"—until drink, a bit of violence, or the infirmities of old age bring their careers to a close. Most, however, return to the church and settle down to a day job of some kind, often for familial as well as economic reasons.

9. Reverend Moore states: "Experience is my big advantage, like Paul, but he was on the scene before, now I'm here. You see, I don't *need* to handle money—went through a quarter of a million in a few fast years. I don't *need* to sin any more because I've been around, traveled all over, had all the women, cars, clothes any man could want . . . so there was nothin' left for me to do but live right. It's the one thing I hadn't done up til my conversion in '48."

In the blues role itself a number of interesting and perhaps unique features stand out. The first and foremost feature or fact to be considered is that a contemporary urban blues performer, in order to turn a profit and keep a large following, must travel far, fast, and constantly. The big boys are always on the road or taking a short vacation; there are no in-betweens. And owing to the geographic factors, the road is long and hard. B. B. King's itinerary for November and December, 1962, speaks eloquently for itself:

November	21	Rhythm Club, Baton Rouge, Louisiana
	22	Stardust Club, Longview, Texas
	23	High School, West Helena, Arkansas
	24	Fairgrounds Night Club, Muskogee, Oklahoma
	25	Stevens, Jackson, Mississippi
	26	Club Handy, Memphis, Tennessee
	27	Madison Nite Spot, Bessemer, Alabama
	28	Club Ebony, Indianola, Mississippi
December	2	Cobra Club, Midland Texas
	4	MB Corral, Wichita Falls, Texas
	5	Baptist Auditorium, Hot Springs, Arkansas
	6	El Dorado, Arkansas
	7	Drive In, Texarkana, Arkansas
	8	Townsend Park, Pine Bluff, Arkansas
	10	Dallas, Texas
	11	Club 66, Shreveport, Louisiana
	13	Clovis, New Mexico
	15	Gin Pleasure Spot, Lamarque, Texas
	16	East County Club, San Antonio, Texas
	22	Drive In, Camden, Arkansas
	24	Moulin Rouge Club, Gladwater, Texas
	28	Academy Bridge, Denver, Colorado
	29	Arcadia Bridge, Pueblo, Colorado

According to Sonny Freemen, drummer with B. B. King for the past three years, the standard tour alternates east to west, west to east, with one-night stands in the South forming the bulk of each trip. Aside from occasional forays into the Chicago area and one-week stage shows at the three principal theaters— the Howard in Washington, D.C., the Apollo in New York, and the Regal in Chicago—most of the band's time is spent on the road, and half of that in the South. The South provides the basic bread, and appearances in the clubs, ballrooms, and theaters of the major cities add the butter.

To keep a career going, then, even the most successful bluesmen have to travel to their audience. In a sense this generalization holds for the city and "industrial" blues groups in Chicago who move around the city to different clubs during the week in order to make ends meet financially. Concert artists, salesmen, jazz groups, and baseball teams also travel, to be sure; but all these professionals have a home base where they spend a substantial amount of time, and none of them makes a regular habit of scheduling appearances in eight different states on eight successive nights with nothing but a bus for transportation.

This constant and grueling travel generates a number of severe conflicts among the roles that an adult male is normally expected to fulfill. Most blues singers and the musicians in their bands are married, but work out an arrangement of one kind or another to diminish the tension inherent in the musician/husband situation. Very often a laissez-faire policy is adopted—"I know she's not sitting around waiting for me to come home for a few days, and she knows that I've got other women around the country, but we usually don't talk about it at all when we're together." A common practice is to call home a day or two before returning, so that embarrassing incidents can be avoided. "Man, I *always* call first. Johnny [pseudonym] walked in on his, and he still hasn't gotten over it. Why he thinks she's gonna be true to him, I don't really know—doesn't make sense to just show up and expect everything to be cool when you've been away a couple of months."

Some bluesmen do assume fidelity and try to insure it by sending for their wives whenever they are in one spot for more than a few days or perhaps by marrying a woman who, in one way or another, is self-sufficient. Note that B. B. King's wife brought her mother along when visiting her husband in Chicago, probably as a companion to fall back on while Mr. King is busy meeting his many blues obligations. According to B. B., "we trust each other;" and he tells a pleasant story to illustrate the fact. A woman called on the phone one day to complain bitterly and at length about the lack of support for her child. When the woman finished her harangue, Mrs. King replied matter-of-factly, "You must want to speak to Mr. King; *I* didn't give you no child." The lady hasn't been heard from since.

Another blues singer, who shall remain nameless, maintains an interesting arrangement. He is married and calls his wife every other night on the phone. "Sometimes when I call I'm married, and sometimes I'm not—depends on her mood." The girl vocalist who travels with the band doubles as his girl friend. Home, however, is where his mother lives, and his first allegiance is to her; as he puts it, "A mother will never divorce you," implying perhaps that his wife is about to take action. The vocalist is a religious girl and would like him to settle down, presumably with her. None of the parties involved is happy with the present state of affairs, and the singer shakes his head in despair over the demands that the women in his life make upon him. But what can a traveling man do?

He can sing the blues. The traveling life and its attendant woman troubles (or role conflicts, if you prefer) provide of course the source material for the most typical blues lyrics and, more important, enable the singer to deliver those lyrics night after night with absolute conviction.

Although a wife invariably occupies a subsidiary or assimilated position in a bluesman's role set, fatherhood can be a more serious consideration. When a child comes along, it may mark the turning point in a career. Jimmy Witherspoon insists that he is a changed man since his baby daughter arrived. "I used to be real wild, I mean—I was a *bad* one, you know, but now the biggest kick in my life is changing diapers. I'm not kidding, I don't do many one-nighters any more, and the money has to be pretty good before I'll leave home for a week or two. Juicing, fighting, women—all that stuff broke up my first marriage, but that's all changed." Spoon carries a raft of pictures of his little girl in his wallet and likes to talk about her charms to anyone who shows the slightest interest. It should also be added that he sings solos in the local Baptist church whenever he is home and takes pride in the fact that his father-in-law is a minister. J. B. Lenoir also indicates that children were an important factor in his semi-retirement. During a long visit we had at his home I saw him lavish affection upon his little girls, bouncing them on his knee and implanting big wet kisses one after another, as if to punctuate the answers to my questions. Willie Dixon has an even larger brood of children and now restricts his activities to lyric writing, A and R work at Chess Records, and an occasional European tour. The subject deserves further investigation, but I think that the obligations of fatherhood weigh heavily on a bluesman's mind; he avoids becoming a father if he can; but once he does, his career and life style may have to be adjusted accordingly.

The attributes of the blues role itself are complex and difficult to describe in any systematic fashion. The confusion here stems largely from two factors.

First, a blues singer's personality and life style represent a heightened model or type of Negro masculine behavior in general. The bluesman is in a sense every man: the country bluesman is an archetype of the migrant laborer; the city bluesman, a stereotype of the stud, the hustler; the urban blues artist, something of an ideal man or prototype for his generation as well. For example, the credentials for becoming a bluesman or soul singer are listed in order of importance by Al Hibbler as: having been hurt by a woman, being "brought up in that old-time religion," and knowing "what that slavery shit is all about." Many other performers list much the same requirements, yet these essential characteristics are shared by most young Negro men living in Chicago, and a large number of these men can and do render the blues lyrics of the day in a manner that could pass professional standards. The pool of potential bluesmen is large—the old story of "many are called, but few are chosen." Why does one man among the hundreds who have the necessary credentials and capacities choose to sing blues for a living? More in-depth interviews and some personality testing might provide the answer, but at present I can only speculate in terms of ambition, persistence, endurance, and similar motivations.

The second factor that makes a role analysis difficult is the inseparability of the man himself from the role: the bluesman's work is his life and vice versa. Once a man has chosen the blues life, not only are familial roles (husband, brother, son, if not father) either shunted aside or assimilated to the blues role, but the day-to-day existence of a blues singer is one of constant attention to people and details. Aside from the two governing or pivotal attributes of the role—singing the blues and traveling— there is a long string of less institutionalized obligations to be met. The singer is friend, advisor, confidant, and employer for the musicians in his band and other members of his traveling entourage, the bus driver, manager, souvenir salesman, female vocalist, and whoever else may be along for the ride. He is friend, father confessor, and a humble hero to his followers, who visit with him after and between shows, usually to reminisce and express their appreciation for a particular song. The extra-performance communication between a bluesman and his fans seems to be fairly patterned in terms of privacy. I can think of two or three occasions at ballrooms when a well-known blues singer had been standing or sitting at the fringe of the audience for some time waiting to go on stage, yet not a single person had ventured to come forward and shake hands. A few people would wave or shout their greetings, and the singer would nod or wave back; but face-to-face communication was at an absolute minimum. Backstage or in the dressing room, however, a small but steady trickle of fans will come to pay their respects, but in public it seems to be a common understanding that the singer must initiate any interaction. A converse rule, however, is that the singer is always available. Backstage at the Regal, dressing rooms are invariably open; phone lines to the hotel rooms where bluesmen stay are never closed, even in the early morning hours; the do-not-disturb sign is rarely, if ever, found on the door. The factors contributing to this state of affairs are: the singer's knowledge that to remain popular he must remain accessible, a man of the people; the relaxed warmth and intimacy of the performance itself, which seem to make further contact unnecessary; the audience's knowledge, whether conscious or not, of the artist's availability and a corresponding devaluation of autograph seeking and the like (such tangible souvenirs or mementoes are obtainable from vendors anyway).

In addition, the urban bluesman usually makes a point of polishing the man-about-town halo effect, alluded to earlier, by attending many post-performance parties, by visiting the local night clubs where he may sing a number or two on request, and in general by keeping up with the swinging set in every town and city he visits.

Every bluesman does much, if not all, of his own public relations work, chatting with disc jockeys, consulting and contracting with promoters. As one singer summed up the situation in a moment of frustration: "This is an ass-kissin' business. You *got* to be nice to *everybody!*"

Aside from an occasional visit to a bowling alley with a friend or two in the band, sporadic attempts to keep up with a correspondence course, the flying lessons, and a short vacation or two at home during the year, all B. B. King's activities are blues-oriented—even these possible exceptions can be so construed. Vacations are likely to be spent poring over records for refurbishable material and in preparation for the next recording session; a pilot's license will ease the travel burden; bowling with the boys has the non-avocational aspect of increasing group solidarity to recommend it; and so forth.

After it is realized that B. B. King's interests are far more diversified than those of most bluesmen, the summation of roles under the blues rubric becomes impressive indeed. The reader should begin to grasp what is meant by the initial assertion of the role's all-encompassing nature. The president of the United States, Albert Schweitzer, the dedicated priest, the top executive, the true scholar, the country doctor—all may perhaps be more devoted to their work and enveloped by it; but the urban bluesman still stands out as an exceptional instance of specialization. Even within the more restricted kindred realm of expressive roles labeled "artistic," the urban blues singer seems to be in a unique and intermediate position between West and non-West: unlike that of his Western contemporaries, his first obligation is to his public rather than to a private muse. Although the artist in tribal society[10] may also be primarily a public servant, the extreme specialization characteristic of the blues role is nowhere attainable to the same degree in the pre-industrial world. The incessant travel, the manipulation of the same form and even the same songs night after night and year after year, the sacred foundation of secular expression and easy transition from a creative role to a belief role, the intensive specialization, the extensive public and interpersonal obligations —all combine to define the contemporary blues singer.

These features suggest that a more intensive and rigorous investigation of the blues role could add immeasurably to our knowledge of expressive roles in general. In the foregoing discussion, the essence of the role—that is, blues singing itself—has not been so much avoided as surrounded. The encirclement continues in the following section on the blues audience. To penetrate the core of the blues role, however, a great deal of effort must be spent on dissecting the patterns of expressive symbolism utilized by the performers. Lévi-Strauss' analysis of shamans and sorcerers,[11] Moreno's concept of psychodrama and spontaneity,[12] and Kenneth Burke's dramatism and rhetorical analyses contain useful theoretical tools for the analysis of form and content.[13] Bringing theory and data together is, as usual, the immediate and difficult task to be faced in future research.

From observations and conversations at blues clubs around Chicago and on the basis of short interviews conducted with ninety-seven persons attending an International Blues Festival at the Ashland Auditorium, I have found it possible to make a few estimates and generalizations regarding the composition of the blues audience. Approximately one-third of the persons at-

10. Marian W. Smith, Ed., *The Artist in Tribal Society* (New York, 1963).

11. Claude Lévi-Strauss, *Structural Anthropology* (New York, 1963).

12. J. L. Moreno, *Psychodrama* (New York, 1946).

13. *A Rhetoric of Motives* (New York, 1950); *Counter Statement* (Chicago, 1957); *The Philosophy of Literary Form* (Rev. Ed., New York, 1957).

tending the blues festival on the West Side were from Mississippi, assuming that the eighty-five who gave us information on place of birth are a representative sample. This substantial segment of Mississippians is rather surprising and may even be an under-estimate—those few who avoided or refused to give a place of birth may have wanted to disguise a Mississippi background, and a few others may even have distorted the facts slightly to cover up a down-home origin, especially when questioned by a Negro interviewer.[14] The respondents from Mississippi, Arkansas, Tennessee, and Alabama account for more than 75 per cent of the sample. Certainly less than 10 per cent of those present were born north of the Mason-Dixon Line, and I suspect that most of the audience has lived in Chicago less than a dozen years. These estimates would vary slightly if we were to sample the audience at a South Side performance—fewer from Mississippi, more long-term Chicago residents—but the over-all pattern would remain the same.

At these festivals and at Regal Theatre stage shows, the numbers of men and women are about equal; but at the local clubs there are always more men than women, especially during the week when the only women in a club may be the waitresses and barmaids. On the other hand, it seems to be the women who buy more of the blues records[15] and listen more faithfully to the blues disc jockeys. In other words, the male segment of the blues audience likes to go out to enjoy the music, whereas the female segment brings the music into the home but will attend an occasional Saturday night event.

The native categories—the basic criteria and preference patterns of this audience—are easily illustrated with a typical exchange of queries and replies. Asking the average blues fan, "What is the difference between good and bad blues?" an interviewer usually received a puzzled expression for an initial

14. All three Negro interviewers found the place-of-birth question a touchy one. The two white interviewers encountered few difficulties in this area. Birthplace is certainly more of a key status marker within the Negro community than outside it.

15. Phil Chess estimates that women account for about 80 per cent of the company's blues record sales.

response and an eventual answer something like: "No difference, baby, I mean there's no bad blues; if a man doesn't have
soul, you dig, he's not a blues singer, he's just singing." If the
question were rephrased as, "Well, what kind of blues do you
like best?" the conversation would often run as follows. Fan:
"B. B. King is my man, and Bobby Blue Bland, and of course
Ray Charles is the greatest." Interviewer: "What particularly
do you like about King and Bland?" Fan: "They're mellow,
man. None of that nasty gutbucket stuff, you know." Interviewer: "What do you mean by 'mellow'?" Fan: "Well, B. B.'s
cleaned up the blues; they've refined it, so it's smooth and easy
—no harps, moaning, or shit like that. Those guys have brought
the blues up to date—made it modern." Note also that when
responding to questions on taste and preferences, blues fans,
musicians, and singers alike frequently begin, "I like 'em all."
This may be followed by a "but" and some specific preferences,
or the respondent may refuse to play favorites and continue
along the line of "everybody's got something to say."

For most of Chicago blues fans, once it has been established
that a singer is soulful, the distinction between clean and dirty
(or new and old) is the only criterion of any importance. There
exists a minority group—usually middle-aged women and older
people generally—who still like the dirtier down-and-out styles
of Muddy Waters and Howlin' Wolf. For the most part,
however, the audience at an Ashland Auditorium blues festival or
at one of the Regal Theatre's blues shows favors singers that
bring back memories of the "old country" (the South) without
forcing their listeners to identify themselves as lower-class,
farmer types, or recent migrants from the South. The clean-
dirty distinction of course bears a close resemblance to the
urban-folk dichotomies made by scholars and critics, though
some country singers with a more sophisticated style are not
necessarily considered dirty and a few urban musicians are
unregenerate.

Among blues singers and some of the more discriminating
listeners, other styles of blues singing are sometimes distinguished. When pressed to go beyond the soul—no-soul and
clean-dirty dichotomies, musicians will often point to different

types and degrees of commercialism. It is recognized that singers like Chuck Berry, Fats Domino, and Bo Diddley can be called blues singers but are really showmen first and bluesmen second. Their appeal rests primarily on novelty songs, catchy lyrics, and visual appeal. The commercial labels, rhythm and blues and rock and roll, are used in connection with performers of this type.

Cry singers may also be considered a part of the blues community. McKinly "the Soul" Mitchell is Chicago's best-known performer in this category and appears frequently at blues clubs, shows, and festivals. On the national level, Little Richard and James Brown are probably most famous. The climactic feature of a typical cry singer's act comes at the point when he falls on one knee and asks the audience, "Did you evah cry?" or another question about suffering and soul that can be answered with an affirmative shout. This technique stems directly from earlier experience with spiritual groups. Mitchell swears that when he is in top form grown men will actually weep during this particular portion of his ritual, but my experience has shown that it is usually groups of young women who are most moved by his cries.

Fans and musicians alike invariably have difficulty knowing where to place men like Sam Cooke, Brook Benton,[16] and Chuck Jackson, who sing with a blues and gospel feeling but are rarely accompanied by a blues band. From interview to interview they are referred to variously as pop, blues, or soul singers.[17]

In fact all these "categories" are imprecise, relative, and connotative. The label "rock and roll" may designate one group or class of singers for one informant, and the next person may restrict or expand the term to include a much different set of performers. Similarly, a fan's idea of dirty blues singing will depend upon what reference point is selected as clean or modern: if Sam Cooke is clean, then B. B. King may be dirty; if King is considered modern, then Howlin' Wolf is likely to be considered old; and if the Wolf is taken as a paragon of

16. Usually referred to as Sam Cookes and Brooks Benton (See footnote 3, Chapter V).

17. See Appendix C.

"electrified, powerful, streamlined" blues, then cousin so-and-so back home *really* sings dirty. Whatever the words or labels used, however, a blues fan's classification of a given artist or an expression of preference is likely to be made on the basis of three dimensions: soulfulness, dirtiness, and commercialism.

Blues audiences respond at the beginning of things. At the start of a number that is immediately recognizable you will hear a burst of applause mixed with oohs and ahs and shouts of encouragement: "Sing your song, baby," "Tell it like it is," "Play your heart, man, play your heart." At the beginning of a vocal chorus or an instrumental chorus, or at transition points between choruses, or even immediately upon recognizing a standard phrase, lick, or physical gesture that identifies a particular performer, an audience will register its approval in no uncertain terms. In many instances it almost seems as if responses precede stimuli, but noting this illusion is just another way of saying that a blues fan's satisfactions are instantaneous and evaluative pauses play a little part, at least in the ongoing musical process.

A blues audience presents the analyst with a ready-made program analyzer, a device used by Robert Merton in measuring the impact of propaganda materials.

> How, then, can we help the audience to recall their responses to particular aspects of the material? Should the interviewer mention specific scenes or episodes, he would be determining the focus of attention. Moreover, the interviewer's description of the scene would also influence the respondent's account of his experience. The Program Analyzer serves to eliminate these limitations.
>
> While watching a film or listening to a radio program, each subject presses a green button in his right hand whenever he likes what is being presented, and a red button in his left hand when he dislikes it. He does not press either button when he is "indifferent." These responses are recorded on a moving tape which is synchronized with the film or radio program. Thus, members of the audience register their approval or disapproval, *as they*

respond to the material. Reasons for and details of these reactions are later determined by the type of focused interview to which we have referred.[18]

Blues fans rarely manifest their disapproval. As many a listener responded when asked the difference between good and bad blues, "Bad blues is not blues." Studied or overt indifference is difficult to detect, since those individuals who are likely to be found in a blues situation are in a sense already committed.

This is an ideal commitment pattern that I have described, to which can be added many inconsistencies and deviations. The audience at a blues festival will often give token applause to a singer after a particularly stirring performance, and the clientele of a blues club may demonstrate its affection for an artist as he leaves the bandstand at the end of a set, but such responses are extremely rare and usually occur only after an exhortation from the master of ceremonies, club owner, or a drunk bystander. At a large blues gathering, a number of individuals will be found who are practically oblivious to the music and are primarily concerned with finding old friends, new friends of the opposite sex, or are simply seeking good company, a mellow scene. The blues fan, however, as an ideal type, is devoted to the genre as a whole and has no doubts as to its validity. The blues tell a story to him, and every artist has a slightly different story to tell. His reactions, then, to particular blues artists can be ranged by degree only along a spectrum of commitment, since disapproval or indifference is quite foreign to his orientation.

The deceptively simple criterion for commitment is soul: if an artist has it, he can do no wrong; if he doesn't, it's not blues. "Soul" may be partly defined as a mixture of ethnic essence, purity, sincerity, conviction, credibility, and just plain effort. Using this definition or one like it, bluesmen say that white singers like Frank Sinatra and Tony Bennett have soul. Similarly, Robert Merton, talking about the factors that facilitate mass persuasion, finds that Kate Smith's soul as perceived by

18. Robert Merton, *Social Theory and Social Structure* © 1957 by the Free Press of Glencoe.

her listeners was the primary reason for her success in selling war bonds during an eighteen-hour radio marathon. "In short, it was not so much what Smith *said* as what she did which served to validate her sincerity. It was the presumed stress and strain of an eighteen hour series of broadcasts, it was the deed not the word which furnished the indubitable proof. . . . The marathon took on the attributes of a sacrificial ritual."[19]

For many Negroes, life is one long sacrificial ritual. The blues artist, in telling his story, crystallizes and synthesizes not only his own experience but the experiences of his listeners. It is the intensity and conviction with which the story is spelled out, the fragments of experience pieced together, rather than the story itself which makes one bluesman better than another. The big men (Ray Charles, B. B. King, Bobby Blue Bland, Jr. Parker) and the older "boys" (Muddy Waters, John Lee Hooker, Lightnin' Hopkins) deliver their material directly with an important but subtle use of gestural or dramatic adornment. They have been around; the deeds which validate the words are largely taken for granted. Younger artists, like the cry singer McKinly "the Soul" Mitchell, or Al "T.N.T." Braggs, may work themselves into a frenzy, grappling at the microphone, making the entire body quiver, clutching at the air, peeling off clothing, building to a climax of physical exertion. This frenzied approach to validation of the word is analogous to that of some comedians—Jerry Lewis and Red Skelton come to mind—who build a following as much on the basis of energy expended as on the humor of their patter. Some disc jockeys also gain credibility and sympathy from white teenagers by creating a feeling of intense exertion with their neurotic ravings, groans, and shouts. Interviewing proponents of the frenzied approach, I am struck by their quiet, controlled, almost shy demeanor; yet put in front of a microphone, they almost literally tear themselves apart to get across to their publics. As Merton has indicated, in an age of sophistication, cynicism, pseudogemeinschaft, and anomie, words and music which are neither backed by the gold of experience nor accompanied by inflated action have only limited

19. *Ibid.*, p. 109.

credibility. It is interesting that at present each of the three best-known and most experienced touring bluesmen carries along a younger man of the inflated action school to warm up the audience: Bobby Bland is preceded by Al Braggs, Joe Hinton serves in the same capacity for Jr. Parker, and B. B. King now has Elmore Morris to take care of the gymnastic preliminaries.

Although one of the current trends in jazz, what critic Martin Williams has called "the funky hard-bop regression," lays heavy stress on soul—gospel chord progression, heavy blues chromaticism, call-response forms—jazz, since the last war, has clearly become an art music and its audience is largely appreciative rather than committed. Applause is reserved for solo conclusions and the end of pieces. Occasionally dynamic peaks within a solo will stimulate shouts of encouragement, but single characteristic phrases or an opening melodic line never elicit shrieks of approval as they do in a blues performance. B. B. King walks into the spotlight, picks his guitar once, and bedlam reigns. Paul Chambers begins a bass line, and drums and piano fall in as they please; Miles Davis emerges from behind the piano and slowly constructs a solo which receives polite applause at its conclusion. The contrast is clear.

The distinction between audience commitment and appreciation also differentiates folk and urban traditions, as a parallel example from the white country-music field should demonstrate. Bluegrass bands have recently been discovered by the college set, and country-and-Western groups now appear with increasing frequency in campus auditoriums. The college audience, for example, at a concert given by the Country Gentlemen at Indiana University, responds jazz-style or appreciatively, applauding after solos and numbers. The country folk react on the basis of recognition—blues style, at the beginning of things. Observations made at a performance by Reno and Smiley in a barn near Bean Blossom, Indiana, bear out this analogy between blues and bluegrass in their natural settings almost to perfection. Whenever the fiddle player would step to the microphone and deliver the two rising pick-up notes that signaled the beginning of his chorus, he received warm applause. When he left the microphone after his solo, the audience usually, but not always, remained quiet, eagerly anticipating the opening line of the next soloist. As in a blues situation, a particular bit of fancy phrasing or an artist's idiosyncratic gesture is likely to elicit a more enthusiastic response than a piece in its entirety.

Here we are confronted with the central problem once more; to puzzle over audience responses is to probe again at the elusive core of the urban blues role. We think we know a little something about art, music appreciation, criticism, sound for sound's sake, aesthetics, and other notions associated with the Western concert hall, but what are the concomitants of musical commitment? There are really no blues critics—the very title seems either self-contradictory or altogether empty of meaning. The best blues singers seem to be both more than and less than artists, as we usually use the term. The man himself is somehow more important than his music. Why do single phrases elicit greater responses than whole selections? What semantic burden does one of those phrases carry? What is a bluesman doing for his audience? What sort of ideology or aesthetic supports the bluesman in his work?

CHAPTER VII

SOUL AND SOLIDARITY

I SHOULD LIKE TO discuss in more detail the concept of soul and its many dimensions, because in this notion of an "unspeakable essence" we have the foundation of the ideology which both guides and is embodied in any contemporary blues ritual. The word "ritual" seems more appropriate than "performance" when the audience is committed rather than appreciative. And from this, it follows, perhaps, that blues singing is more of a belief role than a creative role[1]—more priestly[2] than artistic. The preceding discussion of bluesmen and preachers supports this shift in perspective, as does the Saturday-night and Sunday-morning pattern of the Negro weekend. Bluesmen and preachers both provide models and orientations; both give public expression to deeply felt private emotions; both promote catharsis—the bluesman through dance, the preacher through trance; both increase feelings of solidarity, boost morale, strengthen the consensus. In brief, according to Clifford Geertz's exposition of ideology, it is apparent that both singing and preaching, in the Negro community at least, have a strong ideological aspect. In his paper, "Ideology as a Cultural System,"[3] Geertz takes great pains to divorce the term from its current pejorative connotations and then directs his attention to the problem of analyzing

1. S. F. Nadel, *The Theory of Social Structure* (Glencoe, 1957), p. 53.
2. Ralph Ellison, *Shadow and Act* (New York, 1964), p. 257.
3. In *Contemporary Ideology*, D. Apter, ed. (New York, in press).

ideologies in terms of rhetoric, figures of speech, and the manipulation of symbols into strategic and stylized formulas for dealing with problematic situations.[4]

A particular ideology can be viewed and analyzed in at least two different ways. It can be interpreted in terms of the socio-psychological conflict, stresses, and strains that give rise to it (this is the usual approach), or in terms of ideological thought, the formulation and interworking of symbols. In the blues, or in any other musical expression, we might subdivide this latter approach, speaking of ideas about the music on the one hand, and the rhetoric inherent in the music itself on the other. The following elucidation of the soul mosaic or associational cluster is prefaced with a brief recapitulation of the relevant situation. References to the dynamics of soul music and lyrics are scattered throughout, but the primary objective is simply to set out the connotational dimensions or components of the concept as it is employed today. Ask any bluesman or fan straight out what the blues are all about, and the answer nearly always pivots on the word "soul." It would seem worthwhile, then, to milk this word for all its meaning, even though we must construct a catalogue of Negro culture to do so.

The situation which gives rise to the soul strategy really needs no elaboration. Pick up any document dealing with the Negro problem, and the central message whether explicit or implicit will be the same: the problem of self-hatred, the lack of self-esteem—the lack of self, for that matter; these form the pervasive and frightening theme, and the variation on it is a deep-seated distrust of others—black as well as white. These factors and their countless corollaries have been a long time in the building, and it is no accident that the current concept of soul began to take shape a year or two after the Supreme Court decision of 1954[5] which focused attention on these problems.

The soul ideology ministers to the needs for identity and

4. Cf. Kenneth Burke, *The Philosophy of Literary Form* (Rev. ed., New York, 1957).

5. Ray Charles first began mixing jazz, blues, and gospel together in 1954, and his successful synthesis established the pattern for much of what is called soul music today.

solidarity. Question to Little Jr. Parker: "What does your audience expect from you?" Answer: "They expect what you are." Question: "Why is it that nobody dances much when the band plays for dancing, but when you come on stage people move out on the floor?" Answer: "The blues is based on somebody's life; it hits 'em in the heart and the love comes out. You think of your last love, or the girl you're with, or the troubles you've had; and they want to be close to whoever they're with, so they dance." These explanations and illustrations will be expanded below but the essential points should be clear.

The components of soul which follow are derived from interviews with blues singers, observations at blues rituals, and a *Hotline* program on radio station WVON, "home of the good guys"[6]—that is, home of the blues, soul, and solidarity. *Hotline* is a public-opinion program which gives listeners a chance to comment on various issues by phone. Moderator Wesley South accepted my short "script" on the topic, "What is soul, how do you define it, who has it?" but added a religious twist to the proceedings by speaking of theologians and asking ministers to call in at various points along the way. Hence, many of the thirty-three self-selected commentators hewed to religious lines in their definitions and comments. Seventeen women and sixteen men (three of them clerics) offered their opinions, including one man who simply quoted a stanza from one of Shelley's poems.[7]

6. I am told that there are "white good-guy" stations in other cities, but in this context the "good-guy" designation carries specific implications.

7. This stanza is from Percy Bysshe Shelley's *Queen Mab*, Aside from the poet's scorn for "earthliness," his concept does seem to be in tune with current usage:

> Sudden arose
> Ianthe's Soul; it stood
> All beautiful in naked purity,
> The perfect semblance of its bodily frame.
> Instinct with inexpressive beauty and grace,
> Each stain of earthliness
> Had passed away, it reassumed
> Its native dignity, and stood
> Immortal amid ruin.

Many of these comments are included below, and all are of interest in one way or another.

In this itemized presentation, components are listed in no particular order, although those referents which overlap and interact extensively are juxtaposed.

"*The breath of life.*" As far as the original religious center of the current conception is concerned, the glosses for "soul" are similar to those found in the dictionary, viz., "1. an entity which is regarded as being the immortal or spiritual part of the person . . . 2. the moral or emotional nature of man, 3. the spiritual or emotional warmth, force, etc., or evidence of this: as, the painting, like the artist, lacks *soul*, 4. vital or essential part, quality or principle." Meanings like these are common enough in the Negro community, but religious definitions given by participants in the *Hotline* program have a marked fundamentalist and sensory or "tactile" slant. For example, "I believe the soul is what leaves the body when a person dies . . . the hearin', the feelin', the tastin'—I believe that all goes to make up the soul." Almost all religious comments referred to Genesis and other Scriptural examples: "and then He stood them up and He breathed the breath on them which made them become a living soul . . . which could mean that the breath of God is the soul of a man"; or "the soul is the spiritual part of the body; the soul is the part that goes back to God"; or "the soul dwells in the body until the breath is taken out, and after which the soul comes out of the body and I don't know where it goes or where it langles until the day of resurrection." This "breath of life" or "God's gift" approach was most common, but a few persons stated or implied a non-separatist notion; "Man himself is soul, 'cause when the breath is put into man he became a livin' soul . . . anything that breathes, he's a livin' soul. It's just life"; or "I don't think man has a soul—I think he *is* a soul."

"*Our souls, our bodies* . . ." The phrasing in these religious definitions often has a bodily element that seems somewhat paradoxical or is inconsistent with the definitions found in dictionaries. This body emphasis lends itself to extra-religious definitions as well. The comments from three female *Hotline* participants are illustrative:

> Soul is the part of every individual's body and it's in the makeup of their spiritual body.

> I mean I feel that soul is your heart. And I feel that how that come about, you know, long, long time ago when the old people was expressing soul that they meant their heart. [Wesley South:] You mean the heart that beats, this big piece of muscle in our chests? Yes, that's what I think soul means, I mean, and it's you know, well they'd say, "I feel it in my soul," and I feel they feels it in their heart, you know, the good and the bad.

> If you're havin' some soul food, like E. Rodney Jones says [Jones is a WVON disc jockey—he called in later in the evening to advertise his soulful show], we havin' our greens and neck bones and blackeyed peas, we havin' some soul food because we're feeding our souls, our bodies.

Clearly, these women are concerned with a rather concrete and physical sort of spirituality, and this same body emphasis can be found in many discussions of soul.

Kenneth Burke's reaction to a musical play staged by a Negro group in New York (*circa* 1938) reflects this mode of thought:

> I had been witnessing a work which revealed at times a remarkably complete kind of biological adaption (for I hold sound art to be precisely that). Here were ways of shuttling indeterminately between bodily processes and their "spiritual equivalents" which could repeatedly provoke, under new guise, "internal-external correspondences" as correct as may be felt, say, in the Processional and Recessional of the orthodox service.[8]

"*Grits and greens.*" The reference to soul food above is also typical, and indeed I have often had the feeling that

8. *A Grammar of Motives* (New York, 1945), p. 365.

traditional Negro cuisine may have greater symbolic than nutritional value at the present time, so often are analogies drawn between food and sex or between food and music. The titles of jazz compositions and record albums dealing with food have proliferated in recent years, even though the music so labeled tastes pretty much the same in most instances. Purvis Spann, "the all-night bluesman" at WVON, expresses his musical preferences: "I don't want no lettuce sandwich on toast; I want hog maws . . . grits . . . collards . . . potato pie" and so on down the line. Jr. Parker explains why all the young men who sing blues don't become professionals: "Anybody can boil up some greens, but a good cook—a good one—has a special way of seasoning 'em that ain't like nobody else's. So anybody can do it, but it's only somebody who can do it their own way." At another point in the interview: "I like a lively audience—they holler back and give you support and that's real nice; like when a wife cooks up a real good meal, you blow her a kiss (smack) or a compliment, and she'll come back with somethin' even better next time. Feels like that on stage—you want to please them that you can." Recall also the conclusion of Jr. Parker's *Drivin' Wheel:* "Here's where you get your steak, potatoes and tea," which Al Braggs elaborates into an extended sex/food metaphor. Cleanhead Vinson refers to his old gal Sue as "not the caviar kind, just plain old kidney stew," and metonymic substitutions of this kind are scattered throughout blues lyrics, old or new. Louis Armstrong likes to sign his letters, "Red beans and ricely yours." Finally, we have the noun "nitty-gritty," derived from "grits," meaning roughly "the basics, the essentials" and hence a partial synonym for soul.

"Keep on pushing." Soul also has to do with staying power—having survived, you carry on. According to some blues practitioners, the only way you can measure soul is by "what a man's been through" a general standard that incorporates Al Hibbler's criteria "being hurt by a woman" and "knowing what that slavery shit is all about." A great many of the songs that are considered particularly soulful are based upon themes like "Pushin' on," "You can make it if you try," "Keep on keeping on," "You'll make it through," and similar slogans of persist-

ence in the face of adversity. In the humanities courses that were part of my undergraduate curriculum, we would have been quick to identify this aspect of soul or the concept of soul itself as a demonstration of the wisdom-through-suffering theme; indeed, one of the more aggressive angles in the soul ideology being pieced together here is that Negroes have a dearly bought experiential wisdom, a "perspective by incongruity," that white America can only envy and certainly never share. Soul is the higher value that, in retrospect at least, may justify all the terrors, anguish, and degradation of the preceding centuries.

"You can make it if you try." And for many Negroes the trying is more important than success or failure. In this connection an exchange between the *Hotline* moderator (Mr. South) and a high-school student who called is most instructive and given here in full.

It seems to me that when you [commentators] speak of soul, you're gettin' off the point, because I go to Phillips, and around the school when the teenagers speak of soul they mean put all you have into it. And what I've been hearin', people are gettin' on the Bible, and that doesn't seem like what it should be.

South: What should it be?

Well, when you speak of soul, let's say like a musician, when he speaks of soul he means he's puttin' all he has into the music—make it sound *good*.

South: Suppose he puts all he has in it and still it doesn't sound good?

Well, he has a lot of soul.

South: He still has soul.

Right!

Some bluesmen, and of course the cry singers, express the same sort of opinion. Answering a question on audience expectations, Freddy King says: "They expect work, they does, *hard* work. And if you're workin' hard and enjoyin' it, they'll enjoy it too."

"*How you feelin'?*" Strong emotions and feelings are soulful, especially when shared with others. The same woman who spoke of "feeding our souls, our bodies" said: "It's the freedom sentiments or feeling. And I feel like this, if you feel the way I feel, soul is just what you feel. And the way I feel, our souls are just the way we feel, our feelin's and our sentiments, because without the soul you won't have any feelings or sentiments." Also two comments from men: "And when you hear some people use soul, and I do believe that means soulful, like appealing to the deeper emotion of a person." "I believe that soul is actually the inner man, and I wouldn't say that soul controls the emotions or that emotion controls soul. I believe they work in there together somewhere."

"*Talk that talk.*" The vocabulary of soul, the argot of the ghetto, is rich, extensive, and difficult to discuss short of compiling a full lexicon. The titles of songs provide a neat focal point, however, and Jr. Parker's remarks are particularly apropos. On the placard that advertises Parker's current show, he and Joe Hinton are pictured in characteristic poses and the titles of their best-known songs are linked together in the middle of the poster so as to form a statement: *There Oughta Be a Law* (Hinton) about *The Things I Used to Do* (Parker) '*Cause You Know It Ain't Right* (Hinton), and *Strange Things Are Happening* (Parker) *But That's All Right* (Parker). The people that this poster hopes to attract will know not only the titles but the lyrics of these songs as well. The interweaving of the phrases is full of implications, mostly sexual, for any soul brother or soul sister who sees the placard. The fans like to interpret and utilize these phrases in conversation, so that key expressions from well-known blues lyrics often become common parlance over night. For example, many people noted that just after Jr. Parker stopped touring with the Bobby Bland package show and went out on his own, Bland had a big success with a song called *I Pity the Fool.* Their interpretations of this title were "confirmed" soon after when Little Jr. announced his financial independence in the first lines of his identifying song, *Drivin' Wheel:* "My baby don't have to work, she don't have to rob and steal." Parker's fan letters—about a dozen or so a week, mostly from the kids, who are not his primary audience—often have titles artfully embedded in them, and occasionally a "little girl" will string together a dozen titles or snips of lyrics to communicate either her admiration for Parker or her own troubles.

The communication channel is open in both directions of course, and most blues lyrics borrow more from current slang than they contribute to it. Jr. Parker sees two ways to produce a soulful song: first, by simply recording accurately your own reaction to some trouble with your wife or girl friend— "what she said, and what you said, and how you felt"; and second, by overhearing conversation or gossip of some kind and putting together the high points of it. In general, blues singers and lyricists reshape and disseminate those new expressions which are coined from year to year to redefine the same old situations.

The transformation of colloquial expressions into blues lyrics and the poetry of those lyrics have yet to be taken beyond the anthology phase into thoroughgoing analysis—an analysis for which the models and methods of Kenneth Burke are particularly well suited.

"Walk that walk." The body emphasis, the effort, and the aforementioned language are all related to a concept of appropriate and often hyperbolic body movements which in turn may dictate a certain style of dress. Cry singers invariably appear in José Greco outfits, removing coat, tie, and sometimes the shirt, as their stunts become more strenuous. (This sort of striptease or "soul baring" symbolizes the idea of getting down to the nitty-gritty.) Female vocalists wear spangled floor-length sheaths that restrict their feet to tiny steps but emphasize their glorious hips and behinds. Disc jockeys have charactertic gaits and accoutrements. Every blues singer has a lyric or two that describes the motion of his beloved. Howlin' Wolf: "And when she walks, her flesh it shakes like Jello." John Lee Hooker: "I

love to see you strut, up and down the floor." Jr. Parker: "When my baby walks, it's like a leaf shakin' on a tree."

More important than lyric tributes, however, are the gestures, movements, and stances that identify each bluesman and underscore his vocals. The kinesic punctuation of a blues rendition is an intimate part of the style and, like the poetics, much in need of further study. I suspect that specific gestures— for example, B. B. King's finger wagging, finger in ear, hands at sides—correlate very closely with particular types of content. Again, as Burke notes, Negroes have come close to achieving an ideal sort of music drama in their church services and blues rituals—"a kind of performance in which the visual and auditory aspects of an event would be completely integrated, so that the tone of the voice and the flexions of the body would seem interchangeable."[9]

"*It don't mean a thing if it ain't got that swing.*" Timing is a variable that runs through walking, talking, singing, dancing, preaching, joking—the whole gamut of soulful behaviors. Without a well-developed sense of timing, of how to phrase or place notes vis à vis the pulse, a sure knowledge of when to pause, where to accent, how to hold and bend a note, a word, or a limb, and so forth—without these qualities, there is no soul worth mentioning.

"*That same old thing.*" Sex, like rhythm, is controversial and omnipresent. From the chanting that induces union with Christ in the fundamentalist churches to the closing strains of Ray Charles' orgiastic best seller, *Tell Me What'd I Say*, the sexual undercurrent in soul music runs strong enough to bowl over the most disinterested observer. The persistent myths of Negro super-sexuality and hyperpotency stem perhaps from the candor, the style, the ritualistic manner with which sexual matters are often treated rather than from any difference in capacities. Differences between middle-class and lower-class codes further complicate the myth-debunking problem. In any event, my only assertion here is that notions of sex, soul, and love are tightly intertwined in the strategy and almost consubstantial.

9. *Ibid.*, p. 363.

"*It's me and you, I and thou, call and response.*" The word "soul" itself is more of a positive term than a dialectical one,[10] since there is really no oppositional word or conceptual equivalent like "no-soul." But the positive term is derived from dialectical operations. The patterned greeting behavior already noted involves a series of moves and counter-moves aiming toward a higher synthesis—brotherhood. Similarly, "signifying" or "playing the dirty dozens"—a game in which insults are exchanged in rapid succession—is a give-and-take affair. The psychological mechanisms involved are complex: the insults involve parents—especially mother—siblings, personal inadequacies; feelings of hostility, aggression, catharsis, and camaraderie are engendered in both participants and onlookers.[11] Signifying, however, is as much a part of the soul vocabulary as greeting banter. The rap (line or pitch) that a man makes to a woman and her replies to his advances are other instances of a highly evolved thesis and antithesis formula. Still others might be mentioned: for example, a couple of winos rambling down Indiana Avenue in the heart of the Indianapolis slum would engage passers-by with the line, "What's the word?" the reply being "Thunderbird." "What's the price?" "White folk's price." "Who drinks the most?" "Colored folks."—and so on through a half dozen questions and answers.

The greeting, signifying, rapping, and Thunderbird dialogue are all dialectical strategies for situations and are part of the larger soul strategy focused upon identity and solidarity. A soul brother is one who can initiate or respond with just the right line or gesture and can fully appreciate the statements and counterstatements of others. The word "member" is sometimes substituted for "soul brother," and to belong to the club you must

10. *Ibid.*, pp. 107–111. Actually, Burke would probably see the term "soul" as an "oxymoron," since it encompasses many opposites and defines a paradox, the Negro's acceptance of life in all its bittersweetness, joyful-sadness and painful-pleasures. Baldwin, Ellison, Bennett, and other realistic-romantics have noted this indefinable quality but Jr. Parker's poster sums it up best—"Strange Things Are Happening," "But That's All Right."

11. Roger Abrahams, *Deep Down in the Jungle* (Hatboro, 1964), Chapter IV.

know the games, passwords, pledges, and interplay by heart.[12] In the current phraseology, those who don't have this requisite knowledge are "not ready," the implication being perhaps that someone who has not defined himself as a Negro and accepted his past is not really free—hence, not ready for tomorrow.

The same type of dialectic is found in sermons, comedy routines, and of course in music. The ubiquitous magic formula of call and response has been outlined above and need not detain us long here. I am not ready either to defend or to attack Alan Lomax's broad hypothesis concerning song structure and social structure,[13] but it is nevertheless obvious that there are strong parallels between patterns of social interaction and the interplay between voice and instrument in every blues. A great deal of work has yet to be done on the call-and-response pattern before tighter correspondences can be made between the music and its socio-cultural context. Yet, after listening repeatedly to Sonny Boy Williamson's harmonica weave in and out of a blues lyric, one can almost substitute words for notes. Many of B. B. King's most expressive guitar phrases also seem to be saying something. It would be most interesting to explore with these men and a sample of their audience the possible verbal equivalents of certain instrumental phrases in one or two of their most popular recordings. The usual transcriptions of blues lyrics give only one side of a conversation.

Similarly, there is much to be derived from an analysis of the shape of content in the fifty or so recordings of the Reverend C. L. Franklin and his flock, the vaudeville routines of Pigmeat Markham and friends, and audience seminars held by that nasty but lovable old lady Moms Mabley. The similarities and differences in all these strategies offer a fascinating field of study for those interested in rhetoric, style, and the dialectics or mechanics of soul.

"*This nonmachine tradition.*" Lerone Bennett, Jr., sees the "folk myth of *Soul*" as the Negro's spiritual gift to America.

12. Woodie King, Jr., "The Game," *Liberator* 5 (1965): 20–25.
13. "Song Structure and Social Structure," *Ethnology*, I (1963): 425–51.

From the womb of this non-Puritan, nonmachine, nonexploitative tradition have come insights, values and attitudes that have changed the face of America. The tradition is very definitely nonmachine, but it is not anti-machine; it simply recognizes that machines are generative power and not soul, instruments and not ends.[14]

T-Bone Walker likes to knock off a solo on the electric guitar with the instrument held behind his head. B. B. King, like T-Bone before him, never lets an evening go by without playing a few fine choruses one-handed. Jimmy Smith likes to pull out the stops and play the electric organ "no hands." Jimmy McGriff actually climbs on top of the organ and plays it on all fours. Other instances of man over machine, though less dramatic, perhaps, could be listed on page after page; every jazzman or bluesman worthy of the name has mastered and transformed his instrument to suit his own special purposes. Contrast this sort of mastery with the mastery of the symphony musician, who strives to play his instrument as it ought to be played, so as to produce the tone that the instrument was designed to produce, and you will have another idea of what soul is all about. Automation may not be such a big threat to the soul brother; he's used to playing "no hands."[15]

"Something initially pure." One of the more eloquent definitions of "soul" on the *Hotline* program came from a young lady:

> Now, to the word "soul." When I think of the word "soul," stripped of all reference, I think of something, anything, initially pure. When applied to man, which is our first reference, soul in man would then apply to the heart of man which is initially pure. When you refer this word to anything else, you can't help but go back to its origins: the relationship being between man and himself.

14. *The Negro Mood* (Chicago, 1964), p. 53. Obviously, this nonmachine tradition hasn't yet changed the face of America appreciably, but we can hope that it will.

15. C. E. Wilson, "Automation and the Negro—Will We Survive?" Part II, *Liberator* 5 (1965): 11–15.

So if you apply it to food or music or what have you, you're getting at the very same thing, the heart of it, which is initially pure . . . Whenever I hear the word "soul," no matter what it's related to, right away I have that very good feeling that here we are going to have something very fine, something pure, something that hasn't been in any way distorted.

Later in the evening, Purvis Spann, the "all-night blues man," singled out this definition as the one he liked best, introducing his program with the following remarks.

Y'all wanna know what soul is? Stay tuned to me for about the next hour. I'll tell ya, if I don't completely satisfy your curiosity I'm gonna knock a big dent in it. You better know it, 'cause I got nothin' but some soul for you . . . this mornin' child. [Plays a Ray Charles record.] Just listen to him—that's soul—that's pure. When you're thinking about pure things you're thinking about the soul of things, and I'm thinking about pure blues. [Puts on Muddy Waters' *That Same Thing* and intersperses comments with the music.] Not watered down—not diluted—not dehydrated—oooohh, but the real nitty-gritty, I'm talkin' about pure soul.

Muddy's pure lyric is also interesting for its subtle sexuality:

What makes men go crazy when a woman wear her dress so tight?
What makes men go crazy when a woman wear her dress so tight?
Must be the same old thing that make a tomcat fight all night.

Why do all of these men want to run a big-leg woman down?
Why do all of these men want to run a big-leg woman down?
Must be the same old thing that make a bulldog hug a houn'.

O, that same thing.
O, that same thing.
Tell me who's to blame;
The whole world's fightin' about that same thing.

What makes you feel so good when your baby get a
    evenin' gown?
What makes you feel so good when your baby get a
    evenin' gown?
Must be the same old thing that made a preacher lay his
    Bible down.

"*Tell it like it is.*" Although this sounds like a command, it is used as a commendation for a basic point well made or in response to a new insight. I am reminded of Bobby Bland's asking the rhetorical question at the conclusion of the guitarist's solo in *Stormy Monday:* "Ain't that the truth?" For "Sincerely yours," "Truly yours," Louis Armstrong substitutes "Red beans and ricely yours"—the soul tradition feeds on truth. The comments of the boy from Phillips High School are also relevant —as long as a man is trying hard and is sincere in his efforts to express himself, he has soul.

"*The esthetics of folkways.*" Another young man gave his *Hotline* definition an anthropological twist.

I think that soul today is used primarily in the Negro communities, and it's also beginning to be used more in the white community. I think it has more of a social connotation rather than a religious connotation, referring to some of the esthetic ways of Negro folkways. [South:] Such as what? [Young man:] Well, I think that maybe pertaining to Negro foods, some of the dance, some of the dances that we have, referring to more of the esthetics of folkways.

Bluesmen frequently mention other kinds of soul. B. B. King's reference to Japanese koto music is a case in point. Almost all blues musicians agree that Frank Sinatra and Tony Bennett have soul. Although some are at a complete loss to explain the phenomenon of a white man who sings with that feeling, others point to Sinatra's Italian background; Al Hibbler, for one, thinks that his troubles with Ava Gardner made the real difference. Willie Dixon, reminiscing about his stay in Israel with Memphis Slim, observed that the radio in his room there brought him "all different kinds of soul music; in the morning there'd be one kind, and at night another, and around six there was some stuff sounding just like blues, same notes and all, but a different language." His travels have convinced him that other countries have their own versions of soul, and most musicians seem inclined to agree with him.

"*Who am I?*" In order to tell it like it is, a practitioner must first follow two more fundamental commandments: "Be what you are" and "Believe in what you do." In a blues career the identity commandments are generally followed automatically; but the blues singer's self-assurance is a rare commodity, and for the audience, the man in the street, the questions "Who am I?" "What are you?" have considerable force. The comments of two middle-aged and probably middle-class men on *Hotline* are interesting.

> I believe that as Negroes we have been depicted as having more soul feelings than anyone else in the world seemingly, and I believe that we have also been exploited along those lines. And I believe that now they're stretching the thing to a point in adding it over into the jazz idiom, although I suppose that deriving it down through the spirituals and field songs and folk songs along that line and going over into the jazz things that we are supposed to be still considered as depicting ourselves through those mediums [slightly incredulous tone of voice] . . . maybe we should look at it from more or less the spiritual angle. You see this soul thing deals with a mysterious object, something we can't see.

> On the question of soul, you might say I'm a young observer of all things. This question tonight has aroused my curiosity and has also left me puzzled. Soul is more or less, so far as I've ever heard the word, has been referred

to with connection to religion. But to hear people stand and talk about it, it makes you stop and wonder. How can they say exactly what soul is, especially concerned with religion . . . today you hear mostly, when you hear the word "soul," the first thing you think of, it's somehow connected with the Negro, or connected with jazz, or well just lately with the Civil Rights movement and . . . well, take Dick Gregory for instance, every now and then you hear him drop a line about the soul brothers, and well naturally, I won't assume that everybody thinks as I do but this is the first thing that comes to me—that it's being referred to the Negro. But, to the original statement I made, it's just puzzling. I won't be satisfied until I get some concrete proof as to just what it means.

Here are two men who equate soul with a fuzzy sort of "negritude." They recognize a tradition, more or less, but are either querulous (first speaker) or skeptical (second speaker) and leery of being stereotyped. The concept of soul is "mysterious," "puzzling," "depicted," "somehow connected with the Negro," and hardly reassuring or reaffirming in its implications. Soul, for some Negroes, perhaps a substantial number, is not a working strategy for the situation, but rather a part of a confusing situation for which a new strategy may be needed; neither of these commentators gives us much of an indication as to what that strategy should be. There are certainly alternatives to the soul orientation, however, and these will be suggested in the following chapter.

"Getting together." "I won't assume that everybody thinks as I do," says the "young observer of all things." But in a most basic sense this assumption of common understandings, a common experience, shared modes of thinking about and expressing that experience is exactly what is meant by soul— "our feelings and our sentiments," as one woman put it. She made a point of telling us how she arrived at this opinion: "But we should also have a model for a man, and we have a moral and emotional part of man's nature, an' this is what we found in our discussion, just a group of our lady friends gettin' together."

Another woman placed a rather mystical accent on sharing: "In my estimation, I believe that soul is the energy or the mind of human beings. And how this is transformed into activity, I believe, is really incarnation of one person's idea into another makes him the soul of the other person."

For all its ambiguity, this last interpretation of soul provides a fine insight into what happens at a blues ritual. B. B. King, Bobby Bland, Jr. Parker, and Ray Charles are the incarnations of soul; they do transform the collective "mind" into representative activities. A good blues lyric is a representative anecdote, the distillation of a problem, the naming of a malaise. Today, a good rendering of an urban blues lyric is also a representative antidote, ritually acted out, for the malady named. The naming-and-curing ceremony is a grand synecdoche (literally—from the Greek—"a receiving together"), and this dramatized figure of speech is effective to the degree that the man stands for his people, the people for their man—one for all, and all for one.

The foregoing list of elements or connotations—the ideas people have about soul—is neither systematic nor complete and does not really lend itself to summary generalizations or terminological pronouncements, if only because "soul" is best defined in action. I can only hope that the reader's feeling for the blues can be enhanced somewhat by juxtaposing the components of this soul strategy with the events described in preceding chapters, but the ideological elements interact and cohere differently, gain additional meaning and force with every public reenactment. Reminded, perhaps, of the *Hotline* discussion a few weeks earlier, E. Rodney Jones opened the proceedings of a recent Chicago blues festival with the following appeal: "Do you want a definition of soul? Well, you're going to get it tonight, right here on stage. I want everybody to raise their right hands and repeat after me, 'I hereby bear witness to the blues!' Do I have a witness out there?" Seeing and hearing is believing, and there is no substitute for bearing witness.

With this admonition in mind, we can move this discussion toward a conclusion by returning to the denouement of a Bobby

Blue Bland performance at the Trianon Ballroom. The hour was late, and Bobby had just finished the second show of the evening following a format similar to the hypothetical pattern suggested in Chapter V, replete with the one-two punch of *Stormy Monday* and *That's the Way Love Is*. During this latter song, a long conga line took shape in response to Bobby's affirmative shouts and the band's enthusiastic support—the only instance of communal dancing I have seen at any blues gathering.

Thoroughly mellowed by a full evening of soul, people begin to move toward the exits as Bobby thanks everyone for coming out and moves to the edge of the stage to "talk that talk" with his well-wishers. E. Rodney Jones emerges suddenly—his first appearance of the evening—goes through a brief but hearty reunion ritual with Joe Scott (they were schoolmates in Texarkana, Arkansas, I'm told) and takes the microphone to announce an unexpected guest—the comedian Dick Gregory. While Gregory makes his way forward, another one of "the good guys at WVON," Purvis Spann, rambles out from the wings, conspicuously attired in sweatshirt and sneakers, to lead the congregation in singing the WVON station break a few times— "double-you-vee-oh-en, fot-teen-fif-tay" (WVON, 1450 on the dial)—with some hog-calling thrown in for good measure, "Sssssuuuee." Gregory is introduced again, and ambles out in his trench coat to a big ovation. He lights his cigarette and tells a couple of jokes appropriate to the occasion and worth paraphrasing:

> You know we finally got the papers downtown to stop using the word "Negro" over and over again whenever they report a crime. But they've got ways of getting around that now. They let you know it was Negroes who did the job anyway. Like in this report of a supermarket robbery last week; they said the safe with $10,000 in it was open but the money was untouched. The only thing that was missing was forty pounds of chit'lins and one six-pack of Pepsi-Cola. And a witness said she saw two men leave who had kerchiefs over their faces and around the tops of their heads too. The fuzz [cops] found a copy

of *Jet* with Moms Mabley on the cover at the scene of the crime. Now you'd never guess who pulled off that job, would you?

I'm sure you've all heard that Elijah Muhammad has just suspended Malcolm X from public speaking, but I'll bet you don't know the real reason he got busted. It wasn't because he was happy about Kennedy gettin' what he deserved and all that. No, somebody caught the big X at a Baptist church eating chit'lins with a white woman.[16]

Gregory joins Spann and Al Braggs to have their pictures taken at one side of the stage while E. Rodney Jones huddles with Joe Scott momentarily before turning to the microphone and asking Bobby to sing *The Feeling Is Gone* one more time. Bland agrees (this is the fourth version of the song in one evening) and puts his arm around Dick Gregory as he sings. The comedian listens intently, puffing on his cigarette, then leaves with a handshake and sympathetic smile as Braggs comes forward to sing the last verse. He imitates Bland to perfection, every nuance, inflection, and mannerism exactly in place, while the man himself stands at his side and beams his approval.

"And how this is transformed into activity, I believe, is really incarnation of one person's ideas into another makes him the soul of the other person." That's what the lady said. This fresh instance of Braggs-Bland unification will serve as an illustration of the malady-remedy, anecdote-antidote generalizations ventured above. The lyric, as usual, names the problem: instability of male-female relationships.

When I needed you to stand by my side
All you did was laugh while I cried.
And now you want me, to take you back in my arms.
Oh, it's too late, baby,
I'm here to tell you that the feelin' is gone.

16. This was, of course, some months before Malcolm broke officially with Elijah Muhammad and began to fuse the soul ideology with the spirit of African nationalism. It is also worth noting that Gregory has become progressively more militant since that time.

Yet, it is not too late, and the feeling is forcefully present, filling the hall with togetherness rather than separateness. Braggs, Gregory, the "good guys" from WVON, the band, and the audience are all standing at Bobby's side, helping, encouraging, empathizing.

> I remember, the look on your face,
> Oow, when you told me, that I was being replaced.
> Now you're beggin' me, you say you wanna come back home.
> Oh, it's too late, baby,
> I'm standin' here to tell you that the feelin' is gone.

Bobby is quite literally being replaced by another man—or is reincarnated, if you prefer—but this time he feels pride, not pain, as Braggs steps into the spotlight to deliver the last verse.

> You told me to hit the road, and I did just that.
> Now you find out that you need me, but I ain't comin' back.
> And now you say you want me, to take you back in my arms.
> Oh, I say it's too late, baby,
> I'm here to tell you the feelin' is gone.

The lyric anecdotes give one side of the picture; the symbolic actions on stage show us another side. B. B. King, the bluesman proper, takes a more independent stance before the public, but he too makes the same drastic point from time to time, as when he finishes a long tale of his woman troubles and feigns a collapse, "going down slow," only to have his sidemen rush forward to support him. They lift him to his feet, and he immediately bounces back with another number at a brighter tempo.

Those women have put us in a bad situation, say the bluesmen, and so we'd best stick together for strategic purposes. But what are those purposes? The constant show of brotherhood is obviously an end in itself, but in what way, if any, is masculine solidarity a solution to the many forms of conjugal instability? To put it in functionalist terms,[17] what are the consequences of the blues brotherhood? I have no straightforward answers to these questions. Part of the trouble lies in translating from culture to society, from the anecdote-antidote pattern on the symbolic or cultural level to the facts of life on the social level. Perhaps the show of solidarity is just that—a show or statement of what *ought* to obtain in day-to-day, man-to-man relations; whereas outside the soul setting or ritual-entertainment world, it's still every man for himself. Perhaps the action on stage only indicates a hardening of the battle lines —the men mustering their forces so as to slug it out on equal terms with the women. Possibly these functions and others are being served simultaneously.

Reviewing the elements in the soul ideology, the full range of lyrics, blues performances *in toto*, and the party line at WVON, however, I think it is possible to interpret the soul and solidarity syndrome as a key phase in an incipient movement or perhaps as a complex response to the civil rights movement. This interpretation rests initially upon a few broad assertions: American society is in the midst of a revolution, and the crisis is forcing basic cultural readjustments on the part of both blacks and whites; the black masses have only very recently been emotionally affected by the current "revolution"; most of those in the ghettos, though they read or hear about it, have yet to receive any concrete benefits from this revolution; Negro men are especially disadvantaged, from almost any point of view, and at the very bottom of the American socio-economic heap; the spokesmen for these people—bluesmen, ministers, comedians, disc jockeys—are much more interested in freedom and self-respect than in integration per se and, perhaps because of their vested ethnic interests, even a little afraid, consciously or unconsciously, of absorption or disappearance in the white mainstream. If assertions of this sort have some validity, then the soul movement readily takes on a strong nativistic and revitalizing tone. The concept of nativism implies, to this

17. Robert K. Merton, *Social Theory and Social Structure* (Glencoe, 1957).

analyst at least, a reaction, an affirmation of the old values in response to new stresses and conflicts. It may well be that the soul movement represents a retrenchment or retreat, corresponding in some respects to what is currently called the white backlash. If realities are too grim to cope with, if aspirations remain unrealizable, or if the price placed on first-class citizenship seems to be exorbitant, defining oneself as a soul brother may be a way of saving face. There is this nativistic aspect to soul, and it may be dominant at present; but the related concept of revitalization, with its emphasis on sweeping reform and establishment of a new order based, in part at least, on the old values, is becoming more applicable to the soul movement with every passing day.

The Black Muslim movement offers a most convenient reference point, since it represents an excellent example of the revitalization process described by Wallace.[18] Both Muslim and soul movements are attempting to achieve the same end—self-respect; but aside from the core feature of brotherhood, the means employed by the two groups are diametrically opposed. Cloaked in an Islamic and Zionist ideology, the Muslim program is based on a complete, harsh, and puritanical negation of the Negro lower-class stereotype. It is this stereotype of course that the proponents of soul hope to refurbish, reshape, and revive. For the Muslims, "the collard green is a weed," "the pig is a poison animal," and both are strictly taboo; for the soul brothers, "hocks and greens sustained us during slavery times, and they're the source of our strength today." Bobby Bland pleads for cooperation, tolerance, increased understanding, togetherness; Elijah Muhammad hands down the rules and dogmas that contribute to a sense of purification and superiority. The soul strategists try to turn old liabilities into new assets; the Muslim ideologists continue to mint a new currency altogether, although the coins are clearly stamped with the Protestant ethic. Contrasts of this kind could be multiplied at length, and a thorough comparative study would be most rewarding, for the Muslims are unalterably opposed to all the tenets and manifesta-

18. Anthony F. C. Wallace, "Revitalization Movements," *American Anthropologist* 58 (1956): 264–81. See also *Culture and Personality* (New York, 1961).

tions of soul, and, judging by Gregory's crack at what was once the Muslim leadership, the feeling is mutual.

The basic common denominator of brotherhood brings us back to the question raised above: "What are the consequences of male solidarity?" More men than women make the conversion to Mr. Muhammad's movement; the Fruit of Islam, a fraternal paramilitary order, is the backbone of the organization. Its slogan and *raison d'être* is "We must respect and protect our women," for they in turn are the trees which will bear fruit in the future. Brotherhood in the Muslim setting contributes directly to marital and familial stability, although the willingness of most Muslim men to hold down a steady job is the decisive factor.

Purvis Spann, whose commitment to soul is beyond reproach, has been campaigning over the airwaves on a very similar platform. Although the protection plank is not stressed, the respect theme runs strong and the code of decency seems to be based on working-class norms; married women should never work under any circumstances, but should stay home and take care of the children; men should bring their pay checks home, although it's all right to deduct a little spending money for a night or two out with the boys; men should offer their seats to ladies on the bus, shouldn't use foul language in the home, and so forth. Other disc jockeys at WVON echo Spann's line from time to time, but it is difficult to determine whether this is simply a pitch to the ladies, a fad that will pass, or the first phase of an explicit reform program.[19]

19. Radio Station WVON might easily spearhead a "practical revolution" in Chicago if the management were so inclined. Since its inception about a year ago, it has become a force in the Negro community and its programs provide a running documentary of the developments in the soul movement. The station once took an important step in the direction of political action with a marathon "sleepless sit-in" to raise funds for the Mississippi Summer Project. A four-day around-the-clock evangelical vigil by the "good-guys" (Spann was the last to collapse) was very successful. Were similar campaigns to be conducted on matters of local concern, the impact might be much greater. The disc jockey Magnificent Montague also took part in this project during his all-too-brief stay at WVON. He moved on to Los Angeles where his soulful slogan "Burn, baby, burn!" was apparently taken up as a battle cry during the insurrection.

Blues lyrics with a normative cast also seem to be gaining rapidly in popularity. In addition to *Yield Not to Temptation* and other songs already described, Bobby Bland's *Your Friends* has some interesting lines:

> Don't let your friends turn you against me, baby,
> Because they ain't giving you one red copper cent.
>   (repeat)
> I said, when I leave you this time, baby,
> I just want to know who's gonna pay your house rent.

>   (spoken) I'll say it one more time.
> Don't let them turn you against me, baby;
> This time I'm gonna let your conscience be your guide.
>   (repeat)
> Oh, but when I leave you this time, baby
> I just want to know, will your friends stand by your side?

> Your friends say that I'm no good,
> I hunt women like a dog hunt a bone.
> But I can't be doin' too much wrong, baby;
> Every week I bring my paycheck home.

> So don't let them turn you against me, baby;
> And I know you're blind and you just can't see.
> I said, I said you better get hip to all of your girlfriends,
> Whoa; they're just tryin' to get next to me.

Bland analyzes; in *Back Door Man* Howlin' Wolf only brags:

> I am a back door man.
> I am a back door man.
> Well, the men don't know,
> But the little girls understand,

> When everybody's tryin' to sleep
> I'm somewhere, makin' my midnight creep.
> Every morning, the rooster crow;
> Some men tell me, I got to go.

It is certainly too early to remove the quotation marks from "the soul movement." An amorphous set of grass-roots sentiments has only begun to be codified and communicated to the large potential source of converts,[20] and there are a few major obstacles and traps that may prevent the style and content of Negro culture from ever finding solid political expression. But, as Burke has noted, "Aesthetical values are intermingled with ethical values and the ethical is the basis of the practical. . . . Probably for this reason even the most practical of revolutions will generally be found to have manifested itself first in the 'aesthetic' sphere."[21] Because Negro aesthetic values already have a concrete, ethical, and practical bent, this point of view (shared by LeRoi Jones and others) gains added power.

The values embodied in the urban blues can easily be tapped and utilized by a man with a plan. Already the soul ideology has given a somewhat different vocabulary to some of the civil rights activists. Dick Gregory and friends do not phrase their appeals for civil rights support in terms of white-christian-democratic-constitutional morality and social justice. White liberals and educated Negroes may be mobilized by these ideas, but these same ideas are less than inspirational when beamed to the ghetto. The soul brothers seem to be saying: "Let us fight for our rights, not because it is a disgrace for a democratic society to include twenty million second-class citizens, but because we value our cultural identity and wish to be able to develop it and express it without fearing punishment from the white majority."

Many Negroes are apparently unwilling to sell their soul to the devil or to discard the blues in their quest for freedom. Quite the contrary. James Baldwin reconciled himself to being a black man as he listened to his Bessie Smith records in Switzerland. Ray Charles, Bobby Bland, B. B. King, Jr. Parker—all the bluesmen—are performing the same indispensable service for the blues people today. To say, "B. B. King is my main man," is to say, "I take pride in who I am." With this self-acceptance

20. These are the two preliminary stages in Wallace's six-stage revitalization process.

21. Burke, *op. cit.*, p. 234.

a measure of unity is gained and a demand is made upon white America: "Accept us on our own terms." The blues will continue to tell us—all of us—what those terms are. This, I take it, is at least one of the important messages carried by the title of Baldwin's most recent dramatic work, *Blues for Mr. Charlie*.

CHAPTER VIII

ALTERNATIVES

THE FOREGOING ANALYSIS of the urban bluesman in cultural context leads, I think, to some intriguing and fundamental questions concerning the future. Are the blues a sad symptom, an embarrassing relic of slavery days, as so many mainline Americans insist? Are they destined for oblivion in the promised great society? Are the goals of Negro identity and white acceptance incompatible or complementary? Must Negroes assimilate to succeed, or must the American definition of success be reevaluated? These are not either/or questions that can be answered in black-and-white terms. But, rather than contemplate the possible gray blends of the future, I should like to conclude this study with some unqualified assertions and obvious alternatives.

Contrary to popular belief, Negroes are the only substantial minority group in America who really have a culture to guard and protect. The small but crucial retentions of African tradition, the slavery experience, the post-slavery history of oppression, the reemergence of the non-white world, and America's refusal until recently to allow integration—all have combined, for better or for worse, to give the Negro a different reality, a different culture with which to master that reality, and a unique perspective by incongruity on American society that may be this nation's outstanding and redeeming virtue.

Like it or not, however, a Negro culture exists, and its

191

existence ought to be recognized by all concerned, no matter what their policy or proposed solution to the American dilemmas. The failure to recognize this culture and a reluctance to work with and within it account in large measure for the failures of the Black Muslims, the civil rights groups, and the warriors on poverty, none of whom have been able to reach the ghetto majority, much less effect any basic changes in its way of life.

As any rational human being must, I detest slum conditions, welfare colonialism, foul schools. These institutions do, after all, constitute the perpetuative core of Negro culture as it exists today. But I suspect that as these conditions are remedied—*if* they are remedied—more and more Negroes will become aware of the excessively high price that has been paid through the centuries for their distinctive status today. They will cherish and defend this cultural identity, and they will see in their "entertainers" the primary carriers of an irreplaceable tradition. Unwilling to cast them aside in a quest for homogeneous middle-class anonymity, they will rebuild and revitalize a culture that will give these figures the profound and unambivalent respect that is their due. The stereotyping of the bluesman as a drunken bum moaning in the gutter, the preacher as a money-grabbing charlatan, comedienne Moms Mabley as a dirty, sadistic old lady, the matriarch as castrating, selfish bitch —all will be rejected or reversed in the light of more realistic appraisals. Thoughtful and thorough studies of Negro radio, Negro preaching, and especially Negro comedy are long overdue. Even the hustler—we hope an extinct breed in the future— may be seen retrospectively not as an anomic criminal but as a tragic hero who once battled the forces of evil: brutal cops, corrupt judges, the whole decadent big-city system of "law and order."

Until such time as the negative aspects of Negro culture have been banished by community self-help and quality education, until the positive aspects are accentuated in a resynthesis of the cultural mazeway, I will continue to dispute those who insist that Negroes have no worthwhile culture and will give qualified support to Norman Mailer and any other "existentialists" who contend that Negroes have *the* culture.

Although the romantic and orgasmic elaboration of Mailer's thesis in "The White Negro" is often just plain silly and has been justly maligned, the thesis itself is sound.[1] The urban Negro male today may be Everyman tomorrow. He has learned to live with the threat of irrational violence; and we too must develop a life-preserving stance toward the vast, impersonal, and constantly growing forces of annihilation that hover over us. He is "fatherless"; and as the pace of our unplanned, unchecked technological "progress" accelerates, our "fathers" can no longer provide adequate models of what it means to be a man either—each succeeding generation will find itself in a radically changed environment. The Negro is useless and expendable in terms of the economic system. Now we can foresee the day when an elite staff of engineers and laboratory technicians will create and nurse the machines that supply all our material needs while the rest of humanity stands idly by, bored and unproductive. Alternatively, we must learn to entertain each other. The Negro lives in a state of compressed humanity, the ghetto; as the population continues to expand, if not explode, our living space must become similarly constricted. The Negro has had to come to terms somehow with a hostile majority of a different color that surrounds him; we are rapidly coming face to face with the same situation. The Negro in America is learning to combat and solve these problems. The solutions that he finds will perhaps be those that the American in the world must borrow for himself in the not too distant future.

As Malcolm X saw so very clearly, "integration" is neither the issue nor the answer. Freedom is the issue. Freedom is never given or granted—it is won. Freedom is founded upon choice. Choice, in turn, rests upon trained, truth-seeking intelligence and a profound awareness of real alternatives. These qualities depend to a frightening extent upon the success or failure of the much talked about pre-school program, Operation Head Start. Will the children (Negro and white) be allowed to maintain real "ratio-nality"?[2] Will opportunities, life chances and choices be

1. Norman Mailer, *Advertisements for Myself* (New York, 1960), pp. 302–21.
2. Again I should like to suggest that Marshall McLuhan's best insights point to a thorough revision of our whole educational system.

open, or won't they? I don't think it is unrealistic to assume that the continued revitalization of Negro culture I hope for and the fate of the nation itself depend upon the answer to this question. If the "operation" in the slums gets out of political hands and into the hands of the people, America must brace itself for a genuine Negro renaissance and/or a real Negro revolution in the 1980's that will make the movements of the 1920's, 1940's, and 1960's seem pale by comparison. If the operation fails—if it represents nothing more than half-hearted "compensatory education for cultural deprivation"[3] and a misguided effort by white men to make Negroes over into their own ugly image—then I don't want to be around to face the consequences.

At present the Negro is marginal in the sense of being on the sidelines, out of it, a victim pleading for recognition of his humanity. Lerone Bennett, James Baldwin, the protestors, the demonstrators—all plead with fervor and eloquence; but what white America wants—though it may not know it, deserve it, or accept it when it comes—is more extensive proof of that humanity, evidence that Negroes can stand on their own feet.[4] If the cultural resynthesis and revitalization which I envisage, and which are already underway, actually come to fruition, then such proof will become available in superabundance. And a different sort of marginal man will emerge as well, the kind that Thorstein Veblen described with such remarkable acumen.[5] These marginal men do not subsist on the fringe of one culture or another, but are caught between two value orientations that

3. Benjamin S. Bloom, Allison Davis, Robert Hess, *Compensatory Education for Cultural Deprivation* (New York, 1965).

4. Eric Hoffer has forcefully articulated the semi-conscious view of many whites who see "the Negro problem" as the Negro's problem rather than their own. ("The Negro Is Prejudiced against Himself," *New York Times Magazine*, Nov. 29, 1964, p. 27.) Ill founded or not, this view must be dealt with; the Negro "striver's" imitation can only flatter this perspective, and it is my feeling that militant self-helping soul brothers stand a better chance of cracking the cocoon of white complacency. Can we hope that worms will become butterflies in the process?

5. Thorstein Veblen, *The Portable Veblen* (New York, 1948), pp. 474–79.

compete on fairly equal terms for their allegiance. By refurbishing a set of Afro-American values—indulging in a little black chauvinism if necessary—Negroes can equal the terms and thereby make available important new choices and alternatives. The "diverse individualities among Negroes," whose emergence Hentoff and Ellison have recognized, are often the products of this latter sort of marginality, as are Hentoff and Ellison for that matter.

Marginality has its dangers: some people struggle with their ambiguous position and transcend it, whereas others refuse to make choices and are trapped by it. Marginality was certainly a motivating factor for Marx, Freud, and Einstein (and for Durkheim, Proust, and Lévi-Strauss in France), men who grappled with conflicting German and Jewish ways of life at an early age and whose minds were consequently shaped into a skeptical and inquiring mode of thought ideally suited to the formulation of the ideas that have shaped and continue to shape our century. Other German Jews were unable to transcend their marginality, suppressed the cultural conflict, assimilated blindly, and, it might be argued, were thereby at a significant disadvantage when warped Nazi minds began to search for a scapegoat. There may be a lesson in this for the Negro, for us all.

Earlier in this century Negroes were lynched and mutilated daily in America, sometimes by the dozen. Astonishingly few voices were raised in protest. Stanley Edgar Hyman, deploring the symbolic and ritual vacuum in American life, says:

> Our public ceremonials on the order of ticker-tape parades and political rallies are collective without being cathartic, as our barroom brawls are cathartic without being collective. The only culture trait we possess which might fairly be called a full ritual communion—collective, purgative, and overwhelming—is the lynch mob, and it is not one we should like to encourage.[6]

Improbably but nevertheless possibly, white America's only ritual may be revived and systematized as a final solution to the

6. *The Promised End* (Cleveland, 1963), p. 273.

Negro problem before this century draws to a close. Neither yellow arm bands nor impressionistic nose evaluations will be needed. Although the Negro has been kept an invisible man, he is all too visible in this respect. Should our efforts to police, contain, and develop the non-white world according to our own narrow design prove futile (and American paranoia rise proportionately), should the investors and creditors push their panic buttons, should the drop-out, delinquency, crime, and riot rates climb geometrically as America's major cities become predominantly Negro (in from five to ten years)—then white America may react in desperation, cling to its appalling innocence tenaciously, and eliminate the Negro in the name of law and order. Improbable? Yes, but not an idle fantasy.

There is a fantasy, a dream, an ideal, a plan current today which is based on the notion that the Negro problem can be solved by making the Negro white, by assimilating and integrating him in the same manner that every other immigrant has been assimilated and swallowed up in monolithic America. Right-thinking whites and the traditional Negro leaders have gone to great lengths to make the plan work, to translate the dream into some sort of reality. The guiding lights of all the better-known Negro organizations try to be very respectable, very good, very acceptable to the best of their ability. Even Elijah Muhammad—hardly an assimilationist—and his patient, self-righteous followers feel that they are too pure in heart for politics. They will wait for Allah himself to set the record straight. But other men of God—Martin Luther King and company—are also attempting to convince people who feel that Negroes are subhuman that they are really superhuman. King preaches a non-violent brand of Christianity that is unfortunately quite alien to the Western tradition.[7] A little less patient than the Muslims and more humble than self-righteous, his followers hope that the holy trinity—the President, Congress, the Supreme Court—will finally be able to rework the Constitution and the American conscience to the point where black men

7. I would have less scorn and much more respect for Reverend King were he to practice what he preaches and encourage his followers to return their draft cards or register as conscientious objectors.

will be granted first-class citizenship. But whatever King's future accomplishments may be (and Harlem is not Selma), an end to segregation is one thing; achieving a lasting sense of one's humanity as a black man or a white man living in America is another and more difficult problem.

Unless a third alternative is recognized, the white man's peculiar mixture of fear, guilt, arrogance, and innocence as well as the black man's bitter blend of anger, cynicism, and sense of inferiority will linger on for many generations to come, contaminating and ultimately destroying this nation, even after the cruel facts of segregation are no longer at issue. Freedom cannot be given, dignity cannot be granted; but a deeper understanding of another way of life—perhaps even a profound respect for cultural differences—is possible. In the world of today and tomorrow it is necessary for survival. No nation on earth has yet achieved a lasting and productive cultural pluralism, and creative marginality of the Veblenesque variety has correspondingly been in desperately short supply. The problem of the Negro in America is inextricably meshed with the problem of America in the world; and, as many confused prophets before me have noted, anything can happen, ranging from catastrophe to a golden age.

If the unrealized American potential for productive pluralism and meaningful marginality is to be realized, more Negroes must identify themselves. They must struggle with their past and accept it—all of it; they must honor their heroes and prophets, past and present; they must define with greater care who they are now and what they want their children to become; they must consciously decide what they will continue to accept from the Western tradition and what they will reject; and, with black men everywhere, they must keep and sharpen their perspective on a white world that would rather absorb them culturally or exterminate them physically than face them as free men. Many more white Americans must understand and accept this process and perspective. They must make a terribly strenuous effort to comprehend the dynamics of Negro culture as they shift and develop through time; and, most important, they must apply the insights so acquired to their own lives.

THE IDENTITY PROBLEM

No DISCUSSION of identity problems can be pursued very far these days without bringing Erik Erikson's well-known schema into play.[1] His ego development outline is particularly useful in highlighting the importance of expressive roles.

Erikson has charted eight cumulative stages or "psychosocial crises" in the life cycle that every individual negotiates with varying degrees of success or failure. The crises are conceptualized succinctly as follows:

1. Trust vs. Distrust
2. Autonomy vs. Shame, Doubt
3. Initiative vs. Guilt
4. Industry vs. Inferiority
5. Identity and Repudiation vs. Identity Diffusion
6. Intimacy and Solidarity vs. Isolation
7. Generativity vs. Self-Absorption
8. Integrity vs. Despair

Data on the first two stages seem to be scarce. To my knowledge, no one has attempted a systematic study of early socialization practices in the black belt. The Negro infant is, however, probably at no great disadvantage compared to his

1. "Identity and the Life Cycle" in *Psychological Issues*, George S. Klein, ed. (New York, 1959)

white middle-class counterpart—he may even be somewhat better off. If, as I am led to believe, later weaning, the high value placed on motherhood, a surplus of mothering females, and more relaxed toilet training characterize much lower-class child rearing, basic trust and autonomy may be achieved with greater success.

At stage three, however, the child discovers that he is black in what appears to be a white world. "Irregularities"[2] in the basic family and the frustration of exploratory and manipulative behavior may also curb initiative. It is largely this situation in many ghetto homes that Martin Deutsch's pre-school "environments" are attempting to alleviate for Negro children. Without this general sort of initiative building, the outcome of the fourth crisis, when school and neighborhood become the child's world, is a foregone conclusion for most urban Negroes—a lifelong stigma of inferiority that is extremely difficult if not impossible to overcome. If we assume, as we must at present, that the Negro child has trouble at stage three, and fights a losing battle with pitifully inadequate schools and rotten neighborhoods at stage four, it is no wonder that Negro adolescents face a profound identity crisis with the odds stacked firmly against them. The statistics on drop-outs and delinquency climb inexorably, and next summer's street disturbances will most certainly not be the last.

One viable identity that emerges from the gang, the bar, or pool-hall clique is our friend the hustler. A hustler knows who he is, and his "repudiation" is practically total. Usually this identity is sound within Negro culture and good while it lasts, but the law and old age catch up with the hustler eventually, and to the extent that crises six, seven, and eight are faced at all, "isolation," "self-absorption," and eventual "despair" would seem to be his lot—unless of course he experiences a marked change of heart and turns to preaching or a similar calling.

2. Here again we must ask whether Negro family patterns, matrifocality for example, are really "disorganized," "broken," and "irregular," or simply regular institutions within Negro culture. There is nothing inherently wrong with "matrifocality," and the burden of proof is on those who say that there is.

But what of other adolescents seeking their way through that crucial fifth phase? Most don't find a genuine identity—in Elijah Muhammad's words, "The Negro wants to be everything but himself"—and many seem to illustrate what Erikson has called "identity diffusion." Experimentation with entertainment roles is endemic among Negro youth. The number of Negroes who have achieved semi-professional status, either consecutively or simultaneously, as athletes, singers, dancers, musicians, comedians, disc jockeys, and preachers would probably defy belief. Every other Negro and his uncle wants to be a master of ceremonies. The entertainment heroes who provide models for young people present a fascinating picture themselves. Are these heroes Renaissance men, avid hobbyists, or simply versatile? Or do they also exemplify identity diffusion? Consider the following list of athletes alone:

Satchel Paige—pitcher, clown, philosopher, actor
Muhammad Ali (Cassius Clay)—boxer, poet, singer, religionist, jive or put-on artist
Sugar Ray Robinson—boxer, dancer, fashion sophisticate, nightclub owner
Roosevelt Grier—football tackle, singer
Harlem Globetrotters—masters of choreography and trickery as well as of basketball
Althea Gibson—tennis champ, golfer
Jesse Owens—track star turned disc jockey
Bill Cosby, Dick Gregory—athletes turned comedians
Red Garland, Dave Bailey—boxers turned jazz musicians

This partial listing gives some substance to the idea that the full range of expressive roles has a strong and perhaps unique attraction for Negroes which sometimes persists even after an identity has been firmly established in one particular area of performance. The interplay between blues singing, preaching, and disc jockeying must also be considered in this connection. Problems of role experimentation and identity diffusion among Negro youth deserve more careful study than they have so far received. Drop-out training programs and teaching might be made much more effective if the impact of entertainment models upon Negro youth were better understood.

A consideration of the urban blues singer in terms of Erikson's three final stages will serve to refocus our attention upon the themes and subject matter of the preceding chapters. Unlike the hustler, who achieves an identity at the expense of further growth, the bluesman's self-acceptance sustains him in the crises of maturity. In fact, dramatized resolutions of these crises are his stock in trade, as illustrated by the "psychosocial modalities" and "related elements of the social order" that Erikson links to the basic stages.

Psychosocial Crises	Related Elements of the Social Order	Psychosocial Modalities
5. Identity and Repudiation vs. Identity Diffusion	Ideological Perspectives	To be oneself (or not to be) To share being oneself
6. Intimacy and Solidarity vs. Isolation	Patterns of Cooperation and Competition	To lose and find oneself in another
7. Generativity vs. Self-Absorption	Currents of Education and Tradition	To make be To take care of
8. Integrity vs. Despair	Wisdom	To be, through having been To face not being

5. B. B. King's career hinges on his being totally himself and sharing that self with others day after day and night after night. He has developed a clear ideological perspective to support this way of life, as is reported in Chapter IV, above.

6. The problems of partnership—of losing and finding oneself in another—figure prominently in all the best urban blues lyrics. The stylized patterns of cooperation in Bobby Bland's performance and his lyrical analysis of sexual competition are described in Chapter V, above. The intimacy and solidarity generated by such a performance are discussed at length in Chapters VI and VII, above.

7. The blues singer's generativity nourishes itself upon the raw materials of the preceding crises—all of them, 1 through 6.

His creations spring from a well-developed musical and poetic tradition (cf. Chapter II, above) and the peculiar experience of being black in white America. B. B. King, the Beale St. Blues Boy, and Big Bobby Blue Bland, as the nominal alliteration suggests, represent modes of being. These are men who "can take care of business," say their listeners, "because they've been through it."

8. As for evaluations of such rare qualities as integrity and wisdom, I leave this ultimately to the reader, but I would like to include Erikson's eloquent criteria:

> Although aware of the relativity of all the various life styles which have given meaning to human striving, the possessor of integrity is ready to defend the dignity of his own life style against all physical and economic threats. For he knows that an individual life is the accidental coincidence of but one life cycle with but one segment of history; and that for him all human integrity stands and falls with the one style of integrity of which he partakes.[3]

In a paragraph on ego strength, Erikson has also given us— indirectly—a beautiful definition of the blues.

> A weak ego does not gain substantial strength from being persistently bolstered. A strong ego, secured in its identity by a strong society, does not need, and in fact is immune to any attempt at artificial inflation. Its tendency is toward the testing of what feels real; the mastery of that which works; the understanding of that which proves necessary, the enjoyment of the vital, and the extermination of the morbid. At the same time, it tends toward the creation of a strong mutual reinforcement with others in a group ego, which will transmit its will to the next generation.[4]

But will the integrity and strong ego of the bluesmen be transmitted to future generations?

3. Erikson, *op. cit.*, p. 78.
4. *Ibid.*, p. 47.

TALKING ABOUT MUSIC

IN THIS APPENDIX I shall outline and discuss a broad analytic framework for talking about the musical experience, since the problem of relating the blues to Negro culture is part of a much larger problem. Many important issues are touched upon in a single phrase; certain crucial problem areas are glossed over with bibliographic footnotes; but I think it is important for the reader to form some sort of appreciation for what a more comprehensive study of the blues or any other musical style might be like.

Any anthropologist interested in music must inevitably be overwhelmed at times by a combined feeling of euphoria and frustration. Music is a cultural universal—every culture has some, and most peoples systematically order sounds in scores of different ways for equally various situations. Elation, however, springs not only from the sheer quantity and variety of music but from its paradoxical position as a culture's quintessential medium of expression, at once highly formalized, abstract, and systematic yet conversely capable of incorporating powerful and primordial emotions. This point cannot be overstressed. Nor can it be easily validated. Beyond the subjective assertion, echoed by many,[1] that music often represents the ultimate distillation of a people's total experience, we can state only that the field to be

1. Claude Lévi-Strauss. *Le Cru et le cuit* (Paris, 1965).

explored is vast and constitutes as complex and demanding a challenge as can be imagined.

The excitement of this challenge is quickly blended and counterbalanced with frustration. To ask questions about the relationship between music and man—to ask why this particular pattern of sound in this particular time and place—one must confront a welter of speculations and uncertainties. Casting aside romantic philosophies and fanciful intuitions, one can offer only the most tentative and tenuous answers. Individuals who attempt to deal with such questions rationally are not numerous. True, there are many musicologists, music critics, and a growing legion of cultural anthropologists; but as for scholars consistently concerned with the relationship between music and culture, I can think of only three: Alan Lomax, David Mc-Allester, and Alan P. Merriam.

Lomax has probably gone farthest in linking all five types of explanation outlined below.[2] Although he is open to criticism for his uncontrolled subjective measurements, grandiose cross-continental comparisons, sweeping generalizations, and heavy-handed Freudianism, his work since switching from an anthological approach to an anthropological one provides much needed provocation in a field that is marked by strict specialization and academic caution. McAllester's *Enemy Way Music*[3] has often been cited as a classic in the field of ethnomusicology—I would say *the* classic. If only equally sophisticated reports were available for a dozen or so other cultures besides the Navaho, a careful synthesis of these studies could probably raise ethnomusicology to a new plateau of understanding. Alan Merriam's many articles, culminating in the best theoretical textbook to date, *The Anthropology of Music*,[4] offer excellent guidelines to worthwhile research.

Occasional writings or public utterances reveal a real interest

2. Alan Lomax, "Folk Song Style," *American Anthropologist* 61 (1959): 927–54. See also "Song Structure and Social Structure," *Ethnology*, Vol. 1 (1962), pp. 425–51.

3. David P. McAllester, *Enemy Way Music*, Papers of the Peabody Museum, Vol. 41, No. 3 (Cambridge, 1954).

4. Evanston, 1964.

on the part of other ethnomusicologists in a truly interdisciplinary approach to music;[5] an occasional unpublished thesis takes a
significant step or two in the direction of music-culture synthesis;[6] an anthropologist occasionally devotes some worthwhile
pages to music and musicians in a monograph;[7] some jazz critics
persistently focus attention upon social and cultural factors that
shape the music.[8] For the most part, however, musicologists go
one way, anthropologists another, and the critics continue to tell
us what they do and don't like.

At this point let me set forth a provisional but sufficiently
general formulation of the ground to be covered if we are to
explain or understand a given musical style.

Kinds of Explanation	Connective Devices	Levels of Analysis
I. Syntactic	Stylistic pattern consistency and congruence; structural studies	Cultural
II. Pragmatic	Situation-behavior descriptions; artist/audience interaction; role and status studies	Social
III. Semantic	Perception and emotion measurements; content analysis; musician and listener as personalities; musical learning	Personal

5. John Blacking, *The Role of Music amongst the Venda of Northern
Transvaal* (Johannesburg, 1957). Charles Seeger, "Semantic, Logical
and Political Considerations Bearing upon Research in Ethnomusicology,"
Ethnomusicology 5: 77–80. Bruno Nettl, *Music in Primitive Culture*
(Cambridge, Mass., 1956).

6. John M. Smothers, "The Public and Private Meanings of Popular
Music for American Adolescents" (Ph.D. Dissertation, University of
Chicago, 1961). George Robinson Ricks, "Religious Music of the United
States Negro" (Ph.D. Dissertation, Northwestern University, 1959).

7. S. F. Nadel, *A Black Byzantium* (London, 1942). Clifford Geertz,
The Religion of Java (Glencoe, 1960).

8. Martin Williams, Nat Hentoff, and LeRoi Jones are noteworthy in
this respect.

Kinds of Explanation	Connective Devices	Levels of Analysis
IV. Kinesic	Physiological observation and testing; paralinguistics and ethno-choreography	Organismic
V. Genetic	The four interpenetrating types of explanation considered through time and space	Historical

The first three divisions of the left-hand column are from Charles Morris via C. E. Osgood;[9] and the right-hand column derives from the Parsons and Shils "theory of action."[10] Since a full explication of such an expansive and loosely joined framework would be an encyclopedic task, the following comments are restricted to a few definitions, suggestions, and a consideration of the blues in terms of each analytic level.

Syntactics. Any musical style may be considered a cultural subsystem or pattern in isolation, to be analyzed independently of any other considerations. Syntactic meaning refers primarily to the inner correspondences, the regularized combination of sounds with other sounds that are distinctive of a particular style. The accumulation of time-tested analytic tools belonging to the tradition of "product musicology"[11] has been brought to bear with increasing effectiveness on this problem of establishing syntactic norms and deviations. The gross defining features summarized in Lomax's[12] "cantometric" scales—tonal blend, melodic shape, phrase length—and the more quantitative and verifiable procedures developed by Kolinski[13] and others—me-

9. Charles E. Osgood, George J. Suci, and Percy H. Tannenbaum, *The Measurement of Meaning* (Urbana, 1957).

10. Talcot Parsons and Edward Shils, *Toward a General Theory of Action* (Cambridge, 1951).

11. Alan P. Merriam, *A Prologue to the Study of the African Arts* (Yellow Springs, Ohio, 1962).

12. "Song Structure and Social Structure."

13. Mieczyslaw Kolinski, "Suriname Music" *in* Melville J. and Frances S. Herskovits, *Suriname Folklore* (New York, 1936).

lodic level, tempo figure, interval counts, patterning—can be used to define both generally and rather precisely what is labeled above as musical "pattern consistency" or style.

Western composers often have interesting notions to offer concerning the basic integrating mechanisms of musical structure, but few of their many ideas have been tested with non-Western forms. Unlike mathematics, music thrives on the defiance of logical rules and regulations; barriers are erected and obstacles implied only to be hurdled or sidestepped altogether.[14] Similarly, copying the information theorists, we may speak of individually or culturally determined musical "goals" and the various paths by which these are attained.[15] Leonard Meyer's *Emotion and Meaning in Music*[16] is most enlightening on these matters, and his propositions take syntactic analysis well beyond the description of melodic shapes and the counting of intervals.

Continuities in the style having been established, the style may be compared and contrasted with other cultural patterns— existential (what is) and normative (what ought to be) values as they relate to music and other forms of expression,[17] systems of religious beliefs, myths, linguistic categories, folk taxonomies, and so forth. This is what is meant by pattern congruence or the lack of it.

Blues pattern consistency or style has never been given the intensive treatment it warrants. Little is done to rectify this situation in Chapter II, above, where gross textural characteristics and broad formal criteria rather than exact syntactic analyses are used to differentiate the various blues styles. A traditional transcription and analysis of representative samples from the regional country blues genres would help to establish a stylistic foundation against which subsequent shifts in style could be more accurately measured. How far removed from the

14. Igor Stravinsky, *Poetics of Music* (New York, 1947).

15. Edgar Coons and David Kraehenbuehl, "Information as a Measure of the Experience of Music," *Journal of Aesthetics and Art Criticism* 17 (1959): 510–22.

16. Chicago, 1956.

17. McAllester, *op. cit.*

older country idioms is B. B. King's current guitar vocabulary? What innovations did the earliest urban guitarists (e.g., Scrapper Blackwell, Lonnie Johnson) actually contribute? How have bass lines shifted through time as this function has moved from the lower strings of the guitar to the left hand of the piano, from string bass to electronic bass? Scores of questions like these can be answered only superficially until someone takes on the time-consuming job of analyzing note by note and phrase by phrase a large body of blues materials.

A more urgent need is for thorough dissection of a few outstanding contemporary blues selections along the lines indicated by Leonard Meyer. What are the probability relationships, the expectations and goals, the harmonic habits, the melodic norms and ranges of permissible deviation, and the techniques for building and releasing tension that shape a typical blues performance? What organizing principles guide the subtle interplay of vocal and instrumental lines in a song like Bobby Bland's *Your Friends?* Again, questions like these indicate an endless chain of ignorance that can be broken only by a painstaking inspection of the music itself. The harmonic standardization of the urban blues form in a twelve-bar unit (and a few equally standardized variations of it) will give the syntactic investigator a particularly fertile field in which to work. It will enable him to concentrate his attention upon the wide variety of melodic and rhythmic techniques that are played off against this circumscribed harmonic foundation in the various substyles and individual performances. Any musicologist who applies Meyer's theory and method to the urban blues will be richly rewarded for his efforts.

Although pattern consistency has been slighted in this study, the problem of pattern congruence has received considerable attention. Lacking more specific syntactic information, I have used the dialectic pattern of the blues form, lyric content, and the core concept of soul as coordinates, linking the blues to statements made by Negroes about the blues and to Negro culture as a whole. These are only three general coordinates among many, however, and a definitive account of the blues ought to specify a much tighter network of relationships between blues syntax and the values, beliefs, and behavior of blues people. But further tightening and specifying also depend upon data obtained at other levels of inquiry.

Pragmatics. At the social level, the emphasis shifts from music to musicians and their listeners. Pragmatic explanations of a musical style will define it in terms of the common features of the situations in which it is used and of the activities which it generates or promotes. Artist-audience interaction patterns, role and status of musicians, the sociology of the small musical group, and similar aspects of socio-musical behavior—all are consistently overlooked in the best anthropological monographs. Ethnomusicologists have done little to fill this gap in spite of the extensive sociological literature from which ready-made research designs could easily be drawn.[18] The theories of dramatism and psychodrama, propounded by Kenneth Burke[19] and J. L. Moreno[20] respectively, are also of immense heuristic value when one attempts work into the heart of any ongoing musical performance.

The broader situation or environmental context of musical action is almost a completely unexplored area. The economic and ecological determinants of a non-Western musical system have yet to be thoroughly examined. Even our knowledge of the technological and economic complexities of the so-called American music business is still primitive, although the recent writings of Nash, Etzkorn, Hentoff, and Shemel[21] are beginning to reveal many of the corners in this mazeway to our inspection.

Pragmatic explanations have been stressed throughout this discussion of the urban blues, but much ground is nevertheless left uncovered. For example, a good supplement to "B. B. King Backstage" would be "B. B. King and Company on the Bus."

18. Robert T. Golembiewski, *The Small Group* (Chicago, 1962).

19. *A Grammar of Motives* (New York, 1945).

20. *Psychodrama* (New York, 1946).

21. Dennison Nash, "The Role of the Composer," *Ethnomusicology* 5 (1961): 81–94, 187–201. K. Peter Etzkorn, "Social Context of Songwriting in the United States," *Ethnomusicology* 7 (1963): 96–106. Sidney Shemel and M. William Krasilovsky, *This Business of Music* (New York, 1964).

Unfortunately, some good opportunities to travel with the band for a few days were missed. Backstage observations and conversations are really no substitute for living the life with the touring group, and the day-in, day-out patterns of cooperation and sources of antagonism within a blues package are largely unknown to me. The running intermission card game beneath the Regal Theatre stage, if studied closely, could add some interesting information here as well. Similarly, the reader would profit from a detailed description of happenings at a local blues bar or one of the many Negro versions of the discotheque which flourish along all the main streets of the black belt. I have chosen to concentrate attention upon the basic urban blues situation, the performance of a touring bluesman at a major ballroom or theater; but ideally all the activities in which bluesmen engage and all the social situations in which blues music plays a part should be taken into account.

The little information I have been able to gather concerning the economics and technology of blues production is reported in Chapter III, above. A more thorough discussion probably dictates taking a job with a record company, since the business operations of blues producers are remarkably convoluted and confused.

Semantics. Music is also a semantic; any style represents a system of unconsummated, implicit, connotational symbols. To paraphrase the bard, it is the consummation of musical symbol systems that is devoutly to be wished. This consummation is probably the primary challenge facing ethnomusicologists and apparently one they find difficult to accept, given the prevailing point of view that it is a serious breach of taste to speak of the unspeakable. Susanne Langer has summarized the situation in typically articulate fashion.

> Everybody knows that language is a very poor medium for expressing our emotional nature. It merely names certain vaguely and crudely conceived states, but fails miserably in any attempt to convey the evermoving patterns, the ambivalences and intricacies of inner experience, the inter-play of feelings with thoughts and impressions, memories

and echoes of memories, transient fantasy, or its mere runic traces, all turned into nameless, emotional stuff.

There is, however, a kind of symbolism peculiarly adapted to the explication of "unspeakable" things, though it lacks the cardinal virtue of language, which is denotation. The most highly developed type of such purely connotational semantic is music. We are not talking nonsense when we say that a certain musical progression is significant, or that a given phrase lacks meaning, or a player's rendering fails to convey the import of a passage. Yet such statements make sense only to people with a natural understanding of the medium, whom we describe, therefore, as "musical."

Perhaps that is why musicians [and ethnomusicologists] who know that it is the prime source of their mental life and the medium of their clearest insight into humanity, so often feel called upon to despise the more obvious forms of understanding, that claim practical virtues under the names of reason, logic, etc.[22]

The problem in consummating musical symbolism lies of course in the fact that a phrase, progression, or total work may hold different emotional connotations for the musician and for each individual listener. Yet it is safe to assume that Americans will perceive and interpret a Beethoven symphony in patterned ways that are distinctly different from those of the Japanese or of any other culture. It can be further hypothesized that within a single community, individuals of a particular personality type, socio-economic status, or ethnic tradition may share certain learned modes of consummation or common denominators of meaning with reference to a particular piece of music. There is no difficulty either in multiplying propositions of this sort or in making them more specific, but the testing of such propositions presents us with innumerable though not insoluble problems.

A great many psychological testing instruments can be used to measure musical aptitudes, perceptions, responses, and feel-

22. Susanne K. Langer, *Philosophy in a New Key* (Cambridge, Mass., 1941).

ings[23] as well as the potentially significant aspects of auditing personalities.[24] The methodological questions appear to be, first, finding tests that are relatively free of linguistic barriers and applicable from culture to culture and, second, combining a few of these tests in a battery that will produce data immediately relevant to a particular problem and susceptible of fairly objective interpretation.[25]

The work done by Charles Osgood and his associates[26] in quantifying complex connotations through the use of a device he calls the "Semantic Differential" may prove to be especially valuable in consummating musical symbolism. A stimulus or concept of some kind—a piece of music, for example—is presented, and persons are asked to respond by choosing from a fairly long list of bipolar adjective scales: active-passive, hot-cold, and so forth. These responses or choices are then recorded on cards and fed to a computer, which spews out all kinds of averages, percentages, and interesting correlational patterns. These patterns represent numerically the dimensions of meaning or modes of interpretation utilized by the group in deciphering the original stimulus. Having performed an experiment of this kind, presenting four pieces of Indian classical music, a Bach *Two-Part Invention*, some jazz (John Coltrane), and a blues guitar solo by B. B. King to more than eighty white college and high-school students, I can report that the amount of

23. Paul R. Farnsworth, *The Social Psychology of Music* (New York, 1958).

24. The literature on personality types is extensive, but the constructs employed in the following references might be particularly useful: Milton Rokeach, *The Open and Closed Mind* (New York, 1960). Carl G. Jung, *Psychological Types* (New York, 1933). Helen H. Jennings, *Leadership and Isolation* (New York, 1950). Murdo Mackenzie, *The Human Mind* (London, 1940). W. H. Sheldon, *The Varieties of Temperament: A Psychology of Constitutional Differences* (New York, 1942).

25. The suggested links between aspects of personality, aptitudes, perceptions, and emotions put forth by one analyst with respect to musical style are bound to be disputed by others in any case. The fact remains, however, that at the present time there is no body of data on which such arguments can be based.

26. Osgood *et al., op. cit.*

work involved is prodigious, but the results are promising and worth the trouble.[27]

Until I have had a chance to obtain a comparable set of responses to the B. B. King selection from at least one group of urban Negroes, I see little point in presenting my initial findings here. Were this device or one like it to be applied systematically, however, using a much wider range of Afro-American musical styles as stimuli, and drawing responses from various segments of the Negro community—high-school drop-outs, middle-class women, an actual blues audience, and so forth—steady progress could be made toward pinning down the different meanings currently attached to the blues by the people who created them. Interviews with blues fans and performers might be expected to uncover some valuable information on blues meanings, emotions, and the blues esthetic. These expectations are likely to be only partly fullfilled: blues performers are a tightly knit group of professionals and reluctant to criticize each other's work. Some are highly articulate on a number of subjects but at a loss for words when it comes to music. Blues fans can usually indicate their likes and dislikes, but they too find it extremely difficult to rationalize or explain these preferences. Speaking of the unspeakable—talking about music—is not an easy thing to do, and any method like the Semantic Differential that can get at the processes underlying preferences is worth trying.

What is all the shouting about during a B. B. King performance? Why do certain sequences of sound provoke screams of delight, whereas others are received in relative silence? The speculative answers ventured in Chapter VI, above, are hardly satisfactory; the general deficiency of specified relationships between blues syntax and blues semantics constitutes a large gap in the preceding account. But this is a gap that could conceivably take a lifetime to close completely. The harmonic standardization of the blues form that gives the syntactic investigator a rare opportunity for productive analysis is paralleled by these overt responses to the blues which will

27. "Musical Meaning: A Preliminary Report," *Ethnomusicology* (Spring, 1966).

provide the blues semanticist with a clear and logical starting point for his research. It is hoped that someone will choose an "in-person" recording[28] of a noted blues artist and set about performing both tasks simultaneously.

Kinesics. It is entirely possible that the most significant aspects of some musical styles are physiological or biocultural. On the organismic level, we are dealing with such distinguishing features as tone production in head, throat, and thorax; degrees of laryngeal constriction and relaxation; the cycles of bodily tension and release; and the motions required to produce music or respond to it appropriately. The fields of kinesics[29] and ethnochoreography[30] will have much to offer the patient worker interested in this level of analysis, since music in many instances can be seen as validating movement in much the same way that myth validates ritual. A detailed breakdown of all the body movement associated with a musical style or specific performance could be of great assistance in segmenting the musical continuum into its significant units, something which standard transcriptions, mechanical or otherwise, almost entirely fail to take into account. Note that we have come full circle and are facing syntactic problems once again.

Ethnomusicologists are not yet adept at non-Western syntactics: musical semantics and pragmatics are sorely neglected, but the kinesic-somatic or body movement aspect of music is not even recognized by many of them. In any musical style we must not only consider the notes syntactically and in abstraction—scores, transcriptions, and so forth are essentially a Western preoccupation after all. There is also an obligation to examine what is done to the notes, to describe accurately the process by which music is actually produced in performance. There is one school of ethnomusicological thought that is devoted to what they call a "performance orientation," but this boils down to

28. *B. B. King Live at the Regal* ABC-Paramount, 509. "In person" recordings by James Brown, Ray Charles, Joe Tex, and others might also be used.

29. Ray L. Birdwhistell, *Introduction to Kinesics* (Louisville, 1952).

30. Gertrude P. Kurath, "Panorama of Dance Ethnology," *Current Anthropology* 1 (1960): 233–54.

mere mimicry of alien styles in practice and has produced little that might be called "kinesic analysis."[31]

What Pablo Casals *does* to a Beethoven cello sonata (his attack, tempo, phrasing, and so on) is still a mystery. When we consider the many non-Western forms, specifically the African and African-derived genres, in which the music is at least partly improvised and either linked to or completely embedded in the dance, the mystery deepens and the need for a solution-finding methodology becomes even more urgent. What makes a jazz or blues rhythm section swing or fail to swing? How is B. B. King able to inject vital feeling into a tired guitar phrase that fans are hearing for perhaps the hundredth time? Some would insist that syntactic explanations can account for phenomena of this sort, but I doubt it. For it isn't so much what a bluesman plays but the way that he plays it that really counts. I discuss these issues and related problems in an essay soon to be published.[32] Until we find some way of talking intelligently about the split-second timing of music-making motions and their conjoined bodily responses, much of the meaning of the blues must either remain hidden or be grasped intuitively from prolonged first-hand experience.

Genetics. The genetic, historical, or diachronic type of explanation in musicology needs no elaboration here. It would seem, however, that important new insights into the processes of style formation and the continuity or change of styles through time rest ultimately upon a more sophisticated treatment of the synchronic problems touched upon in the preceding sections. Once the complexities of a few contemporary blues and gospel styles have been explored and understood in these comprehensive terms, past developments are likely to be viewed from a much different perspective and it may even be possible to predict some future stylistic developments with a fair degree of accuracy.

Music is a rare distillation of human experience, and occupies a relatively inaccessible apex or peak of culture. For this reason,

31. Mantle Hood, *Institute of Ethnomusicology* (Los Angeles, 1961).

32. "Motion and Feeling through Music," *Journal of Aesthetics and Art Criticism* (Spring, 1966).

a musical style and its exponents may ultimately reveal some important and otherwise unobtainable knowledge of the total environment from which they spring. At present, however, we don't know much about the intricate process of distillation, and musical peaks all over the world have yet to be scaled. These mixed metaphors reflect a confused situation. To extract the essence a musical style has to offer, we must approach it initially from every conceivable angle, utilizing all levels of analysis and all types of explanation. Borrowing theories and techniques from other disciplines, we may eventually climb a few of those peaks and repay our accumulated debts with a view from the top.

The barriers separating musicology from the various social sciences and humanities have only really begun to disintegrate during the past decade, and the dialogue that will lead to a new and useful ethnomusicology has hardly entered its first phase. Hence the proffered frame of reference is rudimentary, preliminary, and subject to much revision and refinement. Yet even so crude an outline highlights some of the unexplored terrain. It also points to some of the chapters that are missing from this book.

BLUES STYLES: AN ANNOTATED OUTLINE

THE FOUR MAIN CATEGORIES listed below are in phylogenetic order; each style in the list has developed from its predecessor, although practioners of all styles can still be found. Almost without exception any blues musician has moved through two or more of these basic divisions during his career. The subheadings under II and III are also in chronological order; the headings I. A. 1, 2, 3, refer to regional variations. Key diagnostics and defining features of each category are in brackets. Representative artists from each style or substyle are in parentheses.

Basic Resources—[unaccompanied vocalization] (preachers, work-gangs, peddlers, etc.) Key: [diagnostics in brackets] (typical artists in parentheses)

I. Country Blues [unstandardized forms, unamplified guitar, "strong-beat" phrasing, spoken introductions and endings]
    A. Individual, self-accompanied
        1. Delta area [drones, moans, bottle-neck techniques, "heavy" texture]
            (Bukka White, Son House, Robert Johnson, early Muddy Waters, John Lee Hooker)

2. Texas area [single-string guitar work, relaxed vocal qualities, "light" texture]

(Blind Lemon Jefferson, Texas Alexander, Mance Lipscomb, Lightnin' Hopkins)

3. Eastern seaboard and hill country [characteristics of white folk music common, standard forms usual]

(Peg Leg Howell, Blind Boy Fuller, Brownie McGhee and Sonny Terry, Baby Tate)

B. Group

1. String bands [a guitar or two, plus any of the following instruments: fiddle, mandolin, bass, harmonica]

(Mississippi String Band, Big Joe Williams)

2. Jug bands [jugs, kazoos, washboards, "gutbucket"]

(Gus Cannon, Will Shade *et al.*, Eddie Kelly)

3. Traveling show blues [various mixtures of B. 1 and B. 2, wide instrumental variation]

(Rabbit Foot Minstrels, Silas Green, variety shows, circus bands, medicine show ensembles)

II. City Blues [standardized form, regular beginnings and endings, usually two or more instruments]

A. Piano accompanied—20's and 30's

1. "Classic" female singers ["stride" piano, jazz instrumental responses]

(Bessie Smith, Ma Rainey, Ida Cox, Alberta Hunter)

2. Male singers [boogie-woogie and rolling-bass piano styles with guitar "fills," the "Bluebird beat"]

(Tampa Red, Blind Blake, Lonnie Johnson, Carr and Blackwell, Broonzy, Big Maceo, Memphis Slim)

B. Contemporary—40's to present [string bass and drums added, electric guitar, harmonica]

(Sonny Boy Williamson, Muddy Waters, Jimmy Reed, Howlin' Wolf)

C. "Citified country" [country features but bass and drums added]

(Hooker, Hopkins, early Wolf and Waters)

III. Urban Blues [saxophones added, freer vocal phrasing, arrangements, no harmonicas, etc.]

A. Territories and Kansas City [shouting vocals, big bands, riff accompaniment, 4-beat time flow]

(Hot Lips Page, Jimmy Rushing, Joe Turner, Walter Brown, J. Witherspoon, Louis Jordan)

B. Postwar Texas [electric guitar, more relaxed vocals, smaller bands, generally slower tempos, piano still important]

(Charles Brown, Roy Brown, Amos Milburn, T-Bone Walker, Lowell Fulson, Louis Jordan)

C. Memphis synthesis

1st phase—(Gatemouth Moore, Johnny Ace, Roscoe Gordon, also Jordan and Walker)

2nd phase—(B. B. King, early Bobby Bland, Jr. Parker)

3rd phase—(Freddy King, Albert King, Little Milton Campbell, Little Johnny Taylor, James Davis, Buddy Guy, and others who follow the King-Bland-Parker pattern)

D. Industrial [everything electrically amplified, 2 or 3 guitars plus drums, 1 tenor sax optional]

(Otis Rush, Earl Hooker, numerous club bands)

IV. Soul Music [blues-jazz-gospel synthesis]

A. Basic or heavy [gospel chord patterns, jazz orchestration, responsorial voices]

(Ray Charles, Bobby Bland, recent Little Milton, Aretha Franklin)

B. Frantic cry singers [lyric appeal to young women, gospel fervor, emphasis on action, disrobing, pleading]

(James Brown, Joe Tex, McKinley Mitchell, Joe Hinton)

C. Refined or light soul

1. Male "pop" [string sections, slick arrangements, relaxed vocals, slower tempo, choir optional]

(Brook Benton, Sam Cooke, Jerry Butler, Solomon Burke, Walter Jackson, Chuck Jackson, Gene Chandler

2. "Detroit sound" [firm, danceable beat, medium tempos, "sweet" vocal sound]

(Mary Wells, Dionne Warwick, Marvin Gaye, the Supremes, Major Lance)

3. Groups

a. "doo-wah" types ["doo-wah" background, simple instrumental accompaniment]

(Flamingoes, Swallows, Radiants, many amateur groups)

b. gospel-spiritual types [falsetto emphasis, sacred style and content affinities as well]

(Impressions, Temptations)

Commercial Designations
Rhythm and blues [blues band accompaniment, novelty lyrics
common, some non-blues forms]
(Wynonie Harris, Bo Diddley, Chuck Berry, Little Richard
were once typical, but any artist who reaches a wide, predominantly Negro audience using a relatively unadorned
blues sound qualifies)
Rock and roll [Honking saxes, heavy offbeat, echo effects,
gimmickry, teen lyrics]
(Bill Haley, Fats Domino, Elvis Presley, but essentially any
singer, Negro or white, who reaches a young, predominantly white audience with something approximating a
Negro style)
V. Parallel and/or Derived Styles
Urbane blues [musical sophistication, no amplification, polished
technique, coherent lyrics, original forms]
(Snooks Eaglin, Lonnie Johnson; might include Percy Mayfield, Mose Allison, Louis Jordan, some songs by "classic"
and Kansas City singers)

Folk blues [wide repertoire, more protest lyrics]
(late Broonzy, Brownie McGhee)

Phony folk blues [reinterpretation or re-creation of older styles]
(Odetta, Leon Bibb, Josh White, Harry Belafonte)

Blues in various jazz idioms
(jazz groups of all periods, notable singers: Jelly Roll Morton,
Louis Armstrong, Jack Teagarden, Jimmy Rushing, Sarah
Vaughan, Dinah Washington, Mose Allison, Joe Williams,
Lou Rawls)

"White" blues
1. hillbilly or country and western tradition
(Jimmie Rodgers, Woody Guthrie, Bill Monroe)
2. white American imitators
(Paul Butterfield, Righteous Brothers)
3. British imitators
(Rolling Stones, Beatles)

Some subsidiary and semi-blues styles on the chart require
further definition, and it is also necessary to relate this taxonomy

to the jazz and "white blues" traditions. For convenience, the
spectrum of blues styles may be renumbered (audience composition is suggested in the right column; N—Negro, W—white, M
—mixed, w—small percentage of audience white, and so on) as
follows:

1.	Basic resources	N
2.	Country—Delta	N
3.	Country—Southwest	N
4.	Country—East	N
5.	String bands	Nw
6.	Jug bands	M
7.	"Show" blues	Nw
8.	City—"classic" female—1917–1930	Nw
9.	City—"classic" male—1925–1945	N
10.	City—contemporary—1945–1963	M (mostly N)
11.	Citified country	Nw
12	Urban—Territories and Kansas City —1925–1945	M (mostly N at first)
13.	Urban—postwar Texas—1945–1955	Nw
14.	Urban—Memphis—1950–1964	N
15.	Urban—industrial—1955–1964	N
16.	Soul music—basic	M (mostly N)
17.	Soul music—frantic	Nw
18.	Soul music—refined, male "pop"	M
19.	Soul music—refined, "Detroit"	M (mostly teens)
20.	Soul music—refined, groups	Nw (mostly teens)
21.	Rhythm and blues	Nw
22.	Rock and roll	Wn
23.	Urbane blues	M
24.	Folk blues	Wn
25.	Phony folk blues	W
26.	Jazz versions	M
27.	White—country and Western	Wn
28.	White—U. S.	M
29.	White—U. K.	Wn

"Basic resources" refers to the call-and-response patterns
used in work songs and church music but also includes field
hollers, peddler's cries, songs from children's games, the chanting style used by most Negro preachers, marching band music,

country dance music, as well as the content and phrasing of everyday Southern Negro speech.[1]

The regional country blues styles have been discussed in Chapter II, above.

String bands have rarely been recorded, but a Big Joe Williams album, *Back to the Country*,[2] reveals something like a country group in action. The guitar-mandolin duets and other groups recorded by Ramsey[3] are also indicative. Jug bands and show band styles are not well documented on record either. The Mound City Blue Blower records represent a jazz version of the jug-band sound (no jugs); many of the emerging jazz leaders of the day (Gene Krupa, Coleman Hawkins, Pee Wee Russell) worked with the group from time to time.

A discussion of the blues as played and transformed by jazz men during various periods is a book in itself, but the relationship between jazz and blues has always been intimate and essential to the development of both traditions. Contact has been constant, and indeed no one can really play jazz without first-hand acquaintance with the blues, its chromaticism and its form. There are points on the blues continuum, however, where the two traditions have fused almost completely and, conversely, points where communication between jazzmen and bluesmen was minimal. Beginning with the basic resources shared by both jazz and blues, the key fusion points are 8, 12, and 16. Bessie Smith's mergers with Louis Armstrong, James P. Johnson, Charlie Green (8), the Basie-Rushing partnership (12), and the Ray Charles–Milt Jackson collaborations (16) exemplify these periods of intensive cross-fertilization.

No effort has been made to taxonomize the white country-and-Western tradition (which includes some blues materials), though it is linked in some ways to the classification presented here. A comparison of this kind by an ethnomusicologist well acquainted with both traditions would certainly be most instructive, since many analogous developments seem to have taken

1. Most of these sources are well documented in the *Music from the South* series, Vols. 1–10, Folkways Records.

2. *Testament Records*, T-2205.

3. Folkways Records, FA 2659, FP 654.

place side by side in the two fields in recent years. By stretching the various white blue-grass groups along a continuum, from the Carter family through Bill Monroe to Reno and Smiley, the broad stylistic distinctions between country, city, and urban could possibly be made.

Styles 16 through 22 have been discussed in connection with the distinctions made by the members of the blues community themselves, leaving styles 23, 24, and 25 to be accounted for—urbane blues, folk blues, and phony folk blues.

"Urbane blues" is certainly a dubious category, and is included simply as a niche in which to fit two special bluesmen, Snooks Eaglin and Lonnie Johnson, who might be described as urban bluesmen using country textures—that is, using urban forms but accompanying themselves on unamplified guitar. Their chord voicings are complex, and their single-string melodic lines are clean, sure, and imaginative. Johnson's lyrics are usually his own or a reshaping of traditional material in some new way; Eaglin shows considerable taste in his borrowings from a wide range of singers. Their voices are quiet, unassuming, and show few of the country, city, or urban trademarks. Percy Mayfield considers himself a composer who sings, and he seems to fit this classification as well. Like Johnson's and Eaglin's, his voice is nothing special; but his lyrics are often original, and he has remodeled blues structure in a number of interesting and influential ways, adding a section between blues choruses, contracting or extending the structure to 8-, 16-, and 24-bar forms. If musical sophistication, some originality, lyrical coherence, low volume, and the like are the criteria for inclusion in this class, then some of the more subtle work of other singers belong here as well—for example, Carr and Blackwell, Bessie Smith, Louis Jordan, Mose Allison. But at this point we begin selecting the most original pieces by a host of singers, and the distinction breaks down.

If Eaglin and Johnson fit into any other category, it is folk blues; in recent years they have come from street singing and retirement respectively to play before predominantly white audiences, Eaglin at the Playboy Club in New Orleans and Johnson in clubs around Philadelphia and in Europe. Folk blues artists, however, are either country bluesmen adapting slightly to a concert-hall context (John Lee Hooker, Lightnin' Hopkins) or city bluesmen who have remodeled their presentation to meet pseudo-country standards (Bill Broonzy, Josh White) as defined by the various folk impresarios.

Although folk blues artists have the virtue of actually being "folk"—that is, having been associated during their early musical careers with the mainstream of blues development and the rural Negro community; phony folk singers simply reinterpret older styles without having lived them—for example, Odetta's recent mimicry of Bessie Smith or Bibb's work song efforts. Josh White might also be included here, since he disguises his legitimate connections to mainstream blues styles so carefully that the resultant pastiche is indistinguishable from other re-creators.

INDEX

PHOENIX BOOKS
in Anthropology

PHOENIX BOOKS
in Archeology

PHOENIX BOOKS
in Sociology